Stepping

**Center Point
Large Print**

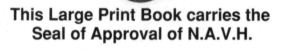

**This Large Print Book carries the
Seal of Approval of N.A.V.H.**

ॐ श्री गणेशाय नमः

Stepping

Nancy Thayer

Center Point Publishing
Thorndike, Maine

This Center Point Large Print edition
is published in the year 2000
by arrangement with
Harold Ober Associates, Inc.

The text of this Large Print edition is unabridged.
In other aspects, this book may vary from the original
edition. Printed in Thailand. Set in 16-point
Plantin type by Bill Coskrey.

ISBN 1-58547-027-9

Library of Congress Cataloging-in-Publication Data

Thayer, Nancy, 1943-
    Stepping / Nancy Thayer.
      p. cm.
    ISBN 1-58547-027-9 (lib. bdg. : alk. paper)
    1. Large type books. I. Title.

PS3570.H3475 S78 2000
813'.54--dc21

                                      00-022283

For Lee . . .

step n. 1.a. The single complete movement of raising one foot and putting it down in another spot in the act of walking, running, or dancing . . . c. The rhythm or pace of another or others, as in a march or dance: *keep step*. 2.a. The distance traversed by moving one foot ahead of the other . . . 4.a. One of a series of actions or measures taken toward some end. b. A stage in a process.—v. *stepped, stepping, steps*. 5. To move into a new situation by or as if by taking a single step.

step—. Indicates relationship through the previous marriage of a spouse or through the remarriage of a parent, rather than by blood . . .

American Heritage Dictionary, 1971.

ONE

I am sitting in an apartment in Kulosaari, a suburb of Helsinki, the capital of Finland. "Kulosaari" means burned island; long ago they burned the trees here to fertilize the land. Now there is no evidence of that burning; the land is lush and green. But it is in fact an island, connected to Helsinki proper by low bridges which look out over an ocean harbor filled with private sailboats and enormous yellow and black Finnish icebreakers. It is an attractive suburb, Kulosaari, gently and compactly lined with fairly new, very clean apartment houses, rows of elegant row houses, small shopping centers, schools, and libraries. Winding around and between the cement structures that house people and their necessities are strips of natural green land: stony moss-covered knolls, sternly jutting gray rocks, birch and spruce and pine trees, berry bushes. Tidy dirt paths for bicyclers, joggers, walkers, wend up and down, through forests, past glades, playgrounds, slopes of hill. Occasionally through the white trunks of the birches the bright blue of the ocean flicks into view. Farther in are the large private estates belonging to various international embassies: it is possible to walk past the Chinese embassy, to stop and study the large permanent glass-covered board they have set on the street with photographs of Mao's living room, dining room, and sleeping quarters. Mao has a long, narrow table covered with papers next to his chaste narrow bed.

Sometimes it is possible to see the Chinese ambassadors leave their mansion; sometimes they even take Bus 16 into Helsinki, as the rest of us commoners do.

I have been in several quite beautiful homes here in Kulosaari, homes of glass and metal, of crisp bright colors and warm wooden floors. I know they exist. My home for the next few months is not, however, beautiful. It is on the fourth floor of the oldest cement block building here, and there is no elevator, and not many of the other electrical luxuries I am so used to. The apartment has four rooms, small rooms, with cold gray linoleum floors and old greasy strips of carpet adhering here and there. In the living room there are two elaborate crystal chandeliers; they are the high point of the place. The walls of the apartment are dirty gray. The furniture is shabby and assorted: a purple sofa and chair worn to an itchy shininess; two green armchairs; a blue rug about two feet square; dusty frilly white curtains ornamented by slick side curtains in a brown and black rectangular design; a sheenless coffee table; a chipped veneer dining table; assorted chairs. In the two bedrooms are two twin beds each, and small chests, all not old enough to be antique but still old enough to be suspiciously sticky. The kitchen, where I sit now, is narrow, with a rickety table covered by an orange and white checked plastic tablecloth. We sit at this table for breakfast, lunch, and dinner; it is next to the kitchen window, which gives us views of the apartment house across from us, and its various electrical power units, and of the autoroute and the cars and trucks and buses speeding on it to and from Helsinki. What am I doing here? I ask myself that question almost constantly.

My husband is a professor, a historian, and he has been awarded a Fulbright professorship here; that's what we're doing here. Or rather that's what he's doing here. I am here because he is here, and our two small children are here for the same reason. Right now Adam, our four-year-old son, is at a sort of preschool at the Finnish-American Society *lasten-tarha*. Our two-year-old daughter, Lucy, is asleep on the other side of the wall, in the children's bedroom. And our other children—my husband's two daughters by a former marriage—are here only as ghosts, as memories. The last time we lived in Europe, Caroline and Cathy were with us, and Adam and Lucy were not yet born, although I was pregnant with Adam then. Now Caroline and Cathy are twenty-two and nineteen, grown-up, one working as a biologist and the other still in college, both living lives of their own. In our case the two sets of children have only slightly touched (in our case *bumped* is perhaps the more accurate word) and passed by on separate journeys, instead of meshing into a fat new nuclear family the way others do. But I think of Charlie's daughters, my stepdaughters, often here in Finland, and I wish they were here. I am lonely in this country of multisyllabic words, isolated in this apartment on this island. The toy kitchen, the strange road signs, the trams and ships, all make me remember Amsterdam, where Caroline and Cathy were with me, when living in a strange country was fun.

Living here is not fun, or only rarely fun; usually it is dreary hard work. We have no car, and the refrigerator is a joke, so tiny and without a freezer, so my life revolves around the simple necessity of getting food for us each day. I do this in the morning because then I can leave my children in the large fence-bound sandy yard across from the set of shops. The "Park Auntie," a severely pleasant woman dressed in warm brown winter clothes, quietly supervises perhaps twenty-five children as they toddle about the yard, fat in thick snowsuits, playing with buckets and shovels and trucks. My children are not especially happy here—no one speaks to them, no one plays with them, they feel odd, like the foreigners that they are—but I can not afford to care. They need to be outside in the fresh air; I need these few minutes of peace. And it costs only about twenty dollars a month—for me it is the biggest bargain in Finland. I hurry to the grocery store and search for inexpensive cuts of meat, and point and nod frantically at the butcher (one pound of hamburger: twelve Finnmarks; three American dollars). The worst part of the grocery shopping is trying to find a fresh green vegetable or a good crisp apple; these are hard to come by in Finland in the winter. The best part comes when I stand at the bakery counter trying to decide which warm and hearty loaf of *limpa*—bread—I should buy. I also choose some yogurt, a tiny carton of milk, and two bottles of Jaffa, the Finnish orange soft drink which I treat my children with during bad spots in the day. Each day I shop with extreme diligence and concern, both because of the expense and because I have to carry all I buy six long blocks home and up four flights of stairs in a red net bag that tugs at my wrists. Once in the apartment, I unpack the groceries and do the laundry, which must be done daily because although we are very lucky to have a washing machine in the bathroom, it is a very small machine, and then sometimes I have some lovely free time in which to read the mail or drink a blissfully solitary cup of tea before going back down the stairs and out into the cold to fetch my children from the Park Auntie's. I bring them home and prepare lunch for all of us, and Adam goes off to his preschool, and Charlie goes off to lecture, and Lucy sometimes takes a nap, and if she does, and if I don't have to walk ten blocks to pick up the cleaning or go into Helsinki on some household errand (vacuum cleaner bags, light bulbs, rain boots for the children), I sit at this wobbly kitchen table, staring out at the autoroute and trying to think things through. At four or five everyone is up and back and home, and I take the children out for a walk, and return to fix dinner, and do the dishes, and then spend the evening playing horsie or witch or hide-and-seek. The Finns are very shy, extraordinarily shy, and there are no children at all in this forty-eight-apartment complex. The women I pass at the Park Auntie's never speak to me; they avoid me as if I

11

were a leper. The Finns I know tell me that I should make the first advance, invite someone over to tea, but I doubt that I will ever manage that since I cannot get anyone to even look me in the eye. So except for official Fulbright functions I am alone, and my children have only me for a friend. It is hard being both a mother and a playmate. I brought few toys, thinking I would buy some here rather than haul them across the ocean, but it turns out that toys are too expensive, two or three times as expensive as they are in the States, and the Fulbright salary is meant only for the lowest level of survival. So it is necessary to stick to imaginative games. I bark and crawl and hide and creep with Adam and Lucy, but my heart isn't in it. They need friends who like to play these games, and I need friends, too. I am lonely here.

Lonely and bored. And wasted and unhappy. I feel trapped in these small, low-ceilinged gray rooms. At night when the heavy outside door at the bottom of the stairs slams shut, it resonates as dully and finally as the door of a prison cell. I twist about here, wanting to find a way up and out. It is not just Finland; it is not just having two small children in a foreign and unsmiling country; it is also that I am thirty-four and have given up a job teaching freshman composition and literature at a college to come here. It's humorous, probably, but teaching freshman composition and literature is something that I do well and love doing. I like the feeling of the students, slightly timid at their first year in college, cynical, optimistic, wriggly, raw; I love it when they first get the resonance of a metaphor or write a decent paragraph. I like working with words and the structures one can build out of words. I like seeing the world go through its cycles, snowstorms and spring blossoms, from the routinely safe and lively boundaries of a classroom or an office. I like talking to other instructors, laughing with them over tea, comparing fan notes from students ("Shit, if it hadn't been for Mrs. Campbell's freshman English class, I don't think I could of wrote a damned thing!"). I like teaching. I don't like it *instead* of marriage and children; I want those, too. Part of my life has been lopped off by leaving my job and coming here; it adds to the sense of isolation and waste.

Still, I sense that as I sit at this kitchen table, or pace about these four small rooms, bumping into the cold gray walls, I am at work on something. I am working something through. More and more I am thinking of the past, as if understanding it will help me with my future. Or with the present; Lord knows I need *something* to help me with my present. I used to secretly laugh at Caroline and Cathy's stories of their mother, Adelaide, screeching around the house, hitting them over the head with the bristle end of the broom, but now I find myself screeching around this apartment, kicking at the furniture and walls. Perhaps, after all these years, I do have something in common with Adelaide, Charlie's first wife: screeching. I screech because I want to teach; Adelaide screeched because she wanted simply to stay home and be a housewife and mother.

Oh, we are different, Adelaide and I, there's no denying we are. I've often wanted to feel, in a grand humanitarian way, like her sister; but I'm not her sister. I don't even know her. I've seen her only two or three times in thirteen years. I wouldn't like her and she wouldn't like me even if we hadn't been married to the same man. She was born and raised in Kansas, as I was, but she was born in 1931; I was born in 1943. She grew up wanting only a house and children and a traditional, secure, conventional life. I grew up wanting everything but that. Well, we have this in common: neither of us got exactly what we wanted. And we have something else in common, too, perhaps—*perhaps*—perhaps we'll both end up being ex-wives of Charlie's.

Is it the children—having small children—that is causing the trouble? I think that's a great part of it. And I wanted these children so. But it's disturbing to think that my marriage to Charlie could end for the same reasons as Adelaide's. No, there's more to it than that. Still, on rainy Sundays here when Charlie and I can't make love or go to an art museum or a nice restaurant together because we have these small, still uncivilized children hanging on our arms, I wonder about Charlie's marriage with Adelaide. Mothersuckers, a friend of mine calls her children. Mothersuckers. The name is appropriate. Children start in the womb and continue on the breast and wean themselves from milk onto one's entire life. Psychologists write of the importance of

14

bonding between mother and child; that word indicates ties, mutual physical entities such as ropes joining the two. A perhaps more suitable word would be *siphoning*. For at least the first seven years of life a child siphons off from his mother everything he can get: love, attention, food, warmth, words, touching, clothes, bouncing, a sense of identity. And so what if Adelaide had been, just like me, at that point in her life when it took all of her power to simply make it through the day, attached as she was by psychological suction cups to two voraciously siphoning creatures? So that she fell into bed with Charlie crying, "Oh, God, please just let me sleep!"; so that she screamed, distraught, "I don't care about your fucking faculty party, I'm too exhausted to go"; so that the only books she read were about duckies or bunnies or elves. Certainly that had to have been part of the reason she screamed so much and hated sex so much and was the bitchy crazy way she was. Although Caroline and Cathy were eight and five when Charlie divorced Adelaide, she was past that exhausting stage when there's never a good night's sleep and one's arms ache from carrying heavy damp bodies.

I don't know. Perhaps it wasn't the children who caused the separation between Charlie and Adelaide; Adelaide always needed her children so much, they provided her with an identity. Those first few years when the girls came to visit us for the summer, Adelaide would call Charlie long distance and sob, "I miss my babies so much I can't stand it. Oh, why

15

have you taken my little girls from me?" Caroline and Cathy, then ten and seven, used to silently slip into the front hall coat closet during such a phone call, and they would sit there hugging each other and huddling together amid the safety of the coats and rubber boots. Charlie would have to coax them out with promises of ice cream cones or new toys, and he'd try to explain for the hundredth time why Daddy and Mommy weren't living together and how it was better for them all this way and that their mother really would not die of missing them.

But she did almost die of missing them. They were all she had; they meant everything to her. I am certain that I love my children as much as she loves hers, and yet God knows I wouldn't want to die if someone would take Adam and Lucy away from me for a few weeks. I'd love it; I'd just sit and stare at the walls and soak in the silence. A curious thought: I've spent so much time in my life—the thirteen years I've been married to Charlie—taking care of Adelaide's children. I really tried my best to keep her children healthy and happy when they were with us, and I still care about their happiness. Wouldn't it be only fair for Adelaide to repay me, to take my children off my hands for a while? Oh, wouldn't it be heaven if she could repay me a bit, if I could ship Adam and Lucy off for a week, knowing they'd get orange juice and hamburgers and be made to brush their teeth and be treated like treasures and taken to movies and the zoo! Margaret Mead, let's redefine "extended family"!

Oh, all this Finnish rain is making me nuts. What foolish thoughts. Adelaide hates me, at least she used to, at least Caroline and Cathy told me she did. I could never understand why. I thought she should like me, be grateful. I always worked so hard, trying to keep her daughters healthy and happy when they were with us. As a matter of fact, I think she ought to write me a thank-you note sometime before we both die. Why not? We've never spent five minutes talking with each other, and yet we've both influenced each other's lives. Adelaide, do it: write me a thank-you note for all that I've done for your daughters.

And I'll write you one, too. For when all is said and done, I'm glad that Charlie married you so that your two daughters could be in this world. I'm glad you had children with Charlie. I'm glad I had stepchildren.

And that's saying a lot. I've come a long, hard way, thirteen years of bare feet on broken glass, to reach that point of view.

Yet it is both more and less than that. With step-parenting, as with most daily life, trivial actions cause melodramatic reactions. I wish my step-daughters were here with me now in Finland because often in the past we have had so much fun together, but at least once in my life I have quite thoroughly wished them dead, really dead, and if they were here now we might possibly not have any fun at all. We've gone through so many variations, Charlie's daughters and I. Nothing is simple, nothing stays. Our relationship is never pure and clear and free.

Perhaps it's all because of me. Perhaps it all has something to do with the fact that originally I am a Methodist from Kansas. Undoubtedly people who were raised in New England or California handle it better, have more fun and less misery with divorce and stepping. Over the years I've collected stories from stepparents; I've listened to stepparents with full attention, hoping that their lives would cast some light on my own situation. I know one step-mother who calls her stepson a goddamned asshole to his face (he's fifteen) and who won't let him in her house, and she is clear and righteous and doesn't fret or feel guilty about that. I know another couple who are friends with and regularly visit the wife's former husband and his new wife, and the man's children and the wife's children are all close enough in age to play football or croquet on the lawn while the four grown-ups sit on the patio and gossip and drink. But I also know a woman whose ex-husband has married a young girl who locks the children in their rooms for hours when she gets angry, and hits them when she gets very angry, and I know another stepmother who simply goes off traveling by herself every summer when her hus-band's children visit so that she won't have to come in contact with them.

In comparison it seems that I haven't been such a bad stepmother after all, certainly not a wicked or evil one. Stepmothers have had such bad publicity; I always identified with Snow White or Cinderella

18

instead of their stepmothers. I wasn't prepared for the role; I didn't choose it.

And that is where I'm at now: this matter of choice. As a good female Methodist from Kansas, I was not trained in choosing for myself. As I look back at my life, it seems that I spent a lot of time accepting what drifted my way, making not-choosing a way of life. This leaves me oddly crippled and very irritable now that I'm at a point where I must make a choice. How did I get to be where I am? What am I going to be? What am I doing in Helsinki, for heaven's sake, thinking of my stepchildren while my own children are out at the Park Auntie's, catching colds in the Finnish drizzle? Is everyone's life composed of such crazily disparate elements? I don't know. I don't know. I think I'll fix myself some Maalva rose hip tea and stare out the window and think of the past. I feel I must know what kind of woman I've been in order to know what kind I am going to be.

I was born and raised in Kansas; that much is simple and easily understood and dispatched. I love my parents, they love me, we write and call each other often. Because they are so busy in their own professions now, they found it easy to let me go, but when I was a child they coddled me, took care that I led a protected and untraumatic life. The one fine good choice I made, if choosing to marry the person one has fallen hopelessly and passionately in love with can be called a choice, was the choice to marry

Charlie. Where Charlie and I are concerned, things are wonderfully clear and good. It is only when children get involved—his children, our children—that things become confused.

Charlie and I were married on a brilliant September day in 1964. He was thirty-six; I was twenty-one. He was a professor and a historian; I was a student. We moved to Kansas City, Missouri, where he taught at the university and I finished my B.A. We bought a house, so small and quaint it could have been a doll's house, located in one of the nicest areas of town, within walking distance of the university. We divided those first few idyllic months of our marriage between the university, our city dollhouse, and the farm.

The farm—we called it that—was not really a farm. No one farmed it, nothing profitable grew on it. It was one hundred acres of rough, rocky Missouri Ozarks land, with small mountains covered with scrub oak and pine and spruce and dogwood and a large open valley sloping down from the mountains to a six-acre pond fed by a rushing stream. We had to drive two hours from Kansas City to get to the farm, and we had to cross a little bridge over the rushing stream to officially enter our property, and so the stream seemed magic, a symbolic entrance, purging us and cleansing us and separating us from anything we did not like.

There was a house there, built by Charlie's parents as a vacation home, and the approach to the house was a circle drive around an enormous oak

20

tree. The house itself was not much to look at, but it was easy and comfortable to live in, with a big living room that had a rock fireplace to keep us cozy in winter and a large screened-in porch to protect us from the myriad insects that buzzed through the humid Ozark summers. There were two small bedrooms and a large bed-sofa in the living room, and a tiny but usable bathroom.

Best of all, the house was really ours. That is, it had never, ever, belonged to Charlie-and-Adelaide. Charlie's parents had made the farm their permanent home a few years after Charlie and Adelaide married, and because the parents didn't care much for Adelaide, and because Adelaide didn't care at all for farms, Charlie and his first wife had spent only three or four nights of their eight years of marriage there. Right after Charlie divorced Adelaide, his father had a stroke and died, and his mother moved back to the small Missouri town she'd grown up in, and the farm became Charlie's. He had sold off some land to give the profits to an older brother who lived in California and never came to Missouri but felt cheated by Charlie's having received the farm, and after that everyone was satisfied. I did some wallpapering and redecorating, and made sure that Charlie and I slept in the room that his parents had had, and sold the perfectly good beds from the guest room, which Charlie and Adelaide had slept on, and fixed that room up sort of for Charlie's girls and sort of for any guest. The house was *ours,* Charlie's-and-mine. Adelaide's ghost was not any-

21

where about. Caroline and Cathy didn't remember visiting it.

The farmland was even more ours, or perhaps, since land never belongs to any one person, but remains solidly, placidly, firmly its own, I should say that the land was even dearer to us. It was rocky, craggy, rough-cut land, the kind that causes you to stumble when you walk. It was populated by rattlesnakes and water moccasins and copperheads, and coyotes and cougars and wolves as well as deer roamed the woods, and although I never saw a live one, a dog once brought me the skeleton, complete with dried canvaslike wings, of an enormous bat, so bats must have lived there, too. The beautiful oak and pine trees mothered poison oak and poison ivy and supported vines as thick and hairy and solid as an ape's arm. There were spiders in the grass and mice and rats in the old barn and muskrats in the pond and God knows what else everywhere. But in all our years there no one was ever bitten by a snake or spider, no one ever caught poison oak or poison ivy, no one was ever hurt there at all. The place was charmed. The property we owned was shaped like a hand when it's cupped, with one large mountain behind and one low side where the stream rushed, and the bright blue pond gleaming in the middle. All possible sorts of birds lived there: robins, sparrows, bluejays, cardinals, owls, egrets, herons, hawks, crows, doves, bobolinks, pheasants, quail, and especially whippoorwills. Every morning, spring through fall, they called across the valley to each other, comically, compulsively, hauntingly, welcoming us to day, lullabying us into night. The place was charmed.

And our horses were there. When we married, along with my other possessions, I brought Liza, my six-year-old quarter horse mare. My parents had given her to me for my sixteenth birthday, when I was furiously in love with horses, and I had boarded her at a farm a good half hour's drive from my house. It was a delight to have her there on our farm, where I could ride her first thing in the morning, last thing at night. Charlie bought himself a quarter horse gelding, a bigger, showier horse, and we spent hours riding together through the woods and over the meadows, hours of silent rocking joy.

The first nine months of our marriage were perfectly happy. Perfectly. During the week I had my studies and the movies, ballets, concerts, theater that Kansas City offered, and on the weekends and long holidays I had the farm. And I had Charlie, Charlie, Charlie, big, blond, strong, brilliant, fierce-bodied Charlie, all to myself. I adored him. I loved him. I believed we would be eternally happy.

Charlie's daughters came to stay with us the last day of June, 1965. Their mother didn't want them to come, and they didn't want to come, and although I had never met them I wasn't crazy about having them either, but of course, loving Charlie, I said nothing. But Charlie wanted his daughters with him for a while, and it was a legally arranged agreement that Caroline and Catherine Campbell were to spend every summer with their father. Legalities

23

are by and large a bore and a hassle, but they do have the effect of being rigidly, simply clear right at the time that human emotions tend to be soggy and mushy and confused.

Early in June, Charlie sent a letter with his monthly child-support check, asking Adelaide when it would be best for him to make plane reservations for Caroline and Cathy. Adelaide had after the divorce moved back to Massachusetts to a town near Amherst. They—she and Charlie and their daughters—had lived there for several years while Charlie taught at the university, and Adelaide had friends there, and knew she could get a job as a secretary at the university.

Adelaide's reply to Charlie's letter was brief: since the girls were so small, she wrote, so young, she thought it would be better if they did not make a long plane trip this year, which after all would involve changing planes alone in Chicago. Perhaps next year it would be possible.

Charlie stomped and raged for a day. Since his divorce it had been obvious that Adelaide was not going to be cooperative. When he sent the girls gifts, he did not receive any sign that the girls had gotten them. When he wrote them letters, there was never any reply. When he called them on the phone, it was usually lunchtime or bathtime or bedtime; and anyway, he was cruel and malicious, Adelaide said, to call them at all; it upset them so much. At Christmas, Charlie had flown back to New York to some convention and delivered a paper there, then

24

taken a day to drive to Hadley to give the girls their Christmas gifts and to take them out to dinner. Since Christmas, Charlie had not had any word from Adelaide or his daughters except for the canceled child-support checks. He had called Caroline in February and Cathy in March to be sure they had received their birthday presents, and the girls had said yes, thank you, but not much else. Charlie said that at Christmas the girls had been subdued, even timid with him, not touching, not talking, hanging back, but when he had gotten in the car to leave they had both burst into tears and little Cathy had run to him through the snow to throw her arms about him, to beg him not to go away again. Since then he had been eager for summer, to have his daughters with him for a long period of time, to reestablish the contact, to try to reaffirm his love.

He was furious at Adelaide's letter, and incredulous that she thought she could keep the girls from him, and hurt that she would want to do so. That night, full of righteous indignation, he called Adelaide on the phone. And got hit with a hurricane punch of hatred and fury.

Of course, she was unhappy, and she was having problems. It is not easy to be divorced and alone with two small children and have to work when all you've ever wanted to do was to stay home and be a mother. Women's lib came unfortunately late for Adelaide. That summer her closest friends were moving away and she had not yet met a man she liked who liked her, and all in all, it was one of those years when nothing, *nothing* was going right. As she said, the girls were all she had; how could Charlie take them from her when she needed them so?

Charlie was unprepared for the fury and the noise and the grief. He sat stunned, saying into the phone, "But—but—but—" I sat next to him, fascinated. I had never seen anything like it except for comic routines on television, where the comedian makes a face and holds the phone away from his car and a high, shrill, senseless voice babbles on and on and on.

The gist of it was: if Charlie really loved Caroline and Cathy, he wouldn't have left them in the first place. Since he had left them, he didn't love them. She, Adelaide, had done her very best to help the girls realize that their father did not love them and that they would be happier without him, just as he was so happy without them. They had managed to start a new life with new friends, and it was absolutely evil of him to try to take the little girls away from a house where they finally felt secure and loved, from a place where they had friends. The little girls had gone through enough pain and heartbreak, they didn't need any more. The three of them were happy together, a real family, and it wasn't fair for him to separate them.

Charlie said, when he could find a space, that he loved the girls and he wanted them to be with him as arranged and he would call his lawyer. He hung up the phone.

Five minutes later it rang. When Charlie answered it, Caroline, his older daughter, was on the line. She was sobbing.

"Daddy," she cried, "please don't take us away from Mommy. We can't live without Mommy. Mommy can't live without us. Please don't make us go there. We don't want to live with you and that lady. We want to stay with Mommy."

And before Charlie could respond, Adelaide was on the phone again. "See! See what I mean! That was your own daughter begging you to leave her alone. I know you don't care what *I* want, but surely your own daughters' feelings mean something, that is if you love them at all. And poor little Cathy's right here next to me crying her eyes out; she can't even talk she's so upset—"

"Adelaide," Charlie said, "I want my girls to spend two months with me this summer. I'm going to hang up now and call my lawyer."

And he did.

Two weeks and two hundred and fifty dollars' worth of lawyer's fees and long-distance phone calls and registered letters later his girls arrived.

Those two weeks were a strange and wonderful and terrible time for me. Charlie confided to me things I had never known before about his first marriage, and if I was relieved at his lack of love for Adelaide, I was worried about and jealous of his great love for his daughters. They had always been Adelaide's "property," Charlie said. Things had been clear-cut for Adelaide: work was his, the house and children were hers. She wouldn't tell him how to teach history or do research if he wouldn't tell her how to raise children. He had actually felt that he might be able to get closer to his girls, to influence their lives more, to give them more affection, if he were living away from them, if he and Adelaide were divorced.

He asked me to help him. He had two large, important projects to do that summer, projects he had gotten grant money for, and we needed extra money because of phone calls and legal fees and round-trip plane fares across half the continent. He asked me to help entertain and take care of his daughters, to make them feel wanted, to make them happy.

I wanted to do more than that. I decided to devote my summer completely to the happiness of Charlie and his girls. I decided that I would keep them healthy, I would keep them entertained, I would keep them uproariously, overwhelmingly happy. They would go back to Massachusetts saying that Charlie was the most wonderful father in the world, and that they had had the happiest summer of their lives, and that I was the most beautiful, wonderful, delightful, intelligent, creative, warmhearted creature that had ever lived, a sort of combination Madonna and Barbie doll. I didn't know what I was getting into.

Caroline and Cathy arrived on the last day of June, and after the drama of it all, their pale little presences were pretty drab. They were to turn out to be stunningly beautiful women, but of course we didn't know that at the time, and it certainly didn't show. Caroline was ten and had buck teeth. Real, obvious buck teeth. But at least she tried to be intelligent and interesting; because she thought she was ugly, she tried to be smart. Cathy, on the other hand, was pretty, in the same classic helpless dumbblonde baby-doll way her mother was, and as a result she often seemed, although she definitely was not, stupid. What a pair they were! Two pale startled little girls, wearing light blue summer dresses, clean white shoes and socks, white gloves. The sight of them, physically real and *there,* filled me with consternation; in a flash I realized that from now on my life with Charlie would be changed, would be confused. I wanted to be nice; I smiled. But for a moment I could not move. It did not matter. Charlie, overjoyed to see his daughters, rushed to hug them to him. And he brought them back to introduce us, and then I was able to move, a hand, a foot, everything, and my new life had begun. I was walking out of the airport with my husband and his children. In the car on the way home from the airport Caroline and Cathy sat in the front seat with Charlie while I sat alone in the back.

I think we were all stunned that first week. I know I certainly was. Immediately after we arrived home, Caroline fished a thick sealed envelope out of her suitcase and handed it to me, carefully, so that her fingers did not touch mine.

"This is for you," she said, not looking me in the eyes. "It's from my mother."

"What in the world?" I said, and stared down at the envelope as if it were a toad. What Adelaide might want to send me was frighteningly beyond the reach of my imagination.

"It's a list of the foods we like to eat," Caroline said.

"I'll show the girls their room and the rest of the house," Charlie said. "You sit down and read the letter, Zelda." His mouth was twitching with a smile.

Dutifully I sat down in the living room and opened the letter.

"Zelda," it began, and I thought, Well, of course, I didn't think she would call me dear . . .

As you know, I am very much opposed to this visit. My daughters are extremely fragile both emotionally and physically, and they have been further injured by all the changes so cruelly inflicted upon them. I am therefore sending you these instructions, which must be followed to the letter, so that my little girls will be returned to me with the minimum of psychological damage.

1. Basic nutrition.

For breakfast, every day, they must have: a full glass of whole milk, a small glass of fresh orange juice, a small bowl of cereal with sugar, two pieces of toast, and one egg, preferably poached or soft-boiled. They may be permitted sweet rolls if they eat their eggs.

For lunch they must have soup, a sandwich, preferably meat, but peanut butter if necessary, a fresh fruit such as an apple or pear, a full glass of whole milk, and potato chips IF they eat their fruit.

For dinner they must have a large serving of a

GOOD meat, not just hot dogs or pizza. They must have liver and some kind of fish at least once a week. Steak, lean hamburger, chicken, or well-cooked pork will also do. Two vegetables with each meal. A salad of fresh lettuce. A potato or rice. A glass of whole milk. Their dessert should be something wholesome, like a milk pudding or custard, and Jell-O with fruit.

At bedtime they may have hot chocolate with cinnamon toast.

They must have vitamin pills. I have packed the bottle that I bought with my own money; if they run out while they are there, they are to have CHEWAMINS and nothing else because that is the only kind they like.

They are not to be stuffed with sweets and candy and cookies.

If they have trouble with constipation, they are to eat raisins before going to bed.

They must eat ON SCHEDULE, breakfast by eight, lunch by noon, and dinner at 5:30, or their digestive systems will be upset.
Cook and serve the food in an attractive and appealing manner so they will want to eat it.

2. Sleep and rest.

They must be in bed by ten o'clock at night, NO LATER, and they should be allowed to sleep as late as they want to every morning since it is school vacation.

After lunch they should have a rest period. It is

31

not necessary that they sleep, but they should lie down or sit quietly for an hour. This is necessary to their health.

3. Other Health Care.
They must brush their teeth three times a day. Only Crest toothpaste is allowed. If they don't brush their teeth, they can't have cinnamon toast. They must have a bath every other day, and if they go swimming in a public swimming pool, they must have a shower immediately afterward. Their hair should be washed once a week with Johnson's Baby Shampoo. They will need some help from you with this.

They must wash their hands every time after using the toilet and before and after dinner. Also after petting any animal.

Their nails should be clipped once a week.

If it is necessary for them to use a public toilet, it is necessary that you first line the toilet seat with fresh toilet paper so that their skin makes no contact with the seat.

If the girls get sick, they should drink fluids and take aspirin—orange-flavored baby aspirin—but they may not take any medication from a strange doctor without my permission.

IF EITHER GIRL GETS EVEN SLIGHTLY SICK I AM TO BE NOTIFIED AT ONCE NO MATTER DAY OR NIGHT.

4. General.
They are not to do any of your housework for you.

Do not take them to see movies which might have violence or anything sad; they are delicate, and anything like that will upset them dreadfully. The same with TV.

If they go swimming, they must be supervised at all times.

They are not to be left with a baby-sitter.

When riding in a car they must wear seat belts.

If they want to call me at any time of the day or night, they are to be allowed to call me. They are to call me every Wednesday night at six so that I can see if they are all right.

They are not to play with boys.

I have sent all their clothes freshly washed and ironed and expect them to be returned in the same fashion. They are to put on clean underwear and clean clothes every morning. Their nightgowns must be washed once a week.

They are not to go barefoot. They might cut their feet on glass or something.

THEY MUST NOT BE YELLED AT OR MISTREATED IN THE SLIGHTEST WAY. They are very good little girls, and never do anything wrong, so they should not ever be punished. They are wonderful, sweet, very precious, fragile children and must be treated as such at all times.

Adelaide.

I finished the letter just as Charlie reappeared in the living room, one fragile, precious pale blonde daughter on each side of him. I stared at them a moment, horror-struck. Nails clipped, I thought, liver, seat belts, vitamins, clean pajamas. I can't handle this.

I must have looked as awful as I felt, for Charlie crossed the room and took the letter from me. He read it quickly, his twitching mouth breaking open into a genuine smile. Then he crumpled the letter into a ball.

"You've read it," he said. "Now forget it."

But I couldn't forget it. The letter had the unmistakable mark of authority on it. If Charlie hadn't thrown it away, I think I would have taped it on the kitchen doors so that I could reread it morning and night. I wanted desperately to do everything right.

It was difficult, the first day or two. The girls had to learn that their flesh would not instantly rot off if I touched them. I learned all about daytime television shows for children. Charlie learned that the girls were really afraid of him, that he would have to regain their trust. Those first few days were completely given over to wooing the girls. We took them to Walt Disney movies, to the zoo, to parks. I had saved all my grocery stamps for nine months and gave them all to the girls, who happily pasted them in the books; then I drove them to the store to exchange the stamps for whatever they wanted. Predictably, their mother's daughters, they chose baby dolls. The stamps were a big hit. We took them to get ice cream cones, we took them shopping. We spoke to them gently, we smiled all the time.

With all the treats and ice cream cones and new toys and Charlie's persistent gentle love and my good-natured friendliness, it went very well. The girls opened up a bit, they stopped answering questions with monosyllabic mumbles and moved right along to complete sentences. But then there were the phone calls from Adelaide.

Now I do not think that Adelaide meant to be divisive; I think that first summer she simply could not help herself. The first night the girls were with us it was only natural that she should call to see if they had arrived safely. Charlie put the girls on the phone, one upstairs in the bedroom and one downstairs in the kitchen, to let them talk to their mother. But after a few minutes, when tears were rolling down Caroline's cheeks and we could hear Cathy openly sobbing upstairs, Charlie took the phone away from Caroline. He sent me upstairs to take the phone away from Cathy, and before I could get the receiver down I heard Adelaide screech:

"*Damn* you! God damn you! How can you take my babies from me? I'm all alone here; they're not in their beds. How do you expect me to make it through the night?"

Charlie talked with Adelaide for an hour that night, trying to calm her down, while the girls hid in the coat closet, crying. Later, years later, Caroline told me that she and Cathy had hidden in coat closets long before that year, hiding away from the sounds of their mother and father fighting. It even became a catchphrase for the girls; in their teens they would say, "When I saw Bob at the movies with Annie, I just wanted to run into a coat closet and cry." That first year, that first night, I tried to coax the girls out, but they only cried harder, so finally I shut the door and left them alone. What an introduction to stepping: the two of them in the closet, and Charlie talking soothingly to his first wife on the phone, and me sitting on the front porch step, watching a lovely summer evening slide away.

Eventually Charlie hung up the phone and got the girls out of the closet and held them and soothed them and we all went out for ice cream, which Cathy ended up throwing up all over the bedroom floor and which I sweetly cleaned up. It was that night, that very moment, that I had my first moment of stepping bitterness— She's *your* daughter, I thought, *you* clean up her vomit. But Charlie was rocking Cathy and giving her sips of 7-Up and we had all had enough drama for the night.

The pattern was set. The days went by pleasantly, so that we all felt friendly by night, and then Adelaide's calls would come and shatter everything. Already I've promised myself that if Charlie and I are divorced and Adam and Lucy go off to stay with him, I'll bring in a lover or go stay with a friend or drink myself into oblivion, anything rather than experience and cause such pain.

On Thursday night Charlie told Adelaide he was taking the girls on a little trip and he would have them call her once a week, on Wednesday nights, as she had suggested. And on Friday morning we all left for the farm. That day rushed by, busy with unpacking and buying supplies and giving the girls horseback rides (very short horseback rides; they were afraid of horses) and walking with them to the pond (which they wouldn't swim in because it might contain snakes or bugs or worms or fish). And suddenly it was Saturday morning, and I was fixing breakfast in my pajamas, and Anthony and June Leyden arrived.

The Leydens were old friends of Charlie's, of Charlie-and-Adelaide's. Anthony was handsome, and clever, and irritatingly brilliant. He taught at the same university, in the same department, with Charlie. In fact he had been instrumental in getting Charlie his job. He was really Charlie's friend. But not mine. First of all, he didn't take Charlie-and-me seriously enough. I felt strongly, seriously in love with Charlie, and Anthony kept making lewd remarks about both of us and trying to feel me up whenever Charlie was out of the room.

And I didn't like June, Anthony's wife, or what Anthony and his wife represented together. Anthony by himself could be gay and clever and funny, but his wife was so prettily, properly, righteously solemn that together they seemed the embodiment of Marriage, Property, Children. Everything tidy, approved of by church and state, locked up.

I had met June several times before Charlie and I were married, and each time was a trial. June had been, and still was, by letter, a close friend of Adelaide's, and even though I hadn't met Charlie until after Adelaide and Charlie's separation, June still disapproved of me, still insisted on casting me in the role of homewrecker. If I saw her, in her dust-free house with her two coy children and her electric washer and dryer and blender and floor buffer, with her small print cotton housedresses and ruffled aprons, as a real-life Leave It to Beaver's mother sort of woman, she certainly saw me, with my long hair and my lack of interest in housey things and my hands all over Charlie, as a sort of Wicked Woman. I thought she was pompous, and she thought I was frivolous, and I suppose we were both right. I was still in a sorority before I married Charlie, I was concerned with insignificant things, such as our sorority's competitive skit for Hippodrome rather than with improving the city's elementary schools.

Now I know: children do weigh one down, one does become responsible, one can no longer do whatever one likes at any moment. Compared to her, I *was* frivolous. But still, looking back most generously, I think she was purposely unkind to me. She saw me as an enemy, a threat. Back then I thought she was a bitch. In the earliest days, just before Charlie and I married, she was forever, certainly intentionally, irritating me.

"Charlie!" she would cry when she saw us together. *"Dear Charlie,"* she'd say, kissing him on the check, totally ignoring me, *"how* are you?" And she'd stare at him with a sympathetic sweetness, as if recognizing his secret sorrow at having to be with me and not with Adelaide.

Or, "Oh, Charlie," she'd laugh, "remember what a great time you and Adelaide and your girls had with us last year when we went on that picinic?"

Or, "Yes, this bread is delicious, isn't it. It's Adelaide's recipe. She is the *best* cook."

Or, "Yes, my children are sweet, aren't they. But then, all children are beautiful. They're the living product of a man and woman's eternal abiding love for one another."

Or, pulling Charlie aside, in stage whispers, "I saw Adelaide today. She's gotten her hair cut and she looks like a new woman. You really ought to stop by and see her; you'd be delighted, I know."

After Charlie and I were married and Adelaide and her girls moved to Massachusetts, June's attitude didn't change. If anything, she became even sterner and less open to me, as if trying to be the messenger of Adelaide's bitterness.

Back then—it seems so long ago, so much has changed—things were really different for women, especially for Kansas women. Adelaide and June were closed into a way of life which meant only husband, home, and children. I was ten or twelve years younger than they (and my mother and grandmothers had all gone to college and held vaguely liberated philosophies); I wanted something different from what they had. I was their enemy, openly announcing that I did not think their way of life significant, satisfying, enough for me. And in a way they were my enemies: specters of what I could be if I once forgot to take my Pill, if I bought a fondue pot or looked at fabric samples. I intended to get a Ph.D., to teach at university level, and I was as eager as any man to read everything, to sharpen my wits in stimulating conversation. Charlie, who had been smothered by routinized domestic life, loved the crazy way we lived, eating at least half of our meals out at all times of the day and night, doing the laundry and cleaning together or ignoring it, making love or horseback riding instead of looking at furniture or rugs or chairs. But when we were with Anthony and June, I was never comfortable. I didn't want to listen to her recipes or stories of children's illnesses or cutenesses. I wanted to be talking with Charlie and Anthony, not with her. We had nothing to say to each other.

Back then things seemed black and white. I did not like June; she did not like me. But I did not protest when Charlie invited Anthony and his family down to the farm on that first Saturday. I suppose I thought that the presence of Charlie's girls in *our* home with me cooking for everyone and flitting about being sweet would make me more acceptable in June's eyes. Charlie cared a great deal for Anthony and tolerated June. I wanted the Leydens to like me. No, I wanted them to love me. I wanted them to think I was absolutely wonderful. I wanted them to bless Charlie-and-me. I should have had more practice at cheerfully flitting. We should have waited a few more weeks to invite Anthony and June down.

It went bad right from the start. We four were all just out of bed, stumbling around the kitchen yawning and trying to wake up, when Charlie saw the Leydens' car crossing the entrance to the farm.

"Holy cow," Charlie said. "There're Anthony and June. They're here already. Can you believe it? Hold the fort, Zelda. I'll go on out and meet them."

"June and Anthony?" I said, panicked. I wasn't prepared for them yet, not at all. "Are you sure it's their car? Oh, Lord, I'm not even dressed. Okay, go on out Charlie, stall them, and I'll—Caroline, would you please watch at the window and be sure Mr. Leyden shuts the gate so the horses don't get out? Cathy, would you make some more toast? I've got to get dressed."

"Squeak, squeak . . ." Cathy said.

"Sorry, Cathy, I didn't hear what you said." I paused halfway into the bedroom.

"I said I don't know how to make toast," Cathy said, staring at the tablecloth.

"Oh well, that's easy, honey. You're seven years old; it's time to learn. Just stick two pieces of bread in those little slots and push the red button down. When it pops up, take it out and butter it. That's all there is to it. Oh, Lord, they're getting out of the car. I've got to go get my clothes on and comb my—"

"Squeak, squeak . . ." Cathy whispered.

"What did you say, Cathy?" Unbuttoning my pajamas, I came back into the kitchen.

"I said I might do it wrong," Cathy said.

"Oh, honey, no one can go wrong making toast,"

41

I told her. "Just stick the bread in and push the lever down. I've got to get—"

"Squeak, squeak . . ."

"What?" I was ready to scream. I could see the Leydens approaching the house with Charlie.

"I might burn my hands. Mother says I must be very careful in the kitchen or I'll burn my hands."

"Oh, Cathy, oh dear, burn your hands, oh wow. Look, Cathy, it's simple. You won't burn your hands, I promise. Just put those two pieces of bread—oh no, Cathy, are you crying because I want you to make toast? Cathy—"

At that point the Leydens came into the house. Anthony took one look at me and began to laugh. He was in fine spirits for so early in the morning. Behind him June stared on with pleased disapproval.

"Oh, happy days!" Anthony yelled at me. "Oh, joy supreme! A sight I never thought I'd be blessed to see, Zelda Campbell in shorty pajamas. You've got great legs, Zelda, but I must admit I'm disappointed in your taste. Blue and white striped pajama shirt with red elbow patches? *Not* very sexy. I would have thought some lace or see-through or at least a ribbon; you haven't been married even a year yet. What are brides coming to these days? I know, they're coming to their husbands, yuk, yuk—"

"Hello, Anthony. Hello, June," I said, trying to look respectable in my unbuttoned pajamas. "These are old college pajama party pajamas. Excuse me, I'm going to run get dressed, and Charlie, you'd better find Cathy and console her. She ran to her

42

room crying. I tried to make her make toast."

"AHA!" Anthony shouted. "The wicked step-mother strikes again!"

Nearly in tears, I smiled wildly at the Leydens and escaped into the bedroom and shut the door tight behind me. Then I leaned against it and took deep breaths and tried not to cry. I didn't want to cry; I wanted to be poised. I wanted to be perfect. But it was only eight o'clock in the morning, and already I felt that my day, my week, my summer, had been ruined. I wanted so much for Charlie's girls and Charlie's friends to like me, to think I was a good and capable person. And the farm was too dear a place to have unpleasant things happen on it.

And after all, what *had* happened? I had appeared before Charlie's pompous friends in unbuttoned shorty pajamas. I had asked a seven-year-old girl to make toast. Neither of those things was disastrous, I decided; surely I was taking this all too hard. I stopped shaking and got dressed. I brushed my hair and gave myself a quick snappy lecture: You're a big girl now, I said to myself, and those people out there are after all only human. It's all going to be fine. I smiled at myself in the mirror. Then I came out of the bedroom, ready to shine.

Charlie and Anthony were pouring coffee and talking at one end of the big room; June was sitting on the sofa at the other end. She had both Caroline and Cathy snuggled up against her and she was saying, even though neither one was crying, "Don't

43

cry, sweeties. It will be *all right*. I know how hard it is for you to be away from your mommy. Remember, if you ever need me, you can call me, anytime. Caroline, you can dial the telephone, can't you? You're big enough to find my number in the phone book. We're the only Leyden listed. L-E-Y-D-E-N."

When I entered the room I felt a sudden wave of doubt wash over me, as if I were in the wrong place. At one end of the room were the *men;* at the other end were the woman and girls; and I didn't fit in either place. Cathy stared up at me with accusing eyes, like a now safe child looking at a tormentor. No one else had seen our little scene, and it had happened so quickly I could scarcely remember it. It certainly hadn't seemed momentous enough to prolong in this way. *All I did was to ask her to make toast!* I wanted to yell. *Cut out the drama!*

Instead I tried to smile and walked over to June.

"There," I said, "I feel better in jeans. Sorry I wasn't dressed when you got here. Where are your children, June; did you bring them?"

"Of course," June said, not looking at me. "I wouldn't have them miss seeing Caroline and Cathy for the world. They ran right out to see the horses. Come on, sweetie pies, let's you and I go out and see Dickie and Dierdre. I can't wait to see you four darlings all playing together again, just like you did—*before*." And June rose, and still without looking at me, took each girl by the hand and led them out the door. Her back was eloquent, stiff, triumphant.

One thing June had, which Adelaide had also,

which compensated for the loss of other things, was a real sense of authority in all things having to do with children. That first year I quivered and wavered, not wanting to come on too strong and frighten the girls. I asked them too often what they wanted to eat or do, and since they were not used to making decisions they only stared and shrank back, and I was frustrated. June was a *mother,* and a real power emanated from her. I have often wondered if I as a mother appear as firmly confident as she did, a real steamroller of rightness. I don't *feel* that way.

Then I stood there, I don't know how long, feeling surprised, and in spite of myself, hurt. I couldn't understand why this woman would want to snub me now. I had been trying my best. I had apologized for not being dressed. I had asked about her children. I had smiled. And she had literally turned her back on me.

I longed to run to Charlie, to throw my arms around him, to say, "Would you please get that woman out of here, out of this house and off this farm!" But Anthony had already teased me about marrying a father figure. I was determined not to appear weak, not to lean on Charlie. And I did feel infinitely superior to June in spite of her snottiness; I was younger, slimmer, prettier, freer, smarter. Noblesse oblige. I could handle her; then I thought I could handle anything.

I went outside to the barnyard, where all the children were gathered, hanging on the fence, snapping their fingers and trying to get the horses to notice them.

"Who would like a ride?" I asked, and immediately June's two children began to yell:

"I would!"

"Me first!"

I saddled Liza, my horse, and gave first Dickie and then Dierdre rides; I kept the halter on the horse and led with a lead rope. It is not an exciting thing to walk around in huge figure eights and circles inside a barnyard with a strange child kicking frantically and screaming, "Giddy-yap! Giddy-yap!" But I continued to do it, feeling a perverse pleasure at the children's pleasure. I wanted to stick out my tongue at June and go "Nyaa, nyaa, ha-ha. I can make children happy, too!"

In a final fit of glory I took the saddle off and put all four children on Liza, and jumped bareback on the other buckskin, and opened the gate, and took the children for a long walk down to the pond and back. They giggled all the way, rolling and clutching each other, and they yelled, "Hi-ho, Silver, away!" and Anthony came out and took pictures, and June was left standing alone. Back at the barn, I gave both horses sugar and apples and felt like kissing them, and did.

Then Charlie announced that he was getting out the rowboat, and Anthony helped him carry it from the barn to the pond and the four children ran and skipped along behind. June had gone to the car and gotten a plastic sack full of wool and knitting needles and carried that solemnly down to the pond

46

with her. She sat at the bank, primly, knitting and reminding everyone in a voice as tiresomely patient as God's to please be careful because the children couldn't swim. Everyone had long boat rides, and Dickie and Dierdre tried to catch a frog and finally succeeded.

"Look, Mom, we caught a FROG!" Dickie yelled.

"Oh, wonderful, dear," June said. "But please put it down now. You might catch something dirty from it."

Anthony and Charlie went around in circles in the boat, arguing over some faculty issue, and the children splashed and screeched on the edge of the water and June knitted away righteously, mouth tight, not speaking to me. I sat in the sun watching for a while, then told Charlie I was going back to the house to make lunch.

I was excited about my lunch. I was eager to serve it. It was my first official lunch-with-guests. I had chosen to serve what the snootiest sorority alums served at their summer luncheon parties: shrimp and avocado salad. Poppyseed rolls and butter. Fresh strawberries and whipped cream. I set the table on the screened porch beautifully, put a bouquet of wild flowers in the middle, and could hardly wait until everyone came up from the pond. I couldn't have—and wouldn't have if I could have—produced a baby on the spot to show June my heart was in the right place, but I *had* fixed a good meal. It seemed a symbolic under-taking, a peacemaking gesture. June would have no choice but to admit that the meal was good.

The avocados were perfect and ripe, sitting on beds of crisp lettuce, surrounded by a colorful group of tomatoes, hard-boiled eggs, and lemons, all ornately sliced. I wanted to photograph the damned things. There were wineglasses and chilled wine for the adults, 7-Up for the children. The rolls were warm in a basket covered with a cloth napkin. The wine rested in a huge stewpot (this was the farm, after all) full of ice. It was the most elegant meal I had yet prepared. It was an offering. I was agreeing to act like a woman, June's idea of a woman, to cook and serve and decorate, and to do it all with goodwill.

June came in first, and when I told her that lunch was ready, she marshaled the children into the bathroom to wash their hands and faces. Anthony and Charlie washed up at the kitchen sink, and then came out onto the porch.

"Wow!" Charlie said, surprised. "This looks fantastic." He pulled me into his arms and kissed me. He whispered into my ear, "Zelda, you are the greatest. I love you."

I leaned on him, soaking in his warmth and touch. In those early years I was an animal. I loved his touch more than anything else in the world; it meant everything to me. We had petted and kissed and stroked and held and rubbed and snuggled and licked each other day and night for nine months. But with the arrival of the girls, without speaking a word of agreement about it beforehand, we had declared a sort of hands-off moratorium. The only time Charlie held me that summer was when we were safe in bed in the middle of the night; no more ravenous screwing on the living room floor in broad daylight. And even in bed the lovemaking was not the same. We went about it more quietly, as if afraid we might shake the house and frighten the girls. During the day Charlie held Cathy or Caroline, not me. We bounced around and chatted gaily to each other like the very best of good clean friends. I went through the days filled with a sort of gay, rational, tolerable pain; at night my dreams were of being in my husband's arms.

So for one minute that Saturday I leaned against Charlie and he leaned against me, and we had to pull back suddenly and grin at each other in helpless acknowledgment of the sexual desire that surged between us.

As I pulled back from him I saw Cathy, coming onto the porch with her clean face and hands, staring at her father and me. And her eyes flashed an unmistakable message: "That's *my daddy*. Hands off. Leave him alone. I hate you. I'm going to get you for this."

I reeled back from Charlie, thinking I was going crazy. No seven-year-old could think that way, I thought then, not knowing seven-year-olds. I was surely being melodramatic; she was just a little girl, not something out of *The Bad Seed*. And I still believe she would not have tried to kill me even then. She just heartily wished I would disappear. Failing that, she wanted to hurt me. It was logical; I had hurt her.

We all gathered around the table and took our places and I waited for everyone to take the first delicious mouthful, and Cathy burst into tears. Within a minute she was into full-scale, uncontrollable sobbing.

"Cathy, what's wrong?" Charlie asked, reaching Cathy and taking her into his arms only a few seconds before junc lunged up from her seat and around the table.

"I *hate* shrimp!" Cathy cried. "Shrimp has sand in it and bones that taste like glass. And I hate that green thing, too. SHE NEVER FIXES ANYTHING GOOD TO EAT!"

After a stunned silence, with everyone staring at me in anticipation, I said, as calmly as I could, "Cathy, I fix exactly what your mother wrote me to fix you girls."

"Mother *never* makes us eat *liver*," Cathy wailed. "And never yucky old eggs for breakfast. She lets us eat Frosted Makes or Apple jacks. And never, never, never shrimp! Never, ever shrimp; it's yucky, yucky, YUCKY!" Cathy went off into another fit of crying.

Charlie finally carried Cathy into the other room. Caroline sat miserably looking at her plate, two tears slowly making their way down her cheeks. I later learned that whenever one sister cried the other one did, too.

June rose, unable to keep the glee from her voice, and said, "I was afraid something like this would happen. I have peanut butter in the car. You do have sandwich bread, don't you, Zelda?"

In the face of this woman who actually carried peanut butter in her car I could only acknowledge defeat. I didn't even have peanut butter in the *house*. I said yes, I did have bread, and I rose and got it and together we fixed peanut butter and jelly sandwiches for all four children. Eventually Charlie got Cathy calmed down and we all ended up at the table again. Charlie and Anthony said, "This is delicious," and June went so far as to say, "Yes, it's very nice," but the luncheon had been spoiled for me, and even the white wine didn't help. I felt that I'd been bad. I felt that Cathy was a brat. I felt that those two rotten minutes had somehow magnified themselves to reflect on and spoil the whole summer, certainly the whole day.

I wanted to tell Cathy to go away, to got out of my marriage, out of my life, off my farm.

But of course I didn't tell her that. One can't, not to a seven-year-old whom your husband loves. And after a long while I learned what I learned again with my own children: no matter how bad it gets with little children, there is always tomorrow, always another chance. The children are captives. They can't take back their fraternity pin or divorce you or disinherit you and kick you out of the house. They forgive as easily as they fall asleep, and they expect to be forgiven quickly, too.

I didn't know that then. I trudged through the rest of the day, and was delighted to see Anthony and June and their children leave that evening. Charlie and I sat outside with Caroline and Cathy, listening to the night sounds: frogs belching, birds twittering, creatures skittering in the bushes to bed, and the valiant whippoorwill serenading us all. I did dishes while Charlie put the girls to bed, and then I reluctantly went in to say good night.

Both girls looked so small and sweet in their thin cotton nightgowns, with their gold-stamp baby dolls tucked in bed next to them. I kissed Caroline on the forehead, and then Cathy, as I had done every night they had been with us. The air still seemed heavy, not relaxed, so (saying to myself sternly, *You're* the adult; *she's* the child!) I said, "I'm very sorry I fix things you don't like, Cathy. Why don't you and Caroline help me shop for the groceries from now on? You can tell me what you do like."

Cathy stared me in the eye. "Okay," she said grudgingly, not giving an inch. She didn't smile. "I want my daddy, not your food," her stony face seemed to say.

But Caroline, sitting up in her bed across from Cathy, suddenly volunteered, "Oh, Cathy is *always* picky about food, even at home. Mother says she's an exasperating child, and Gram says she'll never get a husband."

I felt as encouraged as if my sternest professor had just interrupted my presentation to say, "*Very* good point, Mrs. Campbell." I smiled. I relaxed.

"Well, I was a picky eater when I was young, too," I said. I sat down—on the far end—of Cathy's bed. "I never used to eat pineapple, but I love it now. But I don't think I'll ever love sweet potatoes."

"*I'll* never love spinach!" Caroline said, wriggling her nose and entire body with enthusiastic hate.

"And *I'll* never love onions!" Cathy piped up.

It seemed I had hit on a favorite topic. We sat for almost an hour that night, the two little girls and I, discussing gleefully turnips and coconut and cod liver oil, and other things that we would never love. I was secretly pleased that neither girl named me.

Charlie had to come in and break it up and insist that the girls go to sleep. I was glad. They had been getting silly—"*I'll* never love poop with mustard!"—but I hadn't known at that time that sometimes with little kids you have to stop silliness as quickly and firmly as letting down a garage door. For a while, wanting to please, not knowing how to escape, I had been their captive. But as I left the room I was content. At least, I thought, at least we're all friends now. At least there won't be any more of this sneaky fighting.

I had a lot to learn.

TWO

October third in Helsinki, Finland, and two rather remarkable things have happened. First, it snowed here today. Not heavily enough to cover the still green grass, but enough, with the wind, to make walking the children to the Park Auntie's very uncomfortable. I felt guilty leaving them there, especially since Lucy has a cold, but they were so glad to be outside, running around, getting dirty, that I had to let them stay. It was best for the children in all ways, I decided: they need to be outside, and I love—thrive on—this short time alone in the apartment. Sometimes I write letters or scribble in these little children's workbooks which I found at the grocery store, sometimes I do housework, always I do laundry in the tiny machine in the bathroom and hang it to dry on our two-foot-square balcony or on the cords strung above our tub. And always I think, think, think. When Charlie and Adam and Lucy are here, I shut part of my mind off and act like a good wife and mother. Only when I'm alone do I open that secret door and let my fantasies and desires clash and clatter with my reason.

The second remarkable thing that happened today is that I received a long-distance phone call. The overseas operator had an accent, and I kept misunderstanding, kept saying, "No, no, Dr. Campbell is not here now," before I realized with a jolt that the call was for me.

"Zelda?" It was Stephen's voice coming as clear as if he were in the next room instead of thousands of miles away. "Zelda? Is that you? Is Charlie there? Can you talk?"

"Yes, *yes*," I cried when I managed to get my breath back. "I mean, yes, it's me; no, Charlie's not here; yes, I can talk. Why are you calling? Is something wrong?" And I suddenly had a vision of our beautiful old farmhouse, now rented to a visiting mathematician, in flames.

"No, no, everything's all right. Everything's fine. I just miss you. I miss you terribly. Zelda, this won't work. It's all wrong.

A surge of joy passed through me at the words, and I felt wonderfully warm, wonderfully happy. And oddly triumphant, too: I hadn't missed Stephen at all these past three weeks. I had thought about him during the times I unlocked the crazy closet in my mind, but I hadn't missed him desperately, I hadn't pined.

"Oh, Stephen, I miss you, too," I said. "But we agreed—nine months is not a very long time to think over such a major change in all our lives—"

"Nine months is *too* long," Stephen said. "Nine weeks is too long. I don't need to think anymore. I know exactly what I want. I want you."

"Oh, Stephen, think of Ellen. Think of Charlie; he's your friend. Think of all the children—"

"They'd survive, we'd all survive. There'd be a month or so of crying and screaming, and then life would continue as usual. Can't you see that it's worse this way, living with Charlie and Ellen when we love each other?"

"But I can't do it now, Stephen, I just can't. I have to have more time to think, I *have* to." My wonderful warmth slid away. I wanted to cry, "Don't, make me plead, don't make me beg, don't make me ask yet another man to let me do what I want and need to do. You're ruining it."

"I'm coming to Helsinki," Stephen said.

"What? What?" I screeched, and in the trans-Atlantic time lapse our voices suddenly echoed and crossed over one another.

"I said I'm coming to Helsinki."

"What? What?"

"There's a conference in New York I can say I'm attending. I know someone there who will cover for me. I already have my reservations. I'm arriving at eleven-thirty in the morning, your time, on BEA #270, on November twenty-ninth. Can you meet me at the airport, or arrange a hotel for me?"

"Stephen, I can't handle this! You can't come here. *Please.*"

I must have sounded desperate enough; there was a long expensive silence, and then Stephen said:

"I promise I won't make a scene. I won't try to force you. I won't even discuss the future. I just want to see you, be with you. I'll stay only two or three days. We'll eat together, hide in my hotel, talk if you want to. I just want to, *see* you, Zelda, I want to touch you again. Low key. No pressure. Is that all right?"

I was weak with fear and delight and sorrow. "All right," I said. "All right."

"Good-bye then till November twenty-ninth. Write me, Zelda, here at the university."

"I will. All right. Good-bye."

"I love you, Zelda."

"Good-bye."

"Oh, I love you, I love you, Chocolate eyes, Chicken Feathers," I would say to my dark-eyed son, to my fine-haired, fair-haired daughter. "I love you, I love you, I LOVE YOU!" I would shout at them in ecstasy, wrestling with them on their beds, nipping at their sweet flesh. "I could eat you up!"

"I love you, Charlie," I would say to my husband so many times during our lives together. And I meant it.

I loved, too, three or four women who were important to me, who were more than friends or mentors. I loved my parents, I loved my two surviving grandparents, who sat blithering away in rest homes. I loved, in a way, my stepdaughters.

But now, for the first time in my thirty-four years, I loved unmistakably, best of all, finally, at long last, ME. It was a great feeling.

I wasn't so sure about Stephen. Perhaps I loved him, perhaps not. That was one of the things I was trying to sort out. How much of it had been a challenge, how much of it was gratitude, how much of it was simply that I hadn't slept with a man other than Charlie for over thirteen years?

We had met Stephen and Ellen several times at university parties, and it turned out that Stephen was the new head of the English department. Ellen had—actually, of course, Stephen had, too, but one always thinks of children as what the mother has because she is home with them—children Adam's and Lucy's ages. Adam and Carrie, Ellen's four-year-old daughter, even knew each other at preschool. Charlie, who doesn't make friends easily anymore, finding books a more valuable way of using time, liked Stephen because Stephen knew so much about books. I liked Ellen because she was so beautiful to look at and because she was like me, a woman who had had "a career" but was now a dedicated mother, happy to have children but finding home life rather confining and dull in spite of the ecstasy. We started doing things together, we even spent one lovely Christmas Eve together, and the friendship of the whole Hunter family was a light in our family's life.

Then Stephen called one September day a year ago to tell me that one of their teachers had had a heart attack, and to ask me if I wouldn't like to teach two courses at the university. Just freshman literature and composition, with mediocre pay, and he could easily get a graduate student if I wasn't interested, but he had heard me say so often how much I missed teaching . . . I felt like someone drowning must feel when he's suddenly caught and hauled up to the air.

I taught Monday-Wednesday-Friday afternoons, and I loved it. It was terribly exciting, each day of it, walking around the classrooms, laughing with the students, trying to dance and jiggle and jangle up the air so that those kids learned something and had fun learning it. I was a good teacher. I had been before, years before, but I was older now, and it was good to know that my abilities hadn't left me, good to know that even if the big, tall, cute basketball stars no longer tried to flirt with me they still paid enough attention to learn how to write a decent essay. I knew I was a good teacher, I knew it in my bones. I was hired part time for the spring semester, and no one at home complained. My teaching somehow energized me for the rest of my life; I smiled through my housework, sang to my children, began to feel more creative in bed.

I would have taught again this fall, but instead Charlie was awarded the Fulbright research grant, and here we all are in Helsinki. I keep telling myself that I'll always be able to teach again, that this is a great opportunity to enjoy another culture, that we should travel while the children are young. But the desire to teach is yet another thing that flutters behind the locked doors of my mind and shakes me by the shoulders when I let it out. I once intended to be a university professor, to head a department of English. I am not sure now whether it's Stephen I want or his job.

It was exhilarating to teach again after so long, and Stephen was always there, complimenting me, reporting on my good work, helping me—it was easy to grow fond of him. And all the more delicious because he was a man that few people could touch. He was a slim, handsome, New England prep school type who had graduated from Yale. He had published a lot, in all the right places, and he moved through the world with the unruffable case of a man who is thoroughly competent at his job and has money in the family as well. His wife was another jewel in his crown; she had been an actress on Broadway and now gave her advice to the university and little city theaters, although she refused to act because acting took too much out of her and she wanted to save her energies for her family. Stephen

Hunter had everything, and he knew it, and now he wanted to create a great, unique innovative department of English, and he channeled everything into that. His smile for secretaries, professors, students, administrators, was charming but brief; he wanted to get on with it. He had a lot to do. People began to think him snotty or overly ambitious, icy, inhuman. I was only a lowly part-time instructor; I enjoyed the envy of others who saw Stephen stop to sit on my desk to chat and laugh with me. I thought he was joking with me on Monday about a new freshman text because we had all taken our children sledding on Sunday. I thought he spent time discussing the department with me because I had good ideas. Certainly many of them were implemented. I thought he was an intelligent man discussing work with an intelligent woman. I was as saddened as I was pleased when it all turned out to be something different.

One March morning I had a frantic phone call from Ellen.

"What am I going to do, Zelda?" she wailed. "Carrie's come down with the flu. She's really sick. Her temperature's been over a hundred and three for hours now and she can't keep anything down and all she wants to do is sit on my lap. And I promised Stephen I'd have an intimate little dinner party for whoozit—that big-deal critic who's flying in today. I made a chocolate torte yesterday, it's in the fridge, but I can't possibly get around to making a whole dinner today. And no one would want to eat here anyway, the entire house smells like vomit."

"Surely Stephen can take whoever it is out to dinner on an expense account," I said.

"No, no, not the first night," Ellen said. "He's really hot shit, and we're supposed to treat him like a king. He's some lonely old widower who lives alone in New York City and loves to be babied when he travels. Stephen really wanted his first night here to be a home spread."

"Ellen," I said, "are you talking about Levin? Samuel Levin? Good Lord, Ellen, if it's Samuel Levin, I'll have the dinner here! Who all's supposed to come? I'll take the kids to a sitter's and make a stroganoff and salad and you can give me your torte for dessert and we'll all be happy!" I was thrilled at the idea of having Samuel Levin in my house and glad to help Ellen. And as it turned out, Stephen thought I'd done it to help him.

My part of the dinner was a success. Marita Nyberg and Dan Smith, the two English department people other than Stephen, were as pleasant and complimentary as any two people could be. Even Charlie was his most cordial. But Samuel Levin had grown old and odd and bitter and cold, and after spending the winter hidden in his apartment writing diatribes against the critics who had criticized his work, couldn't thaw out enough to act even polite. He was a wall of ice for the first half of the evening, until he had enough booze in him—all of our scotch and three bottles of wine—and then he began raging and railing vehemently, while the rest of us sat stunned, pretending to listen.

"Jesus," Marita whispered to me as she left, "he's doing the Hall lecture tomorrow night and not leaving till the next morning. Who's gonna take care of him and listen to more of that shit tomorrow night? Not me!"

As it turned out, only Stephen and I volunteered to take Levin out to dinner Tuesday night after his lecture. No one else would go, not even for a free meal. Carrie was still sick, so Ellen couldn't go, and on my side Charlie simply wouldn't go.

"That was enough for me," he said as we did the dishes after my dinner. "I'll baby-sit tomorrow night and you can listen to that old madman let off his gas."

I argued a bit, but could see Charlie's point. It had been a boring, wasted evening. Still, I felt a little bit of rancor rise inside. How many nights had I spent being pleasant to Charlie's not always pleasant colleagues? Was I not to get equal help until I became a full professor?

Stephen and I took Samuel Levin to a small restaurant only a few blocks from Levin's hotel. His lecture had been, to our surprise and relief, lucid and dense and memorable. He had really pulled himself together for the public appearance, and the applause was deafening. I felt proud being seen leaving with him; me, a part-time freshman comp, instructor, next to him, a fine old man of letters.

Levin's successful talk seemed to mellow him; at dinner he was again talkative, but this time he dwelt on pleasant subjects. He reminisced. He told tales on Eliot and Stein and Pound, and drank and laughed and thoroughly enjoyed himself. Stephen and I could have been anyone else in the world; we could have been mannequins; Levin needed an audience only because it was not socially acceptable to talk out loud to oneself in public. Stephen and I had fabulous meals, courtesy of the Visiting Lecturer Fund, and we drank enough wine so Levin wouldn't feel alone, enough wine to make us wiggle our eyebrows at each other each time Levin belched out his insane laughter.

After the dinner we both escorted Levin to his hotel room. By that time we thought we'd better see with our own eyes that he got safely there.

"Dr. Smith will be by to take you to the airport at ten tomorrow," Stephen said. "Thank you again for coming to lecture for us, Mr. Levin. You were magnificent."

Levin swayed in his doorway, looking up at Stephen. "Don't suppose you'd like to come in for a little nightcap, would you? I've got a bottle of the best in my briefcase. Never travel without it. No, I can tell you two aren't interested in me and my booze and my old raggy tales. You've been making eyes at each other all night. I'm no dummy. You two can't wait to get rid of the old fart and run somewhere and fuck like rabbits. Well, go on, you two, and bless you. Enjoy it. I'd be doing it too if I had anyone to do it with. I can get it up now as well as I ever could—"

Stephen gently pushed Levin into his room, said good night, and closed the door.

I leaned against the wall opposite the door and began to laugh quietly. "Oh, Stephen!" I said, shaking my head.

Stephen took two steps across the narrow hall, pressed himself against me, and began kissing me. The effect of his lips touching mine was like a match held to kerosene-soaked rags: we went *whoosh*. We were ablaze. We stood together there in the hotel hallway, not six feet away from where poor lonely Levin was undoubtedly pouring himself another drink, and we kissed and pushed each other crazily.

When a sensible thought could get through to me—most of my mind was crying, "Get these clothes out of the way! . . . Where's the bed? . . . More, more, more!"—it was: "Why, he's made us horny, that horny old man, he and all that booze." Yet another voice was screeching, "Zelda! Hey! Stop! What about Charlie?" But I pushed the sensible thoughts away. Kissing Stephen was *fun*.

"I'm going to get us a room," Stephen said suddenly, pulling away. His mouth was swollen, and I knew mine was, too.

"What for?" I asked stupidly. Then, catching on, "No!" I grabbed Stephen again, frantic. "No, Stephen, *we can't*."

Stephen stared at me in disbelief, and seeing that I meant what I said, suddenly grabbed me by the wrist and pulled me through an open door into room number 256. He slammed the door shut behind us. My wits were with me enough to quickly survey the room; it was neat and impersonal, untouched. No coats on the hangers or flung over a chair, no sheets turned down expectantly.

"Zelda," Stephen said, pinning me against the door. "I've been waiting months for an opportunity like this. I want you. I want to make love to you."

He began kissing me, pummeling me again. He was so eager, so desperate, so excited—so different from Charlie, who now of course took our lovemaking for granted and moved slowly and assuredly through it all. All my instincts were aroused, in a wild rich mixture: sexual and maternal desires surged together. Stephen seemed both a full-grown man who could take me and a young animal, pushing demandingly at a mother's breast for food and affection.

Early in our relationship Charlie and I had agreed that we wouldn't sleep with anyone else until we told each other that we were going to do it first. It had seemed a fair and logical agreement at the time, especially since I was sure I would never want to sleep with anyone else, and I had never felt any need to test the agreement in the thirteen years we had been married. Now I saw how absurd it was, and a chuckle started deep in my throat. I imagined me wrestling on the bed with Stephen, dialing the phone, pulling down my hose, and pulling up my skirt, saying, "Charlie? This is Zelda." (Puff, puff, pant, pant, heavy breathing, loss of control.) "I just wanted to tell you that I'm going to make love with someone else now. Good-bye!" And then hanging up the phone, and turning to Stephen . . .

But I pushed him away. Too weak to stand without a wall at my back, shaking all over, I found strength to push him away. I wanted him, but not really. I wanted the sense of romance, the sense of danger, the fun, the acknowledgment that I was desirable, but not the serious final commitment of joining my body to his.

"Stephen," I gasped as I stood holding him off with my hands, as we stood there panting and shaking and sweating and glaring at each other like two combatants in a battle, "Stephen, I *can't. I can't.*"

"Zelda," Stephen said, his voice aching and low, "you don't understand. *I love you.*"

Well, I was drunk. I had had too much wine. I drew my arm back and slapped Stephen as hard as I could on the cheek. We both staggered sideways in surprise.

"You wise-ass sleek New England phony!" I hissed. "You vain egotistical fraud. Don't you ever use words like that so lightly. I'm from Kansas; words like that mean something to me. You don't *love* me, don't tell me you *love* me. You just want to *screw* me, that's all. You've ruined everything by saying that."

I burst into tears. I fell back against the wall and sobbed, both my hands hanging at my side.

After a few moments Stephen said, "I'll take you home now."

I went into the bathroom and washed my face in cold water and dried myself on the nice crisp hotel towels. I put lipstick and eyeliner on and smiled at myself in the mirror, trying to look normal, wondering if anything showed, just as I had done so many years ago after dates when I went home to be inspected by my parents' eagle eyes. But it was Charlie who would be seeing me now. I knew I would tell him nothing. So far I still felt virtuous, only slightly drunk and embarrassed.

Stephen went into the bathroom then, while I sat on the end of a double bed and tried to breathe naturally. When we left the room I couldn't resist smiling. To think of all the passion that had gone on there, and we hadn't even paid for the room. We passed Levin's door, half expecting him to open it and leer out at us, but all was silent. No one looked at us twice, and we went down the elevator and through the lobby and out to the car.

The ride home was absolutely quiet. We said nothing. I rehearsed scenes in my mind to tell Charlie: "Levin's Hall lecture was wonderful, you should have been there, but he got soaked again at dinner. At least the food was good. I had escargots for appetizer, and—"

Stephen pulled into our driveway, and without turning off the engine, leaned over and opened my door from the inside.

I put my hand on the door and said, "Good night, Stephen."

And Stephen said, "I love you, Zelda. I've loved you for a long time."

I stared at him for one long moment in dismay, then jumped out of the car and called in my best old sorority voice, "Thanks again, Stephen. Tell Ellen hi. Hope Carrie's better."

Then I walked to the house, slowly, normally, when I really wanted to run and hide, as if something would get me if I didn't hurry.

That was in March. The next day, on my desk, there was a typed copy of a tenderly coercive love poem waiting for me.

I put my head down on my desk and cried. For ten minutes. Then I got up, fixed up my face, and went off to do a slam-bang, cork-popping class for my cute little freshmen.

And I haven't slept with Stephen yet. I'm not sure why. Probably because the perfect opportunity hasn't presented itself again. No more hotel bedroom doors have fallen open for us. We have seen each other several times—six times, exactly, and I could quote every word we said to each other. We have lingered together over coffee and papers in the lounge after the other professors and instructors discussed this text or that student and then, one by one, left. We have had tea together in the school cafeteria. Each time I've been with Stephen I've felt guilty, ashamed, knowing that what I was doing was not as bad or immoral as it was false and hypocritical. I do not love Stephen. But I have loved being loved. Nothing is as entrancing as hearing all of one's best qualities named by someone who has never seen one's stretch marks or heard one screech at the children. Each session with Stephen left me feeling as punch-drunk and gay as the first time I practiced control breathing in Lamaze class and hyperventilated.

Once we stayed after hours in his office and began to embrace. I don't know if I would have said no again or not. I didn't especially want to make love with Stephen, but it was so delightful to have him right there, wanting to make love with me. Fortunately a student, the stupid fool, came wandering right in, without knocking, opening the closed door, looking for the psychology department. He didn't seem to know who we were, in spite of the fact that the door he had just opened read, "Stephen Hunter, Chairman."

Another time when Charlie was out of town lecturing, Stephen came by, and we stood in the back hall, wrestling between the freezer and the basement steps.

"Not *here*," I cried. "Not *here*. This is *Charlie's home*. You can't come in."

Perhaps Stephen took heart because I said "Not here" instead of "I won't."

At the beginning of the summer, when I was sure we were going to Helsinki, I went to the English department to clean out my desk for someone else to use the next year. I took down my posters, clippings, cartoons, and signs from the board behind my desk. I threw most of the stuff in the wastebasket and put the rest of it into a small briefcase I had borrowed from Charlie. I was sad; very, very sad. I didn't want to go to Helsinki, to live on the 60th parallel. I wanted to stay on our New Hampshire farm, I wanted to teach. *I wanted to teach.* I was thirty-four.

I was tired of following Charlie around the world. Stephen came in, and because it was a Saturday morning no one was around, and he simply walked into my office and stood there looking at me until I stopped shuffling papers and looked at him.

"I don't want you to go to Finland," he said. He looked as though he hadn't slept for weeks. "I've been thinking," he said. "I want you to marry me."

I didn't blink. I didn't skip a beat. "If I marry you, will you let me teach?" I asked.

"Let me check the nepotism rules here," he said, and turned to go down the hall to his office.

I threw everything else in my desk—rubber bands, paper clips, little pink broken stubs of eraser, into my—Charlie's—briefcase, and I ran. I was as frightened as I had ever been in my life. I didn't think Stephen would hear me, but he did. He ran out of his inner office, through the secretary's room, and down the hall after me. Perhaps I wasn't running as fast as I could have—I should have taken my light summer sandals off—but he caught me. And shoved me into a classroom and shut the door.

I was already shaky enough emotionally. I was secretly furious at Charlie for getting the Fulbright and dragging me off just when I was starting my own career again. I was feeling very sorry for myself. And here was the man with all the answers in his hands, trying to give them to me. Except that I knew he didn't really have all the answers.

We went into each other's arms. We were on the second floor of the building, and no one could see

70

us through the windows. It was Saturday, before the start of summer classes; the campus was bare. The classroom was as good as a motel room, with the one notable exception of a nice big bed. I was being thoroughly unrealistic. Perhaps everyone gets to be that way every thirteen years, just once. I encouraged Stephen when he kissed me—probably because I knew he'd never risk getting caught screwing another professor's wife in a campus classroom. He was still, after all, ambitious. I encouraged him when he talked to me; I needed to hear his words. He sounded like a fairy godfather, offering me the dress and the coach and the ball. I did not say I loved him. I did say I'd go to bed with him, the first opportunity we had. "No one gets married anymore without sleeping together first," I laughed. I asked him to please keep things normal, for a while, for my sake. I suppose I thought we were playing a game, one I needed to play, something light and refreshing, something without scorecards or goals. I suppose I wasn't in my right mind. I didn't realize how serious Stephen was. I didn't want to think he was serious.

For the sake of normality he and Ellen and the kids went back to Nantucket for the summer and came home just a week before we left for Helsinki. There was never, in the rush of our packing and his gearing up for a new semester, an opportunity for us to make love. At a farewell dinner that Ellen cooked for us, we risked one drunken kiss in the kitchen; it made me feel nearly sick with guilt. Even so, it was quite a kiss. All I have to do now, sitting at my orange and white checked tablecloth in my dreary Helsinki kitchen, is to place my fingertips lightly to my lips and I feel that kiss again, with all its eagerness and promise, and tears spring to my eyes, and I jump up and pace the room.

Now he says he's coming here.

I can't believe he loves me. In spite of all he's said. I have it all figured out: he's handsome and charming and cool, and I am probably the only woman in his life who hasn't hopped into bed with him on request. He doesn't really want to marry me. He merely wants to make love to me, to satisfy his masculine vanity. If he comes here, I should sleep with him. Then he'll go home and I won't have any problems anymore.

I want to sleep with him, I really do. Perhaps it's just because we've had rain for ten days straight now, so the children weren't able to go to the Park Auntie's and have stayed here in this small gray apartment chewing at my heels for entertainment. Perhaps it's just because all the people we meet say, "Oh, Dr. Campbell, what an honor to meet you," while I sit quietly beside him trying to look appropriately proud. Perhaps I'm just bored and jealous.

I wonder, how does one find out about hotels here? Shall I call the America Center across from the Rautatientori and ask them to recommend a nice, clean, reasonable hotel, reachable by bus from Kulosaari, a *discreet* hotel, for lovers to meet?

I have to stop daydreaming. I've wasted the whole

72

morning. I haven't written a letter or vacuumed my gray linoleum floor and its pitiful patches of greasy rugs with the cute little Hoover that came with the apartment. It is a short, squat creature, the European Hoover, resembling quite a bit R2D2 in *Star Wars*, though it's not nearly so helpful. I haven't washed the clothes in the small Hoover 1200 washing machine that takes up so much space in the bathroom that we have to squeeze between it and the sink to brush our teeth or climb over it to get into the bathtub. I haven't even made the cookies I started. I had poured flour and butter and molasses into a bowl and was looking among the spices which the former tenant had left for the vanilla. And found only *vanilian sokeri*. I looked it up in my Fulbright list of foods—vanilla sugar is all that is available here. No real vanilla in Finland. I wonder why. Could it be because the Finns have an alcoholism problem and real vanilla has alcohol in it? It sounds ridiculous, but one quart of vodka costs around twenty dollars here, which might make it worth some yearning soul's while to buy seventeen bottles of real vanilla and drink it all right down. I had been standing in my tiny gray kitchen, thinking about vanilla and how I might easily start swigging it myself if I had it, given all this constant rain and gloom. Then the phone rang, and it was Stephen, and I sat at the table thinking, and now it's time to get Adam and Lucy and feed them lunch.

Perhaps parents wealthy enough to have nannies are able to get respect from their children. Perhaps even at four the children of the rich know enough to walk in politely when invited, curtsy and count to ten in French, then sit quietly and adoringly, knowing that otherwise they wouldn't get to see their parents at all. Perhaps the mother need say only, "The child whined, Nanny, take him away," and the child would never, ever, whine again in his mother's presence.

But we're not wealthy. I've got the Park Auntie on good mornings, but only until eleven-thirty. Then my children are mine again. It always makes my heart leap to see them, and I'd throw myself in front of a truck or moving train to save their lives, but I wish like crazy they'd respect me a bit more. They're giving me an identity crisis.

They don't say, "Oh, look, here comes our darling mommy, who is so clever. She could be teaching at a university or writing a critical paper for a national literary review, but instead she's here, full of smiles, to take care of us. Hi, there, you good ol' mom!"

No, they say, "You didn't put Vaseline on my lips this morning and now they're all chapped," and, "I did poo-poo in my diaper; take it off, take it off NOW!" Or else they cry all the way home because on this early October morning I have dressed them in only an undershirt and turtleneck shirt and sweatshirt and underpants and woolen tights and rain pants and overcoat with hood and rubber boots and mittens and they were cold. The Park Auntie scolds me through a reluctant Finnish mother inter-preter, tells me I must put three pairs of woolen socks on my daughter's feet. My children do not say, "That's okay, Mommy, you've got more important things to think about." They snivel and whine all the way home. They judge me only by their comforts.

Of course, they do not respect their father any more than they do me, which sometimes irritates me and sometimes makes me glad. If anything, they respect me more—no, not respect, they simply choose me more. My husband's professional vita is over fifty pages long; mine is a page and a half. I suppose I could lengthen it by adding:

Diapers changed,	14,600,	1973-1977
Boo-boos kissed,	1,700,	1974-1977
Shoelaces tied,	6,923,	1974-1977
Noses blown and wiped,	1,784,	1973-1977*

The funny thing is that Charlie actually feels offended and rejected when Lucy or Adam cries, "NO! I want *Mommy* to wipe my bum!" Some jobs, such as boo-boo kissing, are more rewarding than others, and I'm glad the children choose me. But I know their choice of me does not indicate respect. It's simply a matter of habit. I am beginning to come to terms with the fact that my children will probably never know *me*, at least not for a long, long time. It's in the nature of the beast. We all want someone there to take care of us all the time, and when we're little we have to

*Reader please note: the children were asked by their father if *he* could perform the tasks, but they invariably requested *my* services, and *my* services only.

have it to survive, and we get it. There must have been days when Jesus cried, "Mommy, kiss my boo-boo!" and when Mary answered, "Okay, sweetie, come here and let me kiss it. And don't play with the hammer anymore, okay? You're giving me a headache." And if God had bellowed, "*I'LL* KISS YOUR BOO-BOO!", Jesus would have whined, "No. Let *Mommy* do it."

I know all that now. I see it happen every day, I see Adam and Lucy treat Charlie in ways a man of his reputation shouldn't have to stand, and feel them treat me in ways that make me want to scream. (Why does it drive them crazy, for example, when I go into the bathroom and lock the door? Why must they then always fall against a chest and bruise their heads? Why do they climb my leg when I try to talk on the phone? Why won't they eat their food properly when Charlie tells them to eat their food properly?) We put up with things from our little children that would make us punch a stranger in the nose, and we don't hate or even dislike them for it. We know they are *children,* they are trying. We can see the pieces coming together; each day they do a little better than the day before. We love our children even when we hate them, and sometimes when they fix us with a particularly nasty sulky glare, we grab them and squeeze them against us and blow kisses under their chins and onto their tummies until they squeal with laughter.

But in 1965, when Caroline was ten and Cathy

was seven, and I had no children and didn't want any, I didn't have an inkling of any of this. And the women who were my friends didn't have children, and the women I knew who had children weren't my friends and never discussed the subject. I honestly thought the women who were mothers were all placidly, smugly, properly happy. I thought that other women were capable of finding instantly a pure, unadulterated happiness merely from being with children. I, on the other hand, still found children boring and bothersome. I was afraid there was something wrong with me, something missing. I was glad Charlie and I had agreed to have no children of our own. I was already quite sure that his two girls would be more than enough.

It was in the sixth week of that first summer when the girls first stayed with us that Charlie said to me, "Come outside. I'd like to talk with you a minute."

It was midmorning. I had finished breakfast—bacon, sweet cereal, toast, honey, cocoa, orange juice, and no yucky eggs—and Caroline and Cathy were watching some ridiculous comedy show on television, and I had just done the dishes. I was thrilled to be invited to a private conversation with Charlie; we hadn't had one, except whispered bedroom ones, for weeks.

I poured myself another cup of coffee and went out the back door into the sunshine. It was a weekday, and we were back in Kansas City so that Charlie could work on his projects. The backyard of our little house was small, but lovely, with a brick patio enclosing a small lily pond with a bench by it under a lyre tree. Grass and flowers. Birds singing. It was August, a hot, humid Missouri day, and I was wearing shorts and a halter top. I sank into a lounge chair and closed my eyes. For a moment I relaxed. I was happy. The sun made me expand; I felt sexy; and then Charlie sat down next to me, pushing against my legs. I sat up and pulled him to me and kissed him. I hadn't kissed him in the daytime for weeks.

Charlie pulled away. "It's bad news, trooper," he said. Before I could guess, he continued, "I'm not going to the party. The girls don't want to be left with a sitter."

I gaped. *The party* was for me the highlight, the Christmas present the *coup,* of the summer. A famous woman intellectual and writer was coming to the university to give a lecture, and afterward the chancellor of the university was holding a small reception-cocktail party in her honor. Only forty people out of the whole faculty had been invited, and "Dr. and Mrs. Charles Everett Campbell" were two of them. Not even Anthony had been invited. I was longing to just look at the famous intellectual woman up close, to see whether she was real, to hear her speak in her own voice, impromptu, instead of off a printed page. I had planned to wear something brown and drab so that she would see instantly that I was a serious student and not just a flighty cutesy girl. I was hoping she would look at me, talk to me, say just a few words, contact me, touch me, pass something on.

"What?" I asked Charlie when I could get my mind to work.

"I'm not going to the party. I'm sorry. I've just had a little talk with the girls. They really don't want to be left with a sitter. It's understandable. They've been here only a short while. They've only barely learned to trust *us*. As Caroline put it, if I wanted to see them so badly this summer, how come I want to go off and leave them with a sitter? And poor little Cathy just broke down and cried." Charlie stopped and took his hand off my arm, and stared away into the grass, looking miserable.

It was the "poor little Cathy" that got to me more than anything else. Poor little Cathy had cold, hard metal faucets in her head, and she could turn her tears on and off at will. I've never seen anything like it except in a bathroom sink. After two or three weeks with us the girls had suddenly seemed to decide they could trust us. At the very least it was obvious that they weren't getting hit or screamed at or neglected, and they were getting lots of toys and clothes and games and treats. But that didn't mean we were all jolly friends forevermore. They seemed to have a score to settle now, a revenge to continually wreak. Caroline, already out of the baby stage and not cute anyway because of those awful buck teeth, chose the intellectual's role of cold-shouldering and cool-mouthing. She had perfected a marvelously steady nihilistic stare; Sartre would have loved her. "Well, then," she would say, "if we don't go tonight, we'll probably never get a chance to go again, at least not with you, Dad." She would never, ever, hold anyone's hand, and she sat on Charlie's lap as rigidly as if her backbone were made of metal.

But it was soft little, sweet little, pretty little, poor little Cathy who was the one to watch out for. She was such a darling girl, all big eyes and innocence, so cuddly and eager to please. But she knew what she wanted, and she knew how to get it. She knew how to handle Charlie like a baker making himself a pie. It wasn't something she obviously worked at, it just came to her naturally; she was born with it. She knew even at seven how to get what she wanted from men. It came to her as easily and surely as a talent for swimming or singing or taming animals comes to others. Perhaps all girls who are especially winsome when little develop this special art. Caroline didn't have it. She used to stare at Cathy with as much awe and amazement as I did. Even now when she compares herself to her sister, she has to laugh. For Christmas last year Cathy received a complete set of ski gear—boots, skis, bindings, and poles— from one boyfriend and a portable stereo for her dorm room from another. "With my luck, I always seem to break up with my boyfriends just before Christmas," Caroline laughed, and I laughed with her. Caroline feels no awe of Cathy anymore, and no envy. She is a smart girl; she will buy her own skis, her own stereo. And perhaps she'll be able to have a better relationship with a man, when all is said and done, than Cathy will. Who can say? Perhaps one can use men and still establish a good mutual love. Certainly Charlie loves Cathy.

And loved her then. She was pretty, she was the baby, she was affectionate. She seemed to understand that I wasn't going to rat on her. What could I say? "I wish you could see the way Cathy looks at me when you're holding her and can't see her face?" I might have been willing to be petty, but not with such vague material. Frankly, I wasn't, with all my twenty-two years, as clever as Cathy with her seven, and more important, I didn't know what game we were playing. The third day on the farm, after Cathy's tantrum over the shrimp and avocado salad and our later friendly silly talk about food in the bedroom, the day after that one nice night when I thought we had all become friends for good, Cathy got to me again.

We had all finished breakfast, and Charlie had said, "Come on, Caroline, I'll show you how to drive the tractor. I've got to mow. You can have a turn after Caroline, Cathybell." He had gone around and around the house, mowing down the grass with his big red brush-hog, with Caroline sitting rigidly but happily on his lap, occasionally steering.

I had done the dishes quickly, then said, "Come on, Cathy. Let's go weed the garden."

"I don't want to," Cathy said, curling up in a chair, looking down at her feet.

Aha, I thought, she's feeling jealous because Charlie took Caroline on the tractor first.

"Well, weeding's not much fun, I know, but I need

81

to do it before it gets too hot. Why don't you come on out and watch me—and I'll tell you a story!" Oh, wonderful, Zelda, I thought, what an angel you are.

No answer.

"Well, what would *you* like to do? Is there anything special you'd like to do now? We could ride the horses. Or go wading in the stream. Would you like me to read you a book?"

No answer.

"Oh, come on, Cathy," I said, still lightly, pleasantly. "It's too nice a morning to just sit in a chair. Why don't you get a nice cold Popsicle from the freezer"—I briefly wondered if Adelaide would be incensed at my offering a Popsicle at nine in the morning—"and come sit outside while I weed. I know a lot of neat stories I could tell you."

No answer.

"Well, if you want to hear a story, or if you want to go for a walk, or wading, or anything, I'll be out in the garden behind the house. Okay?" Brightly. Softly.

No answer.

I didn't know what else to do. I went outside, leaving Cathy in her chair, in her sulk.

The sun was sweet but getting fierce, and I hurried behind the house to weed. I loved my garden, the tiny new peas, the sturdy carrots, the silly radishes, and I was soon totally absorbed in my work. But I had done only two rows, hadn't even started to really sweat, when I was jarred out of my idiotic bliss by the sudden sound of the tractor engine shutting off. I looked up.

There was Cathy, sitting in the grass, arms folded on her knees and head resting on her arms, sobbing. Charlie lifted Caroline to the ground and jumped down himself.

"Cathy? Honey, what's wrong?" He raced up to her, nearly tripping.

She didn't answer. Simply sobbed. I could see how eloquent her tiny narrow back was.

"Cathy? Talk to me, baby," Charlie said. He bent and picked her up in his arms.

"I don't like being lonely. I don't like being left alone." Sob, sob, sob.

"But you were with Zelda. Where's Zelda?"

I don't know. She wanted me to weed the garden, but I can't. Weeds make me sneeze. She went off and left me." Sob, sob, sob.

"Well, you come on and ride the tractor with Caroline and me. I can hold you both."

But of course he couldn't hold both girls and steer, and after a few moments Caroline got off and ran over to join me in the garden. I told her the best stories I could, but I knew they didn't make up for having only ten minutes with her father on the tractor while her sister rode around in his arms for the rest of the morning.

And that was only the beginning. The summer days went by, riddled with small tragedies in which I played the villainess. Cathy's best thing was being sick or getting hurt. If Charlie and I lingered in bed too long together in the mornings—that is, one or two minutes after Cathy woke up—and especially if

83

the door was closed, Cathy would invariably fall and bruise herself or cut herself or have a tummyache. The one time the whole summer that Charlie and I went riding together, for perhaps fifteen glorious minutes, Cathy came down with stomach cramps and spent the day crying in bed. When we went to the drive-in movies to see some Walt Disney special, Charlie and Cathy and Caroline sat in front and I sat alone in the back. If I washed Cathy's hair, I got soap in her eyes, and only Charlie could get it rinsed out.

And through it all I didn't really mind. She loves her father, I thought, she doesn't get to see him most of the time, let her have him every minute that she's here.

But I wanted to go to the party to meet the famous intellectual woman. In 1965 there weren't that many of them, and even fewer came to the Midwest. I knew that just setting eyes on the real woman in real life would be important to me.

"Oh, *Charlie*," I wailed, "it will only be for two hours. Or one hour. We'll hurry."

"Zelda," he said, "I'm sorry. I can't. I can't leave the girls. Not this time." Then, more hopefully, "*You* could still go—"

"Me? Alone? Are you kidding? The *only* way *I* can go is as the wife of famous Professor So-and-so. They're not inviting students to that thing. Oh, *Charlie*." I was sick. But it was true. In 1977, I could have gone alone, even as a lowly student. But in 1965 things were more proper, rules were stricter. Women still wore mostly skirts, and gloves, and their purses

84

matched their shoes, and they didn't go to parties alone, uninvited. I was still mostly only a faculty member's wife. Low on the totem pole. Very low.

"I hate being in the middle like this," Charlie said. "I don't know what to do."

"Oh, Charlie, you've been with those girls, or I have, every minute of the time they've been here. Surely that's not natural. *Two hours* without you won't kill them. And Leslie is a lovely smart girl; Caroline and Cathy will enjoy her, I'm sure. Charlie, it's so important to me, it's not just a *party,* it's like a symbol, a sign—"

Charlie stood up suddenly. "Don't, Zelda. Just don't. Please. I'm sorry, but I'm not going."

I immediately burst into tears. Perhaps they had been building up over the summer. I didn't cry easily then; I didn't think it was fair to Charlie. But I was sick with disappointment, and I was mad.

"Jesus," Charlie said, and walked over and punched the lyre tree on the trunk, hard. "There's nothing like a house full of weepy females."

I jumped up, nearly spitting in my anger. "Don't you *dare* class me with them!" I yelled. I now think that he didn't even think of it himself, but in lumping me with his daughters—weepy females— he lumped me with Adelaide, his former wife, crazy, weepy bitch. And I didn't want to be like Adelaide in any way at all.

At that point I noticed that Cathy and Caroline were standing in the back door watching us, and that made me even madder. I felt as though I had spies in my house who would report every negative detail back to an enemy. (As it turned out, I was right.) That summer, when Charlie and I hadn't been married a full year yet, I wanted the girls to think we never spoke a cross word to each other, that we thought as one. Now here they were, watching us hiss and fight, and the expressions on their faces were unreadable. Surprise? Delight?

I suddenly felt trapped in my own backyard. I wanted to get away from them all, yet I couldn't even go into the house because the girls were standing there, together, solidly, like the bottom half of a Dutch door, barring the way. I turned and went around the side of the house fast, and walked off down the street. I didn't know where I was going on a weekday morning in a nice section of town wearing only shorts and a halter, not even a pair of sandals on my feet. But I had to get away.

Charlie appeared suddenly at the side of the house.

"Zelda," he called, and I looked back to see him standing there, dismayed and angry and sorry and shocked. He was wearing only shorts, and he was so tall and blond and strong that I wanted to run back immediately and press my body against his. In those days we had only to touch each other and a sort of magic balm swept over us, erasing all hurt.

But then a door slammed and Caroline and Cathy ran to their father's side and stood staring at me as if I were some kind of animal loose from a zoo. What a picture they were, those three healthy, big-boned blondes! So obviously related. So inseparably related. The blood racing in all their veins was the same blood. I was the outsider. My ancestry was different from theirs; eventually the girls would both grow taller than I, with bigger bones in their healthy bodies. I was dark and small and curly-haired, and alone. There seemed to be nothing I could do but walk off down the street. We lived in a dignified neighborhood; Charlie wouldn't come chasing after me, I was sure. All right, I thought, at least it's clear now: Caroline and Cathy are my enemies and they've just won a big battle. I hereby retreat. Watch me go.

I walked down the street and around the corner, past all the pretty Dutch colonials and rambling Victorians and their yards with flowers and shrubs and trees. I felt ridiculous, but I kept on walking. In my fantasies several wonderful things happened: Charlie and Caroline and Cathy got into the car and caught up with me and told me how sorry they were, that the girls would stay with the sitter so I could see the famous intellectual woman. Or I walked to the university and cried on someone's shoulder (Whose? The head of the English department then was an old married Catholic who didn't like women in school, who thought they should stay home and cook and have babies), and that someone took me to the party. Or, this as I finally stopped at an elementary school and sank down to dismally sway on a wood and chain link swing, the famous intellectual woman herself would just happen to be out walking on this lovely summer day, having arrived in Kansas City four days early. She'd see me and immediately sense my innate superiority, and she'd come over and sit on the swing next to me and chat. "Leave them all," she'd say. "What do you need love for? You'll never get on with a career at this rate. Why not come back to New York with me? I'll introduce you to people; you can work on a master's at Columbia."

But of course nothing like that happened. I sat on the swing until three boys about Cathy's age came scuffling over to the playground. They kept giving me strange looks and bursting into fits of embarrassed laughter to see me there, a lone grown woman sitting on a swing. But I stubbornly stayed, swinging slightly and staring back at them or at the sand or the basketball goal or the jungle gym. The morning sun rose a little higher in the sky.

The warmth of the sun made me happy. I was still pretty much of an animal. I liked sex, food, drink, the feel of a horse galloping under me, the feel of water surrounding me when I swam. Other things were more confusing: *why* was it so important to me to see the famous intellectual woman? I wasn't even interested in her field of study. So why should I long to see her? I couldn't figure it out. It was all too vague for me. And why did I feel that the girls, especially Cathy, were out to get me? With all the logic and the guilt that a Methodist from Kansas can muster—and that's a lot, the guilt, that is; we're quite good at feeling guilty, though not so good at logic—I decided I was paranoid. Caroline and Cathy were only children. Sweet, innocent little girls. They hadn't said or done anything, really, I thought. They didn't really want to hurt me. It was easier for me then to believe that I was overreacting than to accept the fact that yes, indeed, Caroline and Cathy did hate me. They would have hated anyone who lived with their daddy. They were hurt. That is the truth, though no one likes to say it: they were hurt. They were little girls, and their daddy had left them, and they had to live with a hurt in their hearts. Caroline at ten was old enough to separate me from my role of evil stepmother. She tried to be nice to me because I was nice to her. And in doing so she had to hide the hate she felt for me—would have felt for any stepmother— and it lay there, that smothered hate, and in the end it did her harm, and showed up at a time when it hurt me most. I wish she had let it out on me then, in those first years. Cathy hated me more clearly and purely, and would have made me disappear, if she could have, simply, with a wand, but she loved her father more than she hated me. She could see that her father cared for me. She did not want to make him angry by openly disliking something— someone—her father had chosen. She had to be subtle. She was happy if she could get me in trouble, triumphant when she could glare at me over her father's shoulder and see that I got the message but was too puzzled or helpless to respond.

It might have been better, that first year, if the girls could have arrived with whips and sticks and rocks in their luggage, if they could have spent all their time with us hitting us and screaming at us and calling us names. "You bad ol' Daddy, how could you leave us?" they could have cried, and, "You bad ol' woman, what makes you think you're good enough to live with our daddy? Why do *you* get to live with him and we don't? I hate you!"

If that had happened, the girls might have felt better. Their anger might have exploded and used itself up instead of burning along steadily inside them, gradually decreasing with the passing years, but still flickering inside them and lashing out now and then at Charlie and me. Charlie and I might have felt better, too.

But we were all civilized. Truths were hidden. If we were nothing else, we were polite. We all tried our best, according to our values. And we were confused, we were muddled. Caroline and Cathy and I were alike in one respect: we all loved Charlie. We wanted to make him happy; we wanted to be with him. But we didn't know each other. We didn't love each other. We did love Charlie. Nothing else was clear. We were in a floundering porridgy emotional mess.

And I think, all things considered, that we did pretty well. Eventually I got up off the playground swing and walked back to the house. I smiled and told everyone I would make a picnic lunch; we'd spend the day at the park. I told Charlie it was fine about not going to the party, not to give it another thought. It was such a great sunny day I felt happy, and Charlie was so glad the pressure was off that he was positively giddy, and I could sense that even

Caroline and Cathy were relieved. Poor little girls, they wanted me to be miserable, and at the same time they wanted me to be happy. It was much nicer for everyone when I was happy.

We had only one week left with them, and Charlie tried to make it a birthday-party-carnival-time-lollipopland of a week, so that they would go back to Massachusetts and nine months with their mother with good, warming, sustaining memories of their father and Kansas City. He bought them new school clothes: dresses, shoes, coats, the works. We had to buy an extra suitcase so they could carry all their new dolls and toys and clothes back. I did my part; I didn't touch or kiss Charlie all week (except, of course, in the luxurious privacy of our bed). I was as good and friendly as I could possibly be.

"You look like Mary Tyler Moore," Caroline said to me the night we got dressed up, to go to a fancy restaurant for a last-night dinner. I didn't look at all like Mary Tyler Moore, but I kissed Caroline on the cheek; I understood that she was trying to pay me a compliment, trying to make me happy.

The day we took the girls to the airport, everyone ended up crying. Cathy started it, and this time I could tell it didn't come from her metal faucets. This time she wasn't trying to manipulate anyone. This time it was for real.

"I don't want to leave you, Daddy!" she suddenly wailed as we stood in line at the gate, waiting for them to board the plane. "Please, Daddy," she cried, "come back and live with Mommy and Caroline

91

and me. I want to be a family again." She clung to his neck and soaked his shirt collar.

"I'll come see you soon, I'll call you tonight, I'll write you letters, sweetie," Charlie said, and his voice was choked and his eyes were red and he couldn't keep the tears from coming, even in such a public place.

Caroline stood clutching her new doll and her flight bag full of candy and comic books, clutching them as if someone might suddenly snatch them away if she let down her guard. She watched Cathy and Charlie with an envious haughtiness. She wanted to cry and fling herself and clutch at her father, too, but she was too big. She was the older, the one in charge. Two tears escaped before she brusquely wiped them away on the back of her white gloves.

And I just let the tears go, flow, run. I felt sorry for all of them. For a moment I wanted to cry, "Oh, do go back to Adelaide and the girls; this is too awful to bear!"

But the flight was called and a stewardess came to take the girls on and told them she'd give them stewardess wings and playing cards and pencils and papers for drawing.

I said, "Good-bye, girls," and quickly kissed them again, and Charlie walked onto the plane with them to be sure they were safely settled. He fastened their seat belts. A friend of Charlie's would meet them in Chicago to help them change planes, just as he had done six weeks earlier on their flight down. Charlie came back and the flight attendant fastened a rope barring the way, and we stood together watching out the window as the plane slowly pulled away.

The rest of the day was like a canyon without a bridge. There was too big, too deep, too wide a hole in our lives for us to cross. We were silent on the way home, and dinner tasted bland, and we watched television in a stupor. We didn't make love to each other that night. It would have seemed somehow profane. Charlie called Hadley, and Caroline answered and said they had gotten home just fine and that their mother had painted their rooms and made new curtains and that Cathy couldn't come to the phone, she was crying.

We went to bed early. Charlie turned to face one way and I turned the other. I lay awake deep into the night, wondering if this breach meant the end of our lives together. I was more miserable than I had ever been before in my life. But finally sleep came, and somehow the next day Charlie and I both woke up on the same side of that vast, lonely canyon. We went into each other's arms. Later we ate breakfast and things happened, friends called, days passed, and our lives got back to normal again.

A few days after the girls left, Charlie came home with a present for me, a new, handsome, expensive hardback book of essays by the famous intellectual woman. I thanked Charlie and tried to read the book, but couldn't somehow get interested. I couldn't remember why I had cared so much about seeing her in the first place. I put the book on the shelf and turned away from it. It did not interest me. I wanted only to be with Charlie, to be happy in his arms.

THREE

One brisk fall day in 1965, I was in a wonderful mood. It was October, and the girls had been gone for over a month, but I was still riding on the freedom I felt in those first few years whenever Charlie's daughters left and my house, my life, my time, and my husband became entirely my own again. I had started my M.A. work that semester and been hired as a teaching assistant for two freshman composition and literature courses. I discovered that I loved teaching. It was not just that I now had my own money to buy gifts for Charlie, although that was certainly grand. It was more than that, more profound, it was as if a thick sturdy chunk of life had locked into place for me, as if a puzzle piece had filled a gap: now I knew who I was and what I wanted to do. I wanted to teach English to freshmen. And people were paying me to do it, and other people, younger people, were sitting in classrooms listening to me talk and acting as if they were learning things. It was marvelous. Life seemed to be all of a piece.

I walked from the university to my home that day fairly skipping with a normal everyday glee. The trees seemed to shimmer past me like great gleaming flames. Children laughed from swing sets.

94

The scent of applewood in fireplaces filled the air. That night Charlie and I were going to a jazz concert with friends. Everything was right. Earlier that day I had mailed Caroline and Cathy two enormous funny gay Halloween cards. In my happiness I was generous; I wanted Charlie's girls to be happy, too.

When I got home, Charlie waited until I had taken off my sweater and made myself some tea. We sat down in front of the fire together. Then he handed me some pieces of paper.

"Today's mail," he said. His voice was grim.

The first sheet was a Xeroxed copy of a letter from Adelaide Campbell to her lawyer, Jonathan Pease.

Dear Jonathan,

I am taking the time and trouble to set this all down in writing, although I still don't understand why you want me to do it this way. I don't think you are being a very good lawyer for me.

As I said on the phone the other evening, I want you to sue my ex-husband, Charles Campbell (the bastard) for a raise in child support. I want it doubled.

As you know, I am not receiving any alimony, in spite of the fact that I cooked and cleaned and washed and ironed for Charles Everett Campbell for almost ten years. But I'm not complaining about that. I have a job as a secretary now, and although this means I can't be home when my little daughters need me, after school, or baking cookies, I am making enough money to take care of my own needs. I do not want any money for myself.

But I do want more money for my children. I don't think it's fair that they should be deprived when their father and his new wife have two homes, one in the city and one in the country. They also have two horses. Two cars. And my daughters reported that my husband's new wife has at least thirty expensive dresses and a complete set of leather luggage and diamond jewelry. Why should she have so much and my little girls have so little?

It is true that Mr. Campbell sent the girls home this summer with new clothes. I suggest that if he has so much money to spend buying them new clothes, that money should be given to me. I am their mother, the girls live with me, and I have to wash the clothes and be sure that they're warm and good enough. It is not fair for Mr. Campbell to impress the girls with new clothes and toys. Perhaps he thinks he will buy their love that way, but I assure you he will not.

You said when I called the other night that it might be better if we settled out of court. I don't want to do that. I want to take him to court and I want the child support doubled, and I want him to pay the court fees, and since I will have to fly back to Kansas I want him to pay the plane fare and my expenses. I want to go to court. I want the child support doubled. I have a reliable friend, Mrs. Anthony Leyden, and she will verify in writing that Mr. Campbell's new wife has very expensive clothes. Why should she have expensive clothes when we're living in a rented house? I tell you, I'm mad enough to spit nails, and if you won't take this to court for me, I'll get a lawyer who will.

Please phone or write me immediately regarding this matter.

> *Sincerely,*
> *Adelaide Campbell*

The next sheet of paper was a letter from Albert Dennison, Charlie's lawyer. It was a formal legal letter, telling Charlie when he was expected to appear in court. At the bottom of the letter Albert had scribbled in pen, "Sorry, Jonathan and I both tried to get her to settle out of court, but she won't. She's *mad*. Call me if you want."

"Charlie!" I wailed when I finished the letter. "This is terrible! It's unfair! Those are *my* clothes that my parents bought me last year. They're *old* clothes! And it's *my* car that my parents gave me for graduation from high school! I haven't bought anything new except underpants and shoes since I married you. And one of the horses is mine. And the luggage is mine. And the diamond jewelry is mostly crappy rhinestone."

"I'll tell them that in court," Charlie said. Then, less grimly, "I don't think it's anything to worry about, Zelda. When we were divorced Adelaide got total possession of our house, which she sold at a good profit, and our best car, the new station wagon, and all the appliances, and all but a few pieces of furniture that had been in my family. And she got all our savings, dammit, except for five measly thousand dollars. She got the few stocks I had. I'm paying for a college trust fund for Caroline and Cathy and all their medical and dental bills, and a great chunk of my salary goes to them each month for child support. I really don't see that they can squeeze any more out of me. I'm surprised at Adelaide; she had seemed quite happy with the financial arrangements. And no one can penalize me for what you've brought to our marriage. Jesus, I inherited the farm and have to pay taxes on it. We're barely making it now. If they win more money, I'll have to sell the farm."

At this somber thought we both stopped talking and stared at our hands. I fought back tears; I knew Charlie didn't need any extra melodramatic misery at that moment in his life. But—*sell the farm*. He might as well have said, "We'll just cut off part of our lives, cut off our legs as well, and one eye and a chunk of heart." It was only one hundred scraggly Ozark acres with a ramshackle house. It wouldn't bring much money at all if we sold it. But it meant everything to us, it was our own secret world within the world. To think of selling it, that little piece of, land which had been Charlie's parents' and was now *ours*, made me want to lie on the floor and cry like a child and kick my feet and pound my fists. It made me sad, and it made me mad.

It made me mad to think that this woman I had never met had the right to break into my life and to threaten to take away the things I loved. I felt help-less. And I knew that Charlie, in spite of his calm, felt helpless, too.

He went to court on January seventeenth, a cold Kansas Monday. He drove back to Wichita while I spent the day silently screaming in Kansas City. I went to class, but I couldn't think, I didn't care. I felt I had nothing to say to my students; I assigned them a pop in-class essay so they would have to write for fifty minutes and I wouldn't have to struggle with words. I tried to work in the library, since final exams were just a week away. But nothing seemed important, nothing relevant. I felt as a farmer must feel when he stands outside in the perfect calm, looking up at a boiling green sky with the black twisting shape of a tornado coming closer, wondering how much destruction that tornado would wreak in his life, wondering how much of his life and home it will shatter and smash and hurl away. The hours passed so slowly I couldn't breathe through them. I felt I was strangling. Finally I started grading the in-class essays with a ruthless harshness I'd never felt before. I refused to let my-self leave the library before all the essays were graded. That used up a good three hours. I expected Charlie back about seven. When I left the library it was six o'clock. I thought I had only one more hour to wait. I could not take deep breaths; my lungs had gone quite tight.

I walked out of the library and down the sidewalk, essays and books and notebooks piled in my arms, staring at nothing. A car pulled up next to me.

"Want a ride home?" It was Anthony Leyden, opening the passenger door of his car, leaning toward me, smiling his charming smile.

We hadn't seen the Leydens since the summer. Charlie had seen Anthony at work, of course, had gone out for beers with him and other professors now and then, but the four of us had stopped getting together. Once or twice June had called to invite us over, or Anthony had told Charlie we should come over for a drink, or pumpkin pie, or Christmas cheer, or whatever. But I had always pleasantly, politely, refused. I could see no reason to spend any time with a woman who so obviously disliked me, who had, as the lawyer's later letters had shown, played a major part in Adelaide's discontent. I hadn't felt bitter; I had just not wanted to go. After the letter in October from the lawyer, with the copy of Adelaide's letter, I had felt like biting and pulling hair. "I have a reliable friend, Mrs. Anthony Leyden, and she will verify in writing that Mr. Campbell's new wife has very expensive clothes." What other ridiculous tidbits had June Leyden been feeding Adelaide Campbell's anger? During the days before the hearing Charlie talked to his lawyers and with Adelaide, and it seemed that June had fed Adelaide's anger quite a lot.

At first I had longed to call June on the phone or to confront her: "See my dress? Sure, it's expensive, my parents bought it for me last year. Do you like my shoes? I bought them myself; I'm teaching now, I have my own money. I'm not a drab, dull drone like you, stuck at home in a greasy print housedress that's five years outdated. Is that why you hate me so? Is that why you're trying to take things from me?"

But of course I didn't call her. I yelled a lot at Charlie and at the walls when Charlie wasn't home, but I decided that after all, it wasn't worth it. If I called her it would only give her more food to feed Adelaide; I didn't want to give those women anything of mine, not even my anger.

But now here was Anthony, so charming and sure of his charm, offering me a ride. I lost control.

"Do I want a ride home? With you? Today? You are perverse." I turned and walked away, quickly.

Anthony shut off his engine, jumped out of the car, and ran to catch up with me. He took me by the arm.

"Why shouldn't I offer you a ride today, Zelda Campbell?" He pulled me to him, smiled down in my face.

I couldn't understand it. He seemed to be flirting with me. I tried to back away, and his other arm shot out around me; I was locked in an absurd embrace.

"I know what you're afraid of, lovely little Zelda," he said. "You're afraid that since ol' Charlie bear is away at that meeting, things might get a little too interesting for an unprotected little cupcake like you. You're afraid that if I take you home now, I might try to eat you up. And you're right, sugar bum, you're right. Yum, yum, yum."

My head was spinning. There I stood on the university sidewalk with a professor who was also my husband's best friend nibbling at my ears. Through all the confusion one word surfaced: *"meeting."*

"Meeting?" I asked, pulling away sharply. "You call a court hearing a meeting?"

"Court hearing? What are you talking about, Zelda?" Immediately the monkey business stopped.

"I'm talking about the trial Charlie had to go to in Wichita today. Adelaide's suing him for more money. Partly thanks to your wife's kindly letters of lies to Adelaide."

Anthony looked so totally taken aback that I couldn't help but continue; a gleeful righteous anger spurred me on. "Dear June, your sweet, pure wife. Don't you know she wrote Adelaide and told her that Charlie and I live in a fine house in the best part of town, with a pond and a statue? When it's the tiniest house in the area, the yard is thirty feet square, and the statue is just a poor little brass frog! June wrote her all sorts of crap, my beautiful clothes, the silver in our dining room—Jesus, it's all my grandparents' silver—we have to go to court because my grandparents gave me a tea service! Your wife is a goddamned *fink*, Anthony Leyden. She tells Adelaide lies, she exaggerates what she sees, to keep Adelaide in a stew of envy and anger. I can't stand the sight of her, and I can't stand the sight of you, so back off and let me alone."

"Zelda," Anthony said, "I didn't know. I really didn't know."

"We might lose the farm," I said, and my voice

began to quaver. "We might lose the farm, and I'd have to sell my horse. 'Thoroughbred horses,' June wrote Adelaide. Well, yes, they're thoroughbreds, and good ones, but one was mine before my marriage and Charlie's wasn't expensive. And Mr. Demes farms the bottom pasture and gives us hay from it for the horses in return for the rest of the hay free to himself. Oh, God, I don't want to lose my horse—"

I was beginning to cry. The January cold was starting to seep into my bones, and it had suddenly grown quite dark. I turned and ran down the street, away from Anthony. He didn't come after me. I heard him get into his car and drive down the street, but I didn't turn my head to see him go. I felt bad—Kansas Methodist guilt again—that I had blithered it all out to Anthony. He wasn't, after all, responsible for his wife's actions, and Charlie had probably not wanted to add any tension to his friendship with Anthony by squealing on Anthony's wife. If Charlie hadn't told him, I shouldn't have, either.

I went home sunk in misery. I made a fire and heated up a stew and put on a lounging robe and waited for Charlie. The television weatherman reported blowing snow on the Kansas turnpike. Hazardous driving conditions. I didn't worry about Charlie; I knew he was a good driver. But I thought I would go mad as the hours went by and I still didn't know the outcome of the hearing.

At ten o'clock Charlie came in the door. His face was so drawn and gray I nearly burst into tears.

103

"Charlie—" I went to him and kissed him on the cheek. It wasn't a moment for sexual love at all.

"It's all right," Charlie said. He managed a smile. "It's fine. Nothing's changed. The court ruled against her. They think she's getting enough. I don't have to give her anything more. God, I need a drink. It was a long day and the roads were tough. Icy."

"Oh, but Charlie," I cried, clapping my hands, "that's *wonderful*. We won't lose the farm!"

I hung up his coat; he fixed himself a drink. Then be sat down in his chair in front of the fire and leaned his head in his hands.

"She looked so awful Zelda " he mumbled. "Jesus she's like a fury from an old Greek play. She looks hard and bitter and wrinkled and crazy. That pretty young girl I used to love."

Every time Charlie talked about Adelaide it was as if he were kicking me over and over again in the stomach. It hurt. It took my breath away. Sometimes I had to sneak to the toilet and vomit. But I never told him that; he never seemed to guess. Now I said nothing.

"She always had a temper," Charlie went on, "and it got fiercer and meaner each year, but I never saw her like this. I think she'd kill me if she could. She was so upset when the court ruled against her. She screamed at the judge and at her lawyer and at me. Then she said she wanted my visitation rights taken away, she doesn't want the girls to see me ever again. She was raving. She had dyed her hair reddish, and she looked awful. I felt I was looking at someone I'd never seen before in my life."

Charlie was quiet for a while, and so was I. What could I possibly say?

"She seems stuck," Charlie went on finally, "stuck somehow in her life. She can't move on. She's nourishing herself on her hate and anger, and it's a terrible, terrible food. Four years ago, I know exactly when it was, Caroline was overnight at a friend's and Cathy was asleep in bed. I said, 'Adelaide, we've got to talk. I can't keep living like this. I don't love you anymore, and you don't love me. We're wasting our lives.'

" 'No, we aren't,' she said, 'we've got these two beautiful children to love. That should be enough for anyone.'

" 'It's not enough for me,' I told her.

"She started raging. 'I cook for you, I keep a spotless house, I iron your sheets, I make homemade bread. And cabbage rolls —do you know how long it takes to make cabbage rolls? I iron your shirts. I make a nice home for you, I cook you delicious food. I've given you two lovely little daughters. Oh, Charlie, let's have another baby. I want another baby so much.'

"That's all she wanted, her house and her babies. She didn't really want *me,* she'd never wanted *me,* but rather a provider, a model husband and father. That night she even told me to have all the affairs I wanted. But not to leave her. She liked her life. Her nice house, her nice children, her nice security. She didn't care if we ever slept together again unless I would give her another baby. And we didn't sleep together very much after that. I didn't want to make her pregnant, I didn't want to be even more tied down . . ."

Charlie's voice trailed off. He stopped talking. He took a big drink of his scotch. We sat in silence for a while. I was miserable.

"And now," he said, "I don't think she can handle it. Being married meant so much to her, the superficial, public part. She didn't care how our marriage was in private, as long as she was *married*. God, we had the shiniest kitchen floor in the city. Now, being *divorced*, she can't handle it. It's as if she were trying to build herself a house to hide in, a house made of anger and hate and despair, all that's left of our relationship, instead of stepping right out into the new world. I wish I could help her. But I can't. It's awful for her, it must be awful for the girls. Dear Lord, I wish she would meet some nice man and get married and have some more babies. Then she could be happy again."

"And when do *we* get to be happy again?" I longed to ask. Ever since that day in October when Adelaide's first letter came, we had lived like two people on death row. There had been so many melodramatic letters and phone calls between lawyers and Charlie, and Adelaide and Charlie. Every night when we sat down to eat or went to bed to make love, half of us was waiting for the phone to ring, for a lawyer to say, "Sorry to bother you, Charlie, but there's one more thing—" or for Adelaide to screech and cry. Christmastime was almost ruined. We sent only a few nice gifts to Caroline and Cathy, not wanting to incur any more of Adelaide's wrath by sending too much. We spent two weeks of Christmas vacation on the farm, hiding from the phone, but it was not a merry time. We each kept thinking that this might be our last Christmas on the farm. I rode my horse every day, but not with the careless joy I had once known. And I didn't shower Charlie with gifts, as I had wanted to; I saved the money I earned. I thought that someday we might really need it. And now, when the hearing was over and the farm was safe, it seemed we still were not to celebrate and be happy. I felt that Adelaide's wrathful spirit was living with us like a malevolent ghost, keeping us from living joyfully. Everything seemed tainted. I could forgive Caroline and Cathy for reporting on us, for listing our every possession, but I wouldn't be able to forget that they had done it. A pattern had been set: for years now the things that we would give them would not be simple gifts. If we gave them a lot, we were trying to buy them, we were wealthy and were spending money fool-ishly, money they (Adelaide) should have. If we gave them a little, we were being miserly and mean, we did not love the girls. If we wanted them to come visit us, we were trying to deprive Adelaide of her joy in life. If we didn't want the girls to come, well, of course we did not love them. Nothing, for years, would be clear and good and free. And at least once a year there would be phone calls, letters from lawyers, threats. For a long time, for years, I would not make homemade bread, or talk to women who had children, or keep my kitchen floor shiny. I didn't want to do anything that Adelaide had done. I didn't want to be like her in any way at all. I thought she was a sad, nutty, lost woman.

"If you divorce me," she had said to Charlie, "I will make you pay for it. I'll do everything I can to make your life miserable."

She spoke in clichés, but she tried her best to carry out her threats.

It didn't seem like a very healthy way for a woman to live her life. But apparently it gave her a sort of bitter pleasure. Apparently, for a while, that was one of the greatest pleasures she had.

Charlie and I learned to live with it. We were happy in our work, happy in our love for each other. We even developed a wry sense of humor about it all. After a while it was almost an unwelcome, acknowledged guest in our home. We learned to live with Adelaide's bitterness and with the sudden gloomy changes in our daily atmosphere that the bitterness could bring. We learned to go on living and loving and laughing in spite of it all. It was like having a ghost behind a door. If one buys a beautiful haunted house, if one loves it enough, one keeps it, and lets the ghost rage on.

In March of 1966, two months after the hearing, an international symposium on human relations was held. Approximately sixty scholars and professionals in the field gathered to spend five days at a first-class luxury hotel, lecturing and listening to each other, and participating in discussions and panels. The papers they presented were to be collected into a book: the National Social Science Association's 1966 Symposium on Human Relations. The honoraria and transportation expenses provided were more than adequate; it was a first-class operation all around. Only the best people in their various specialities—anthropology, sociology, general semantics, linguistics, literature, psychology, nutrition, foreign relations, education, journalism, and so on—were invited, and the historian invited was Charlie. Perhaps to make up for the summer when I missed meeting the famous intellectual woman, perhaps simply because we were so much in love and didn't want to be parted for long, Charlie took me with him to the symposium.

It was held the second week in March, which fitted exactly into our university's spring break. We flew to Chicago and then to Boston, where a limousine from the hotel met us and three other participants. We rode for almost three hours, up into the hills of New Hampshire, and Charlie and the other men played intellectual tennis all the way, while I sat in a stunned respectful silence. I was twenty-three, I had just started work on my master's. After those three hours in that limousine I was ready to weep with despair. I didn't see how I'd ever in my life know as much as any one of the four men, or be able to present my knowledge with such careless, arrogant ease.

Just before we arrived at the hotel, the old, bearded cyberneticist reached across and patted my knee in a gallantly lecherous stroke that he could get away with because of his age and his fame.

"Thank God your husband brought you along, honey," he said. "You're just what we all need: a beautiful young woman to make our blood race so we can keep up all this egotistical drivel."

I smiled back at the man, genuinely pleased. I felt he had just given me a role to play, a reason for being there. I determined to look as pretty as I could at the symposium, and to listen in the most complimentary way possible.

The hotel was grand. It had once been a spa, and was pillared and columned and gilded and carpeted and furnished in the most luxuriously decadent way imaginable. In the winter it was used mostly as a ski resort, and it was so huge that the seventy-five scholars and wives and symposium administrators were simply given a separate wing of conference rooms and a separate dining room. The bedroom Charlie and I shared was carpeted in a deep rich red, and the curtains were thick and the sheets and towels were monogrammed with the hotel's initials. It was great fun throwing off that thick, heavy, quilted satin spread and rolling on those expensive sheets with Charlie. Afterward Charlie took some scotch out of his briefcase and we had a little friendly toddy while I sat on the bed and let Charlie's semen drip out of me into a soft initialed towel. Then we showered and dressed and tried to look appropriately serious as we went downstairs to dinner.

The symposium passed by me in a blur: mornings and afternoons spent listening to papers and discussions; lunch and dinner spent trying to be charming and complimentary to the others at my table; evenings—evenings were best—spent simply watching the famous people get drunk and show off or argue or tell long intimate, personal tales. I tried so hard to absorb all that knowledge that my head continually ached, and I faithfully scribbled notes in a small red binder, but what I carried away from that 1966 conference was a knowledge that I couldn't yet assimilate, couldn't yet understand, couldn't yet use.

I learned that many famous intellectuals are silly little babies, full of pride and defenses and wanting more than anything else some sort of woman to take care of their typing, plane schedules, laundry, and sexual needs, not necessarily in that order of importance.

I learned that a naive young woman can deserve the company of a Nobel Prize winner if she's pretty, and young, and willing to listen with a look of total awe on her face.

I learned that at symposia there were several sorts of men but only two kinds of women, excluding the hotel waitresses. There were the smart ones, who were the participants, and there were the pretty ones, who were the wives.

When I first entered the dining room, I felt relieved to see women sprinkled here and there among the men. Back home there had been only three women in a master's program of twenty-two. The odds here seemed about the same, and it didn't surprise me. What did surprise me, what did ever so slowly sink into my thick skull as the days passed and the participants were introduced to deliver their papers, was that there was not one woman participant that I would have wanted to be. There was a sweet, tired, serenely grieving nun, Sister Grace Anthony Morrow, a specialist in linguistics. There was a tall, wide woman from the U. S. Army, specializing in foreign affairs; she was forty-one and single and wore thick glasses and heavy dark suits and had her hair cropped like a man's. There was a German woman, who wore her hair pulled back into a tight bun and who never smiled. She was a specialist in education, as was her husband, who was also at the symposium. They had written several books together, but they never smiled at each other, or touched, or even sat together. They were competitive with each other; sometimes they argued with each other in a language other than English, snapping at each other sharply, quickly, like a pair of rival dogs. There was a small Japanese woman whose lecture I didn't attend. She was older, and she was exceptionally quiet. I don't think she understood English very well. And there was an almost pretty sociologist, a woman who hid herself behind loose dark clothes and glasses that kept falling off. She trembled so much when she stood to present her paper

112

that no one could understand what she said. She took her lunch in her room, and went to her room every night right after dinner, and left the symposium a day early. A famous woman anthropologist had been planning to come, but had fallen ill, and her huge, amusing, genial, womanizing anthropologist exhusband came instead.

I learned that I liked being considered pretty, and I liked being smiled at by men. I liked being cheerful and helpful and warm. I liked having Charlie look at me in a special way, touch me in a special way; I liked having Charlie love me. If a woman had to lose all that in order to reach the top of her profession, I wasn't so sure I wanted to start the climb.

The most attractive woman there was a wife. Other wives were there, of course, mostly following their husbands around saying, "Of course, dear, I'll run back to the room and get it for you," or, "Do you need a pill, dear? I've got one right here in my purse." But the most attractive woman there didn't do that. She smiled at her husband and leaned against him fondly when they were together, but she didn't fetch and carry for him. She was a tall, slim woman in her late thirties who had long blonde hair and eyes as blue and warming as a summer sky. Men congregated around her; she was witty and intelligent and kind. And she seemed wonderfully together, wonderfully self-sufficient. She attended only a few of the lectures, and spent most of the days reading by herself in the hotel's wicker and green solarium. I admired her for three days, almost wanting not to get to know her, not to ruin the spell. I wanted to be like her, obviously beautiful, warm, confident, serene, and obviously, kindly, intelligent. When I finally got up the courage to interrupt her reading in the solarium, I was amazed at what she revealed.

"How nice of you to come chat with me," she said. She put her book down and pulled some bright yarns out of a batik bag. "I've been ignoring my knitting. I love to read, but I've got to get this sweater done."

Her name was Alice. And she had six children. She was enjoying a week away from them; it was a bliss to have someone else cook, not to wake up in the night, but she had to confess that she missed them all dreadfully.

"But—but—" I stammered, and then blurted honestly, "You're always throwing out the most marvelous quotes from Plato or Montaigne! How can you—"

Alice laughed, delighted. "I'm a Leader of a Great Books Discussion Club for teen-agers," she said. "This is my fourth year of doing the classics. After four years things start to stick. It certainly does fool everyone, doesn't it?"

Alice thought that children were endlessly fascinating, and actually pitied the intellectual men for their dried-up, fusty-dusty, nit-picky lives. She liked to cook and bake and make jelly, to sew, to touch and mold textures and colors into something unique and new. She loved being pregnant, giving birth, nursing, playing with the children.

"Oh, I love to read and think," she said, "but I infinitely prefer *life*."

I fell in love with her, a little bit. We traded addresses and secrets and agreed to correspond. It wasn't until years and years had gone by that she accidentally let the secret of her maternal joyfulness slip. Actually, she hadn't intended for it to be a secret, she hadn't really thought about it at all as entering into the picture. What it—her secret was, was money. She was married to a professor, and professors seldom make much money. But she was the daughter of a New England insurance executive and she had lots and lots and lots and lots of her own money. Which she spent for babysitters and household help. Whenever she wanted. So that there was actually a world of difference between her and any other mother who on any given day can not afford to say, "Connie? Come over and watch the children today, will you? I think I'm coming down with a little cold; I'm going to make some rose hip tea and go read a book in bed and see if I can't get rid of it before it gets worse."

But I didn't know that then. I was desperately searching for models, I suppose. I suppose that's why I fell in love with her. Of course I wasn't the only woman, or man, who did. Several of the famous men practically fell over their feet trying to offer her a chair when she entered the room. Two of the most famous men, men so big in the intellectual world that they would have to be called planets rather than simple stars, brought her drinks and

115

beamed down on her with open admiration. Years later I discovered why, yet another secret: Alice had been sleeping with them at the symposium. She had gone to their rooms—on two different nights, of course—and shared a bottle of gin with one and two bottles of champagne with another and screwed them both silly. Alice loved to screw strangers, especially important ones. She always had fun at conferences; she had a powerhouse of memories that she savored like Polish vodka on a cold rainy day.

But at the symposium in 1966, I wasn't aware of all of Alice's secrets; those wouldn't be revealed for years. I was aware of only the obvious: there were smart women; there were pretty women; and the only woman who combined both qualities was a woman who had six children.

"Women are concerned with the interior of things; men with the exterior," a famous psychologist told me gently, benignly, like God talking to a child. "This is only right, only natural, my dear. Think of your body."

I was too dazzled by his mere presence to question or argue. One of the other things I learned at the symposium was that although famous intellectuals might be silly little babies, demanding and egotistical, arrogant and defensive, they could also be wonderfully handsome and rivetingly powerful. Age only made them more distinguished; fat tummies made them seem only more solid, more significantly secure. The Europeans especially had beautiful, expensive, elegant clothes and charming courtly manners. If my mind said, What a prick that guy is, my body still said, Oh, you bet, pant, pant, let's just go stand near him some more and let the radiation jingle over us.

I learned that my body quite often disagreed with my mind. I was just twenty-three. I thought I'd develop more control over my body as I got older. What a fool I was.

So I learned nothing at the symposium that really helped me at that time of my life with my own personal problems. Charlie, of course, always tried to help in his own vague, preoccupied way, but I knew he didn't understand my problem. I could barely come clear about it myself; it had something to do with wanting to see the famous woman intellectual the summer before. It had something to do with being a smart little female Methodist from Kansas.

I had turned twenty-three that winter, and had begun work on my master's degree, and after the first excitement died down and I realized I could easily handle the work, I looked around the department and noticed that all the professors, every single one, were male. And there were only two other women entering the master's program. One was named Sylvia. Sylvia was skinny and homely and intense. She had a wart, an honest-to-God wart, on the end of her nose. Poor girl. She looked like a comic book witch. She wore nothing but gray, brown, or black. She was fiercely unfriendly and competitive. To be fair, I think she was very poor, and this was her only way up and out. Also, to be fair, she knew a great deal more than I, was a much more serious student. I always thought that love was the most important thing; I still do. Love, first. And also laughter. But Sylvia put literary criticism first, with her teeth clenched. She had no laughter, not even for Chaucer. She did not talk to me, not even if I started the conversation. She never sat next to me in class, as if I had something hideously contagious about me. I thought she was more amusing, in her own wart-nosed way, than anything else.

In fact Linda, the other woman M.A. candidate, used to laugh with me about Sylvia behind Sylvia's back. Linda was a real whiz kid, a woman much quicker than either Sylvia or I. Her brain was always racing, zip, zing, zap; she could make analogies and describe similarities between any two poets or dramatists or novelists one could name. She operated on instinct, mostly. And she was gorgeous, in a strident, plump way. She was wealthy. She was like a great big red-haired sex-pot running on a Mercedes 450SL engine. She didn't belong in a master's program. She didn't give a shit about her studies. Nothing was serious to her: she had all that money, and a big diamond ring from a law student, and she was just filling time until her fiancé got out of school and they could have a large expensive wedding. She wrote her papers on topics such as "Metaphors in Ben Jonson's Plays: Scatology, Bugs, Muck, and Gore." She openly flirted with the professors and the other graduate students. She attended all kinds of rallies and sit-ins, not out of concern but out of boredom. She was a high-powered lady, but a high-powered *lady* all the same: there were vestiges of the old South in her wealthy family, and she had been brought up to be a tease, a flirt, a wife, a mother, and a generally good-looking sweet-talking amusing little thing who always kept her white gloves clean. It was almost too had that she was so brilliant; it only made her flighty and discontent with everything. She would have gone nuts teaching the freshman courses I loved; nothing that routine could have held her interest. In a way I felt more sympathy for her than I did for Sylvia: Sylvia would eventually find a job, and would turn out one well-researched and yawningly dull but thorough paper a year. She would be stolidly content. But Linda was like a flamingo on a farmyard pond. She would never be content. Not with anything. It was only a matter of months, I knew, before she'd get herself knocked up simply to get some action, have a new experience, create a little drama, and force a big showy wedding out of everyone before her fiancé finished law school and she finished her master's. Then she'd be home with a baby for entertainment. I wouldn't have wanted to be that baby.

I wouldn't have wanted to be Linda, or Sylvia, and that was the point. Some of the nineteen male graduate students were married, some weren't and liked to flirt, some were smart, some were dumb, but they were all set on some kind of track that they'd seen other men run first. As a Methodist from Kansas, I had already derailed myself enough by marrying a

119

divorced man fifteen years older than I and leaving the safety of my sorority and home. I knew what I wanted to do, but I was rather afraid that the sky might fall in. My best friend from college had stopped working on her master's in psychology in order to have babies and work in her home as a typist to help meet the expenses while her husband went through med school. My own mother was now a successful research administrator for a hospital, but she hadn't begun her work until all of her children were happily in high school or college and so almost out of the cozy nest she'd built for us. My grand-mothers had both gone to college, which had been unusual in their times, and my mother's mother had even published a few essays on the history of Okla-homa and Kansas in historical journals. But both grandmothers had married and had children and kept house all their lives, with church and book club meetings as their only outside activities. When I mar-ried Charlie, my mother's mother said to me, "Honey, I know your parents are upset about your marrying this man, but you just hurry up and have a baby and everything will be fine. There's nothing like a nice new baby to get everyone to make up." And the minister of the church we belonged to, the nice Methodist minister, said to me the week before I married Charlie, "Well, my dear, since you are so set on doing this thing, see that you do it well. Marriage is a sacred trust. It will be up to you as the woman to create a home, a loving atmosphere for you and your husband and your children—"

"I won't be having any children," I had interrupted. "I'm going to get a Ph.D. and teach at a university."

Reverend Walsh had smiled at me—a smile much like, in its benign and knowing way, the smile I'd later get from the famous psychologist. "Oh, Zelda my dear," Reverend Walsh said, "children are the reason we are put here on earth. They are the reason for living. But I won't argue with you now. You will see, I know, you will see. Just remember, it's nice to be educated, but education means nothing in God's eyes. What really matters to God—and to all of us, when we are finally lying on our deathbed and can see things clearly—is that we have tried to live a good, joyous life, loving men and God."

I had loved Reverend Walsh. He had been my minister for as long as I could remember. He was tall and gentle and homely, rather like Ichabod Crane, but he had powers of magic in his hands and voice and eyes, and a mysterious gentle dignity. I remembered him in white robes at Easter, in black robes at funerals, his eyes full of knowledge, his hands full of blessings. There was no evil or malice in Reverend Walsh, and after listening to his sermons for so many years I knew there was no stupidity in him, either. I wanted to believe in him in order to believe in God. It was difficult, painful, to think differently than he did. It was as if I were turning my back on the benedictions of my youth.

Everything at that point in my life seemed against my ambitions. My mother, grandmother, friends,

121

minister, all pushed me toward the old familiar female roles, and although I seldom saw them after my marriage to Charlie, their eyes and words and values followed after me. The English department in a big, sophisticated, beautiful city was not any help; the professors who didn't openly dislike female graduate students didn't encourage them either. And with Linda on one side and Sylvia on the other, I was beginning to feel a little freaky. Alone. I'll go to the international symposium, I told myself that March, I'll go away from the Midwest to an international gathering, and that will give me a different perspective!

And at the international symposium it was all the same story, simply a larger, more glittering stage.

I am envious of my stepdaughters, who are receiving priority now in the job market simply because they're female. Last January, I left my children with Charlie and took the bus down to stay with Caroline in her apartment in New Haven. It was the last semester of her senior year. She and all her roommates were discussing jobs and ideas as much as they were discussing boys. They had jokes about vibrators mixed with save-the-ecology posters on their walls. *Natural History* and *National Geographic* were on the tables and shelves instead of magazines on makeup and hairstyles and manipulating men. Caroline had already turned down a marriage proposal; she just wasn't interested yet.

If we are progressing in queer little half steps, I had silently wondered, from traditional Adelaide

Campbell to confused Zelda Campbell to right-on, freed-up liberated Caroline and Cathy Campbell, what then will Lucy be? Will fashions and ideas do a switcheroo? Adelaide is twelve or thirteen years older than I; I am ten or twelve years older than Caroline; Caroline is twenty years older than Lucy. By the time Lucy is in college, will Caroline advise her to marry or to work?

Of course, it is all a crazy question anyway. If things continue as they have, Caroline won't even care what Lucy does. We Campbell women may be progressing by half steps, but no one is passing anything on. That's the problem with stepping; we keep tripping and falling backward over an old, old grudge.

After the 1966 symposium in New Hampshire, Charlie and I went to Massachusetts to see Caroline and Cathy. It seemed a good thing to do; we didn't get all that many expense-paid trips back East. Also, I suspected that Charlie wanted to check up on Adelaide, just to see how she looked and was acting. After the hearing in January a sudden calm had hit. No more angry phone calls or letters. Only the canceled child-support checks. In February, Charlie wrote Adelaide to explain that he would be in the East for a conference—an expense-paid conference; he made that clear—and that he would very much like to see the girls. What he would like, he proposed, would be to pick the girls up on Friday evening and have them eat dinner and spend the night with us. We would take them shopping Saturday, if it was all right with Adelaide, for shoes or perhaps an Easter outfit, or whatever she felt they needed. We would return them to her in time for dinner Saturday night.

We cringed and jumped around the house for two weeks after Charlie sent the letter, expecting each phone call to be Angry Adelaide and her screaming serenade. But all that came was an envelope addressed to Charlie. He opened it to find his own letter inside. On the bottom of the letter Adelaide had written simply, "All right. A." Charlie didn't know if that simple agreement after all her drama was a good sign or a bad one.

Friday afternoon we rode down from the beautiful old spa-hotel back to the Boston airport in the hotel's limousine. Several of the other participants rode with us, on their way to Logan field and their various planes to their various homes. This time, however, the ride was fairly quiet. The conference was over, the show had ended, the duels had been fought, the egos had been sufficiently exhibited. There was a general feeling of exhaustion all around, and it was true, they all had worked hard. Now they were eager to get home, loosen their ties and belts, kick off their shoes, and sort through the week's mail. Two of the men slept for the whole drive, trying to recover from hangovers and a general lack of sleep. I noticed how sleep changed them, those brilliant, important men. They sagged and slumped and drooled a bit, and seemed vulnerable and totally dispensable. Charlie sat next to me, scribbling notes about something. There were no other women in the car. I looked out the window, enjoying the passing scenery—the mountains, curving roads, great rocks jutting from snow, winter-gray bare-branched trees. I felt sad. I wasn't sure why. Perhaps because both Alice's exuberantly maternal life and the lives of these significant intellectuals seemed equally inaccessible to me.

In Boston we rented a small Dodge Dart to drive to Hadley. It was a three-hour drive, and this time I slept. When I awoke we were just entering the little village of Hadley, a small town almost inseparable from Amherst. Charlie had lived in this area before; he had no trouble finding the right streets.

Adelaide and her daughters lived in a great big beautiful old colonial house that had been divided and made into a two-family house. It was charming. There were trees all around, and nice homes, and I could tell that Charlie was glad.

"I'll go up and get the girls," Charlie said as we pulled into their driveway.

"Fine," I replied. I looked in the rearview mirror and combed my hair and put on lipstick. I had no desire to go with Charlie, although I was curious about Adelaide. At that point I had never met her. I had only seen an old black and white photo that Charlie had of the four Campbells when Cathy was just born. Adelaide's hair had been chopped short and her lipstick had been dark and thick and her eyebrows had been plucked and drawn in a thin unbelievable arch. She had been holding Cathy and smiling slightly. Charlie's hair had been shorter, and he had been much thinner then; together they looked like some family from an old magazine, advertising RCA Victor radios and Ava Gardner movies. The picture hadn't meant anything to me; I wouldn't have known any of the people if I had passed them on the street. At the time it was taken I had been in high school. I could have baby-sat for such a family.

I knew Adelaide was pretty; I gathered that from the old photo and what people told me and from seeing her daughters. But of course I always wondered: was she prettier than I? That is one of the problems with stepping; the children are always there to remind you that your husband loved someone else first. That he had put his arms around her and held her to him and kissed her tears and given her gifts. That he made a home for her, bought her clothes, and especially shared her bed. When I first married Charlie I used to lie awake in agony at night, thinking of him making love to Adelaide. Had be kissed her nipples so reverently, nestled his head in her stomach, nipped and licked the fruity flesh between her legs? If nothing else, he had certainly entered her, strong muscular arms and chest rising above her like a shield. He was very, very good in bed. He hadn't learned all that from history books. I couldn't stand to think of Charlie with Adelaide, but I sometimes could not keep from thinking of it. I was totally in love with him, I wanted to possess him, all of him, his past, present, and future. I wanted to be all his wives, all his children, I wanted to be his mother. I could not bear it that he had been with Adelaide; if tearing the skin off my breasts would have torn away, erased, that part of his life, then I would have torn away my flesh with my own hands. As it was, I lay awake crying silently, biting my hands until they bled, torturing myself with jealousy. As time went on, I grew less jealous of his past, I forgot his life with her just as I forgot any old unconquerable sorrows. But when the girls came to stay, they might as well have brought a thirty-foot red and gold banner and draped it across the walls of our home: Charlie loved and made love to someone else first.

Then, sitting in our little rented car, I waited restlessly. Charlie had gone inside the house. Inside with his old wife and their two children. What were they doing? Smiling at each other? Kissing? I would never kiss him again, ever, if he kissed her. He was in there for so long, so long, the sun seemed to set and rise again and set and rise again. I felt superfluous, the fifth wheel, the odd one. I was not part of that group. They were in the warm house and I was alone in the car, and the March night was sinking in and the car was growing cold.

Still he didn't come. No one came. Because of the division of the house the entrance was on the side, and I could see only one small window, which was dark. There was no movement.

I grew alarmed. What had happened? Had she fired a gun and shot him as he walked in the door?

Had the sight of her again—hair back to blonde now—entranced him so much that he had strode across the room to her and picked her up in his arms and carried her up the stairs to bed? Were they all four sitting together on a sofa, laughing over old family photograph albums? Was she simply screaming and screaming at him, now that he was there in person? Were the girls clinging to the furniture, pleading not to go with us, begging him to leave them alone? What was going on?

I could see only the black window and the neat red brick wall of the house. How thick that wall was, how silent, how blind.

More minutes passed.

I was still sitting in the little rented Dart, twisting in an agony of suspense, when the ambulance came screaming up. It pulled in so fast, so close to the Dart, that the bumper touched; the Dart rocked a bit. The siren snapped off, and two men jumped out and ran past the Dart into the red brick house.

"My God!" I cried out loud to myself. For a moment I couldn't move. I was horrified. I didn't want to know what had happened.

Then I jumped out of the car and ran to the house.

The men had left the doors open. I raced inside, expecting to see—what?—Charlie bleeding, everyone dead?—and saw only a quiet, neat, coolly luxurious living room. No one there.

I heard noises and went for them. Up the beautiful wooden staircase. Down the carpeted hall, into

128

the back bedroom.

And the first time I saw my husband's ex-wife, she was in his arms. Charlie was holding Adelaide as if she were a giant child. She appeared to be peacefully asleep, or drunk; she was limp. A man in a white coat was looking at her eyelids. Another man was talking to Charlie.

"We'll get her into the hospital and pump her stomach," he said. "If it's been only an hour or two, she should pull through without any problems."

Caroline and Cathy stood shock—still in the corner of the bedroom, white, clenched, past crying.

"Charlie?" I whispered.

"An overdose of sleeping pills," Charlie said. "We don't know how many. Caroline said she had three bottles and they're all empty."

My first thoughts, I must admit, were not kind. I thought, *Damn,* what a phony! She didn't mean to kill herself *really;* she just wanted to ruin Charlie's weekend with the girls. My next thought was, Good God, if Adelaide died, the girls would have to live with us.

But she wouldn't die, I knew. She didn't want to die. She had simply been calling for help in the only way she could.

I took one more good look at her: she was blonde and unbelievably pale, and so slim. Marriage and its sensuous pleasures had plumped me out a bit. But she was so slim, so trim and neat and small. Small waist, small hips, small, almost nonexistent, breasts. Little woman, sound asleep, pale Adelaide.

The men took her from Charlie and put her on a stretcher. They strapped her in, covered her body with a blanket, and carried her from the room.

Charlie went to the corner and picked both girls up in his arms and brought them out of the bedroom. He knelt down and stood them up gently, as if they might fall, and with his hands on their shoulders he said, "Your mother will be all right. Caroline and Catherine, I promise you. She will be all right. I am going to go with the ambulance to the hospital. I'll stay with her. But they know how to take care of her there. I promise you she'll be fine. She'll probably be home tomorrow. Now I want you to go with Zelda. Get your overnight bags. Zelda will take you to the motel and get you some dinner, and I'll be there later, as soon as I can. Don't worry. Your mommy won't die. She'll be fine."

The girls stared, said nothing.

"Is that okay?" Charlie asked. "Will you be all right?"

Dutifully they nodded yes, two good children, shock-white, two little blonde china dolls.

Charlie rose and handed me the car keys. "I made reservations at the August Inn, in Northampton," he said. "You can get the girls some dinner there. I'll be there as soon as I can. Do you have enough money?"

"Yes," I said, and took the keys, not touching Charlie's fingers. The skin under his eyes had gone gray. He looked old. "The girls will be fine," I told him.

Then, "Come on, girls, let's get your bags," I said.

We went back downstairs, not touching, three zombies. The bags were packed and waiting by the open front door. We went out into the black night; it felt strange outside, like a new cold universe. As if in those few moments the very air of the world had changed. I settled the girls together in the front seat of the Dart and put their bags in back. Before I could get in, Charlie came out of the house, pulling the door shut behind him. He passed us by without looking at us and got into the back of the ambulance with Adelaide. The doors slammed shut; the ambulance screamed off. I felt betrayed.

Damn Adelaide, I thought.

I got into the little Dart and started the engine.

"Don't worry," I said to the girls as I drove. "Your mother will be fine. Your daddy will come to the motel soon. Everything will be okay." I repeated those words with several variations on the way to the motel. Of course I didn't know that what I said was true but it seemed the necessary thing to say.

Once at the motel, I ordered room service dinners for the girls and two big scotch and water drinks for me. The girls didn't eat their dinners, but I drank my drinks right down. It was a crazy, spacy time, the hours we spent in the motel room waiting. Nothing seemed appropriate—eating, watching television, going to the toilet—everything seemed in bad taste and irreverent. The phone would not ring and the silence was loud. The girls sat on chairs for the first half hour, looking at each other or the walls or at

131

me, and I drank my drinks, but still felt cold and lost and strange. I didn't know how to comfort the girls. It was not time to flip on the Partridge Family. I didn't know what to do, how to make those awful minutes pass.

Finally I said, "Come on, girls, it's cold; let's get in our pajamas and get in bed. We won't sleep, we'll wait for your father, but at least we'll get warmed up."

Dutifully, zombie china dolls, they obeyed. I put on my nightgown, too, a nice unsexy flannel one I had brought just for that evening with them. Then I finished the last of my drink and crawled right into the middle of the double bed with the girls. I sat up and leaned against the headboard of the bed and pulled each girl up, against me. Caroline of course pulled away a bit, put her head on a pillow and wrapped her arms around it. But she let the bottom half of her body lie touching mine. Cathy cuddled up against me, lay half on my lap. For a few minutes it was horribly awkward and our breathing sounded ridiculously loud. Then, I have no idea why, I began to sing. I had sung in church choirs and choral groups when I was younger and my voice was still a nice steady alto. I started singing an old lullabye: "'Skitters are a-hummin' on the honeysuckle vine, sleep, Kentucky babe . . .'" It had a soothing, Southern, comforting slow lilt to it in a deep, dark minor key. My mother had often sung it to me as she rocked me on her lap; perhaps that was why it came to me so easily then, when I was holding two children against me. The music seemed fitting, neither happy nor sad. I sang it three or four times. When I stopped singing, the room seemed stark and empty. So I sang some more. First hymns, all the hymns I could remember, even Christmas songs—the quiet, holy ones. I sang my serious sorority songs. Serious folk songs. " 'Lord, it's one, Lord, it's two, Lord, it's three, Lord, it's four, Lord, it's five hundred miles to my home . . .' "

Of course, in my own way, I was praying.

Cathy cried quietly, head buried in my lap, soaking my flannel nightgown. Caroline lay stone-still, chilled, dry-eyed, staring.

I sang till my voice was hoarse. At least the time passed. At least we were warmed, there under the covers together.

Charlie arrived at nine, two hours after we had checked in at the motel. He said that Adelaide was all right, would be all right. They had pumped her stomach, and she had thrown up the pills, and at eight she had awakened and was resting normally. He had talked to her. He had told her that he would take care of the girls until Monday. He told her he would pay for a plane ticket and arrange for Adelaide's mother to fly up from Kansas to live with her for a while. He told her he would pay for some psychological counseling for a few months. He told her that everything would be fine.

We ordered up some more drinks and dinners from room service, and this time the girls, reassured by Charlie's presence and Adelaide's recovery, ate. They discussed Adelaide and the sleeping pills: ap-

133

parently she had cheerfully helped the girls pack their bags, had brushed their hair and put them in pretty dresses, then told them to watch television, while she went upstairs to rest awhile. The girls had looked in her room only once, and then Adelaide had been sound asleep on her bed and they hadn't wanted to bother her. They thought it couldn't have been more than half an hour between the time she had gone upstairs and the time Charlie arrived; they had gone to her room during the TV commercial.

"We didn't know she had taken sleeping pills, Daddy," Caroline had pleaded. "Not till you came and we ran up to tell her and she wouldn't wake up and we saw the bottles on the floor—"

"It's all right," Charlie said. "You couldn't have known. And let me tell you what your mommy said, girls, at the hospital. She smiled at me and said, 'Charlie, that was the stupidest thing I've ever done in my life. Tell Caroline and Cathy that I'm sorry if I scared them. Tell them I'll never, ever, do it again.'"

After a while the girls got into bed. They didn't sleep, they probably couldn't, with all the phone calls Charlie made. He called Adelaide's mother and told her about the pills, and listened to her scream and cry and rave—Mrs. Fowler was her daughter's mother—and managed to calm her down. He suggested that she come live with Adelaide and the girls for a few months; Mrs. Fowler was a widow, and lived alone. Then he called the airlines and made reservations, and called Mrs. Fowler back and told her when her flight was, on the coming Monday, and that she would have a prepaid ticket waiting for her at the ticket counter. He told her yes, he would also pay for her fare home whenever she decided to leave. He had her talk to Caroline and Cathy for a few minutes. Then he called the airlines and changed our reservations home to Monday instead of Sunday. He called Anthony Leyden in Kansas City to tell him about the emergency. Anthony said he would cover for Charlie's classes on Monday, and would also see to it that my profs and students knew I was absent because of an emergency. Then Charlie called the Ascrofts, who had been close friends of Charlie-and-Adelaide when they were still Charlie-and-Adelaide and living in Amherst. The Ascrofts still lived in Amherst, and it was George Ascroft who had found Adelaide her job at the university and who was partly responsible for Adelaide's moving back to Massachusetts. After Charlie had divorced Adelaide, George and Susan Ascroft had written Charlie to tell him that they thought he was a cad and a creep and a villain, that they thought he was doing a nauseatingly, viciously monstrously evil and unkind thing by leaving his wife and daughters, and that they would no longer be his friend or have any contact with him. But when Charlie called that night, they agreed to meet him for a drink to discuss Adelaide and her problems and what they could all do to help.

Then Charlie called the hospital to check on Adelaide. She was sleeping peacefully, in good condition.

Finally there was no one left to call. The girls fell asleep, and Charlie and I sat up drinking slowly and talking guiltily in the darkened hotel room.

"I don't love her, I don't know her, I scarcely remember her," Charlie said. "I feel as though I were doing all this for a stranger. But I have to help her; she needs help."

"Yes," I said. I knew he was right; he had to help her. Even I would help her, indirectly, however I could, by being good to her daughters. But I hated her. She had made the canyon come back between Charlie and me. She had made all of us, Charlie, me, her daughters, her friends, feel guilty, somehow vaguely, terribly guilty. It was her weakness, but we had to suffer for it. It did not seem fair. But of course I pitied her, too. I pitied her deeply. And I learned from her. Never in my life, I decided, would I let myself become so dependent, so vulnerable. I would become financially and emotionally independent, I resolved, so that if Charlie and I separated I would be able to laugh, to dance, to fly, rather than to mourn or collapse. I lay awake deep in the night on my side of that vast lonely canyon, while Charlie lay sleeping and tossing and moaning on his side. I lay awake deep into the night, and stared at the dark wall of the motel room, while Adelaide slept peacefully, in good condition in her lonely hospital bed.

The next day was again centered around Adelaide. My life with Charlie was completely dismissed for a while. I hung around and waited when necessary, or took care of the girls, or played chauffeur. In the morning Charlie took the girls to the hospital to see Adelaide. I waited in the motel room, thinking of the four of them, blue-eyed blondes in assorted sizes, together, gently talking. I took the girls to lunch and shopping for clothes while Charlie talked to two different clinical psychologists about Adelaide. Then I sat alone in the motel room again while Charlie and his daughters visited the Ascrofts. The Ascrofts; had children Caroline's and Cathy's ages, so the girls were invited to play while Charlie discussed Adelaide with George and Susan. I was not invited. Charlie thought the Ascrofts might be offended if I came along. I sat for four hours pretending to read a book, wondering if my life would ever be simple again. At six I ordered a scotch and water for myself and at seven I ordered another one, and when Charlie and Caroline and Cathy arrived at seven-thirty, I was a little bit drunk. Not happy-drunk. Tired-drunk. Charlie said the three of them had eaten at the Ascrofts' and now wanted to go to a new Walt Disney movie. I was too drunk and hungry and tired and melancholy to want to go, but I knew it was Adelaide's crisis, not mine, and I didn't want to act like a spoiled child who had lost the limelight. So I went. I ate two bags of popcorn and pretended to laugh.

Sunday it was more or less the same: in the morning Charlie and his daughters went to see Adelaide. In the afternoon the three of them went to visit the Ascrofts, who had invited another couple who had once been friends of Charlie-and-Adelaide. I went to a matinee, some foreign film with subtitles I didn't try to understand. Sunday night the four of us had a big dinner together at the Wiggins Inn. It was an expensive dinner, and I didn't enjoy it; the food was good, but my spirits were low. I felt the canyon between Charlie and me widening, deepening, hourly. I was tired of being silent and subservient, tired of not being touched or talked to. I wanted to fling my wine glass dramatically across the room, to yell, "I'm strangling in this stupid soap opera you've got going! I want out! I want to start my own life!" But all I did was to accidentally knock over my water glass, causing all four of us embarrassment.

Monday morning Charlie and I drove Caroline and Cathy to school. Again Cathy cried when Charlie said good-bye. Caroline ran off into the safety of the school without speaking. Charlie and I rode in silence to the airport in Hartford. He had to meet Adelaide's mother, Mrs. Fowler, at the airport and to drive her back to Hadley. Then he and Mrs. Fowler brought Adelaide home from the hospital. I waited—again, I waited, long, blank, drizzling hours—while Charlie drove back to Bradley Field so that the two of us could catch our six-o'clock flight back to Kansas City. I didn't want to meet Mrs. Fowler, and Lord knows she wouldn't have been pleased to meet me. But I would have sold my soul to be able to watch Charlie as he got Adelaide from the hospital. Was he tender with her, I wondered, solicitous? Loving? Did she fall against him and cry? When he entered that lovely red brick colonial with her, did he want to shut the door behind him and stay?

138

It was at the Hartford airport, waiting through that long March day, watching people kiss and hug and reunite, that I thought it. I thought that the only way I would ever have Charlie completely to myself would be for Caroline and Cathy to die. Then the ties would be cut. If Adelaide died, we would have to raise Cathy and Caroline ourselves, and I would never be free. But if the girls died, there would be no more reason for Adelaide to see or talk to Charlie ever again. He would be all mine. Of course I knew I wouldn't kill the girls myself, and at that moment I didn't actively wish them, those two small girls, *dead*, but still, still, thoughts of plane crashes flickered about my mind like a fire playing, and I thought how clean a plane crash would be, how certain, and how final. I would not have willed it to happen, but if it had happened, I am not sure I would have minded. How confused, how jealous, I was.

Somewhere above Illinois, on our United flight to Kansas City, Charlie, who to that moment had been silent, suddenly rose and went back to the rest room. He was gone a long time. When he returned, he was ashen and shaky. It was obvious he had been sick. When he sat down again, he leaned back and closed his eyes. And reached out to take my hand. And held it tight. The canyon between us closed, instantly, with a magnificent jarring crash, like two continents joining after an ice age.

"Zelda," he said, "I'm so sorry. It was hell for me; it must have been just as awful for you."

The sympathetic words made tears spring to my

eyes. "Charlie," I said, "tell me truthfully. Do you want to go back with her? That would solve everyone's problems."

A real smile broke out across Charlie's face. He shook his head. "Oh, Zelda, my love," he said, as if that were the answer. Then, "No, heavens, no. I'd like to have my girls with me, but I don't want to go back with Adelaide. I don't know why I ever married her in the first place. And now she just bores me. Annoys me. I don't even feel sorry for her after this weekend, and that's the truth. I feel irritated. It's as though she feels the only way she can be important anymore is by being weak and pitiful. And her sad little trick will cost me plenty financially, the phone calls, the fare for her mother, the damned psychologist. I hope to hell he helps her. She's got to get straightened out. What kind of model is she for the girls? It's crazy. If I had been run over by a truck, she would have carried on bravely and started a new life. But since I chose to leave her, she can only fall apart. God, what a mess. It makes me sick. *She* makes me sick."

Well, hooray for that, I thought.

We talked some more about Adelaide and the girls. Charlie thought that if Adelaide did anything else so dramatically unpleasant he would get a court order to take custody of the girls. But he thought that with the help of the Ascrofts and Adelaide's mother things would improve. Adelaide had been living in Hadley for over a year now, and the Ascrofts had said that she had been still feeling so shy

140

and bitter toward men in general and toward women because they married men that she hadn't made friends or even dated. She had insisted on the Ascroft family spending Christmas Day, New Year's Day, Easter Sunday, the fourth of July, and so on and so on, with her. She had fixed marvelous meals. It was as if those holidays with their ritual food had provided the only sense of stability and community that she had. The Ascrofts had felt guilty, Charlie said, because for the past few months they had been trying to pull away from Adelaide. She had spent too many Saturdays and Sundays at their house, had invited them too often to hers; they had lost a feeling of family and had wanted more privacy. And Adelaide had become redundant, boring; too quick to find fault with men; bitter, so acidly bitter that they had turned away from her to keep from being singed. Now they realized that she needed help, really needed help, and they were going to do all they could. Mrs. Fowler was going to do all she could. The psychologist was going to do all he could, one hour a week for eighteen weeks. Charlie had signed an agreement to pay for that many sessions. Surely Adelaide would perk up, especially since she cared for her daughters so much.

I was nearly sick myself when I heard how much Charlie would have to pay the psychologist. It meant that our lives—Charlie's and mine—would be dreadfully austere for the next four months.

"You don't *have* to pay for her treatment," I said, and I worked hard to put the question pleasantly and reasonably instead of in one big wail. "Why are you doing it?"

"For the girls," Charlie said. "They are *girls*. And they love their mother and need her there, healthy and stable, to give them love and a good model of a woman. It wouldn't help if I dragged them away from her. They need their mother first. The only way I can help Caroline and Cathy is to help Adelaide. To try to give her back to them since I've taken myself away."

"I see now," I said, and I did. I admired Charlie for it. I thought he was a good man. I knew I was not a good woman; a selfish beast within kept screaming, Get Adelaide out of my life! I can't take this anymore!

It was wonderful when the plane trip ended. Once we set foot in Kansas City, *our* territory, I felt myself expand. For four months we would be poor, but we would be *alone,* Charlie and I, and he would teach and write and I would teach and study and we would have books and each other and still a few trips to the farm. We would be in our own world again, and I knew I would survive the phone calls about Adelaide and her health. When I saw my beautiful city again, and our small lovely house, and my books and papers, and the bed I shared with Charlie, I knew I could survive anything if I could just have those.

Today was a lovely, bright, sunny fall day here in Helsinki. An unusual day. For the past two weeks we have had rain, gloom, heavy gray skies, and then, oddly enough, clear starlit nights. I usually stand on our tiny balcony after Adam and Lucy are asleep and look out at the cold clear sky and hiss, "For crying out loud, why can't you get it right! Be clear in the *day* and cloudy at *night!*" Actually, I think the Finns may prefer the gray sky; it goes better with their color scheme. Things—coats, dresses, boots, scarves, bags—are of an excellent quality here, but drab. The Finns wear black, gray, dark brown, dark blue. I feel like a freak as I hurry along to the grocery store in my pale blue ski parka with its red embroidery and white furry trimmed bood.

What is it about Finland that makes the Finns so dreadfully dull? The polite word is shy, but it's something more. It seems a philosophical choice. Three families we've been with now, and all the adults have been pleasant and interesting, but all the children seem neurotically reserved. They cry if Adam or Lucy accidentally touches his or her knee as we ride, four abreast, stuffed in the back of a Volvo. They stand almost motionless next to the security of their mother for two hours at a time while my children, tired of trying to get a response, play with the Finnish child's toys. Perhaps Finnish children are so shy because Finns don't like children. Finns like things nice and quiet and clean and tidy, and God knows children are anything but that. Also, children, young babies, indicate that people have been engaging in sexual acts. People have been making love. People have been screwing . . . fucking.

143

I think screwing is still frowned upon here in this Lutheran society. Oh ye sinners. Heavy, heavy. The other night at a party, where only adults were gathered, Charlie asked, "Where is the red-light district in Helsinki? Is it worth seeing?" And all of the people in the room, six other intelligent, sophisticated, grown-up Finns, stopped talking and stared at Charlie with a mixture of embarrassed amusement and serious, reproving shock.

"Well, the one in Amsterdam was so gay," I offered, trying to appeal to their sense of sophistication, wanting somehow to bail Charlie out. And they did stop staring at Charlie, but only to look with bland silent disapproval at me. "The redlight district in Amsterdam is even on the tourist guide maps," I continued, smiling. There was no response; no one said, "Ah yes, I've been there, too." I felt compelled to make it clear that Charlie and I were not crazy American sex fiends. I had a bright idea; I would mention Charlie's daughters, who were young and innocent. Then they would understand how unlewd Charlie's question had been. I wanted the staring Finns to know that we—Charlie and I—all Americans—were *good* people. "I took Charlie's daughters to the Amsterdam red-light district one afternoon. It was a Sunday, and Charlie had left for a conference in Barcelona, and his daughters were living with us that semester, and I said to them, 'Where would you like to go? What would you like to see in Amsterdam?' And they said the red-light district. They had read about it in the tour guides. I was worried about taking them there because Caroline was seventeen and Cathy was fourteen, and Charlie was gone, and I didn't know if he would approve, and their mother might have thought I was damaging their innocent minds. So I tried to get out of it. I said, 'If you cook the dinner and do all the dishes tonight, I'll take you there.' You see, they hated cooking and doing dishes so much I thought they'd never agree. Well, they did. And we had great hamburgers and they cleaned the kitchen and I took them to the red-light district. It was a lovely sunny Sunday afternoon. We walked up and down and around the streets, looking in the windows. I must say that the people on the streets stared at us, too; I was seven months' pregnant with Adam then, and I am short and dark, while Caroline and Cathy are tall and blonde. People always stared at us in Amsterdam. Well, it was fun—there were the Algerian sailors, swarthy little men in dark peacoats with the collars turned up, darting into the ladies' doors, and the ladies would pull down their heavy shades: occupied for a few minutes. But there were shops selling baby clothes and pastries or fruit and pleasant residences mixed in with the prostitutes' apartments, and all sorts of people passed us on the streets, old gentle men with dogs, mommies and children. It was really quite pleasant, even gay."

I stopped talking, breathless, somehow hopeful. I was exhausted and a bit embarrassed; I could only hope I had made them understand. Everyone stared at me a moment. Then, "I don't believe Helsinki has a district as such," one Finnish man replied finally. "This is a port city, there are probably some places where sailors go." He said it straight-faced, solemnly, then turned away. The others gave me one last somber look, then also turned away. I took a big swig of my drink. Thank God when I looked at Charlie I saw laughter in his eyes.

Perhaps it is just talking about screwing the Finns don't like. I'm sure they do it and like it; they're human after all. It's probably very complicated. The Finns don't have what one would call a rip-roaring sense of humor, and making love does involve the ridiculous: sweat, grunts, insane gymnastic positions. And it does lead to children; here we are at children again. Yesterday a Finnish mother who had lived four years in the States said to me, "The next time a Finn is rude to me on a bus because I have two small children with me, I am going to say, 'All right, mister, just wait a few years till your taxes are eighty percent because there won't be many people in Finland because no one has children because Finns hate them so.' " It is true that the Finnish families seem limited to just two children; there are few large families. Social censure must be an effective contraceptive device.

I wonder why they are this way, reserved, quiet, drab, gray, shy. Is it their climate, so cold, their Lutheran religion, so harsh, their heritage and proximity to Russia? Now and then, on good days, when it isn't raining, I play Hansel and Gretel outside with Lucy and Adam. First I am the mother and I send

146

my children off to the woods to get nuts and berries, and then I hide behind a tree and become the witch. Hansel/Adam and Gretel/Lucy come walking by giggling in anticipation, and I jump out at them, shrieking, "Hee-hee-hee, such nice plump little children, I'm going to eat you up!" Laughing like a witch, hands curved to indicate long sharp nails, I chase them around the trees and sidewalk and catch them and nibble at their necks while they dissolve with laughter. The children love this game; they want to play it again and again. But the Finns walking by always look on with frowns instead of smiles. It seems to annoy them to see us having such silly fun.

And just last week Charlie and I went to see a Finnish opera, *The Last Temptations*. It is about a Finnish minister who lived in the 1800's, and the subtitle of the opera was "despair, doubts, pride and delusions." The music was overwhelmingly fine and powerful, modern. But the scenery was stark; the costumes, like Finnish everyday dress, were black, gray, dull brown, dark blue; the women's hair was pulled back in severe buns; and the plot was grim. Paavo, the minister, is in despair. His young son dies. The village turns against Paavo and his second wife, Riitta. Paavo dies. I was wearing a bright red dress and I had a wild desire to jump up onstage and start singing and dancing the can-can.

Of course I didn't. But I do so miss a sense of gaiety here. Everyone is so restrained and responsible here. Even Charlie. He's so busy with all his lectures, and sometimes he isn't home until late, and I

147

am often stuck here, alone, while the gray sky turns black at five, trying to entertain my two children, who have here no television, no friends, and few toys. Perhaps that is why I dream of the past. Perhaps that is why I dream about Stephen and secretly smile as November twenty-ninth grows closer.

FOUR

It's almost Halloween. Last night I spent three entire hours making popcorn balls and wrapping them in clear plastic and tying the plastic with orange paper bows. Saturday we are all invited to a Halloween party, and I promised I'd help decorate and bring the popcorn balls. Popcorn balls, what a job! Perhaps especially difficult here in this inefficient apartment, where I have so few pots and pans and utensils and no measuring cups or candy thermometer. It seemed to take hours for the syrup to reach the hard-ball stage and I thought: What on earth am I doing here stirring over a hot stove late at night like a cranky witch? Adam and Lucy are only four and two; they don't *know* that popcorn balls are a customary Halloween treat. But after all, I know, and I like tradition, ritual, ritual food, and it eases the ache of homesickness a bit to celebrate as if we were at home. They don't have Halloween here in Finland, but a Finnish woman who lived in the States for few years enjoyed the custom so much that she has decided to hold Halloween in her own home, every year, for friends and their children. So I spent three

148

hours last night making popcorn balls, and actually I enjoyed it. When I was rolling the balls together, hands coated with butter, picking up the hot candied corn, which I had spread out in the three metal baking pans, I even smiled to myself and dreamed a bit. In just a few years, I thought Adam and Lucy will be able to help me. Last night they were tucked away safely in their beds, out of the way of the possible harm of bubbling hot syrup. But in a few years—a picture came into my mind. An October evening back home. Crisp air and golden leaves. Adam and Lucy and I in the kitchen, working and laughing together, cheating and eating the sweetened popcorn as we worked. Adam would be interested in the candy thermometer, he already likes things like that, and back home I have a candy thermometer. Lucy would be talking—even now she talks incessantly—about school, and the bats and pumpkins and witches her class would make out of orange and black construction paper. We all three would have butter on our hands, we all three would roll up the crackly balls. Perhaps we would be making them for our own party. Somewhere—in the next room, probably, in front of a fire of applewood—a big dog would be sleeping. After making the popcorn balls we would clean up the kitchen—the children would cheerfully help; it was after all my fantasy—and then go in to sit by the fire. The children would lie next to the dog, stroking his black silky coat (he would be a Newfoundland), and I would tell them a Halloween story, perhaps the Legend of Sleepy Hollow, and we

149

would all drink apple cider.

How funny that I didn't fantasize a man around somewhere, in an easy chair by the fire, reading the newspaper, or even in the kitchen, joking with us and helping.

Perhaps I didn't want to spoil my lovely dream by having to decide just which man would be in the chair. Charlie? I don't know. Stephen? I don't know. I do know I certainly didn't imagine Stephen's children, Carrie and Joe, in the picture.

I met the woman who is giving the Halloween party at a Finnish-American Women's Club meeting which I went to out of desperate need to meet someone who speaks English and has small children. Rija is interesting to me for several reasons, mostly because she is so very nice, but partly because she is also a stepmother. And much more a step*mother* than I ever was.

Rija married an American just one year ago. He was a handsome man, in Helsinki on some sort of business, and they fell in love and were married in Finland just four weeks after their first meeting. She is Finnish and loves Finland, but agreed to live with him in the States. He took her home with him to Chicago, and for a while they lived happily. One Sunday afternoon the doorbell of their apartment rang, and when Rija opened it, she saw two little boys standing in the hallway, crying. She called to her husband, who came to the door and said in amazement that the two boys were his sons by a former marriage. He couldn't imagine what they were doing there, but when he saw the little suit-cases full of clothes he began to guess. The children had been abandoned by their mother, and although Rija's husband had very good connections with the government and other police agencies, no one could find out where the mother had gone. They had of course taken the boys in, and Rija, after the first shock had gladly played mother to them. They were attractive little boys, only five and three years old. She decided that she would have a baby herself, now that she had so suddenly accumulated a little family. But before she could get pregnant, some-thing else happened.

Her husband worked for the United States nar-cotics agency; she had known that when she mar-ried him. One night they were all coming home from a drive-in movie. The children were asleep in the back seat of the car. Rija was curled up in the front seat, her head on her husband's lap. They had been married almost seven months. It was dark. Her husband stopped the car, got out to open the garage door of the apartment building. A huge figure emerged from the dark. Rija sat up just in time to see the figure raise a pipe above her husband's head. She screamed, "Michael!" and her husband turned so that the pipe, coming down, broke his shoulder instead of his skull. Rija, insane with fear and anger, grabbed the loaded pistol which she knew her hus-band kept in the glove compartment of the car and jumped from the car and ran to the men. She pointed the gun at the man with the pipe and told him she would kill him if he tried to run. Apparently she sounded serious enough with her accented English; the man did not run. Her husband lay moaning at her feet and her husband's children sat crying in the car and the man with the pipe stood staring at her while Rija stood on a Chicago sidewalk screaming, "Help! Policel Help! Murder!" Finally other apartment lights came on, finally a police car came. She told the police the story; the police checked her husband's identification papers. They took the man with the pipe away. Later she had to go to the police station to fill out papers. She agreed to be a witness at a trial.

Three days later the police informed her that there had been some problem, some accident, the man with the pipe had escaped from jail. She had thought, Escaped from jail? How? She asked her husband, who was in the hospital with his broken shoulder, and he said that he was sorry to get her involved, but in the international narcotics world all things were possible. The next day she took her husband's children with her to get groceries. She came back in time to see part of her apartment on fire. Firemen arrived quickly and put the blaze out, but much damage was done. The next day she went down to the locked garage to get the car, and the car had been destroyed, the fender and hood and trunk and doors hammered in, the windows and windshield completely broken, pieces of jagged glass sticking up. She had called a taxi and taken the children to the hospital to ask her husband what to do, and he was gone. Her husband,

Michael, had disappeared. The police couldn't find him. No one could find him.

Ten days after her husband disappeared, Rija and her husband's two sons were in Helsinki. Fortunately her husband had some money in the bank and her signature was on the account card. The police had been instrumental in helping her get passports for the two boys. Now she lives in a rented apartment with the boys, and she thinks she has enough money to live on for a year. After that she doesn't know. Supposedly people are looking throughout the States for her husband and his first wife. On her worst days, when the boys are sick and whiney, she suspects that Michael and his first wife are somewhere together on a Caribbean island, laughing because they've managed to get someone else to take care of their kids. She thinks they might show up to claim the boys in a few years. But the boys are nice, and handsome. Rija is sure her husband loved them; she is sure her husband loved her. She thinks he will come for all of them if he is alive. She waits. The boys like her. They are happy. She likes them, but she doesn't *love* them, and she certainly isn't doing what she meant to do. Children don't go to school in Finland until they are seven, and she can't afford preschool for them. She is stuck in a small apartment with someone else's children, and it is not what she wants to do. She thinks it's crazy. When I first heard her story, I felt nearly sick with guilt, as an American, and I thought she would hate people from the States. But she doesn't. She

153

says she loved the way her husband treated her, the way he gave her both respect and freedom, and if she could, she would marry another American in a minute. She holds no grudge against the United States; instead she plays Sonny and Cher records constantly, and sends money back to Chicago so that former neighbors will send the children Sesame Street books.

She is giving the little Halloween party to make the boys happy and to bring some American gaiety into their lives. And after all, she has to do something with her intelligence and energy. She speaks seven languages fluently: Finnish, Swedish, Russian, English, French, German, and Danish. She was, before her garbled marriage, an interpreter for businesses. She is also an artist, although it's possible that she doesn't realize yet just how very good she is. When she finishes a canvas, a gallery in Helsinki always takes it, and it always sells quickly. But she doesn't have much time to paint these days. She writes letters to federal agencies in the States asking for her husband or his first wife, and she stays in a small Helsinki apartment and takes care of her husband's boys. They call her "Mother." "Aiti." "Mommy." She didn't tell them to call her that, but she doesn't know how to ask them to stop.

Caroline and Catherine never called me "Mommy" or "Mother," of course, and Lord knows I never wanted them to. Oh, but there was one time, the second summer they were in Kansas City with us. That summer I had managed to get them to meet some other girls in the neighborhood, and they made some good friends, and we were all a lot happier. One rainy afternoon I had taken five little girls, ages seven to eleven, shopping at a big covered mall in Kansas City. We were walking along, looking at windows full of toys or clothes or shoes or pet food, when I noticed further on down the mall a student I had had the previous year. He had been one of my favorite students; I suppose the ones you convert always are. He had begun my freshman lit class disdainfully, a big bad jock totally uninterested in anything intellectual, and he had finished the course with an A. He had started writing poetry himself, good strong stuff; he slipped the poems to me privately, for comments. When one poem was published in the college paper and he got more praise than mockery for writing it, for writing poetry, big football boy that he was, he said he thought he'd switch from a phys ed to an English major. I hadn't seen him after that, not for a full year.

"Girls," I said, after I spotted the young man at the other end of the mall, "I see someone I know. I want to go say hello for a minute. I'll be right back."

I left them looking at a window full of stuffed animals. As I walked toward the football poet, he turned and looked at me, and smiled, and stood there just looking at me. He was handsome even with, or perhaps because of, his broken nose. For the first time I realized that I was physically attracted to him. And that he was physically attracted to me. He was after all only five years younger than

I, and a good foot taller. Much bigger.

When I was next to him I couldn't think of anything to say. What I wanted really was to rise on my toes and kiss him right in the middle of the mall.

"Hello," I finally said. "How are you?"

"Fine. And you?"

"Fine."

We stood and looked at each other and grinned for a while.

"I'm an English major now, you know," he said. "I even got an A from Corbin's course."

Corbin was the toughest prof the English department had. His course was a sort of filter to keep out the students who wouldn't be good as English majors.

"That's great," I said. "But I'm not surprised."

We grinned at each other for a few more minutes.

"Listen, are you busy right now?" he asked. "Want to come get a cup of coffee or something . . . ?"

"Sure," I said. What was I thinking of? I wasn't thinking at all. I walked off next to him, breathless.

We were at the door of the mall, going out to the parking lot and his car, when suddenly five little girls of various shapes and sizes came running up to me.

"Mommy! Mommy!" they all yelled.

"Mommy, I found the neatest skirt!"

"Mommy, I want the dolly in that window back there!"

"Mommy, can I have an ice cream cone?"

"Hey, yeah, I want one, too, Mommy!"

"Hey, Mommy, I found the neatest shirt that

156

Daddy would just *love!*"

The last was from Cathy, who was hanging on my arms and literally pulling me away from the football poet's side. All the other girls, Caroline included, were giggling and snorting and acting generally half-assed because of their joke, but Cathy was deadly serious. She looked me right in the eye and kept pulling at me until I almost lost my balance. She had seen or scented something; she knew something the others didn't know.

"Come on, *Mommy*," she said. "Let's go buy a present for *Daddy*."

She was only seven years old, but her radar was working even then.

There was nothing I could do but laugh. I had absolutely forgotten Charlie's daughters and their three friends. I had also absolutely forgotten Charlie. I felt rather foolish. I also felt rather sad, rather trapped, rather old.

Good-bye, football poet.

"Sorry," I smiled at him. "I forgot all about the girls. I'd better get them ice cream cones." I didn't even think to tell him that I wasn't the mommy of all those girls, that I wasn't anyone's mommy at all.

"See you around," the boy said, and went on out the big glass door into the hot summer day.

"Pretty funny joke," I said to the girls, and they all cracked up again, giggling hysterical giggles and holding their sides. I bought them all ice cream cones.

I think that was the first, last, and only time they

called me "Mommy"; I *know* it was. They had a mommy already, after all; they didn't need another. And physiologically it was only barely possible for me to be their mother. I was twelve years older than Caroline and fifteen years older than Cathy. Also, they looked nothing like me, nothing at all. They were so tall and big-boned and blonde and I was so short and dark and small. I couldn't have been their mommy. And I don't believe I ever did the things that mommies do. I didn't worry constantly about their health, for one thing. Dentist and doctor appointments were Adelaide's responsibility, though Charlie paid the bills. Perhaps only three or four times during all the years they came to stay with us did I ever have to get up in the night to help them when they were sick. During the day—that was a different matter. Their mother had impressed upon them just how very delicate and precious they were, and apparently one of the favorite ritual games in their house was illness. Caroline and Cathy both described being ill with as much enthusiasm as they showed for Christmas. Being ill meant lying in bed, and being completely waited on and pampered, and having presents and medicine and solicitous remarks, and having the TV set in the bedroom all day. I never liked the game much from my vantage point; I got tired of carrying endless glasses of 7-Up to the bedroom. Mainly my reaction was one of secret distaste because I knew that usually the girls were faking it. There would be no rise in temperature registered on the thermometer, no cough, no vomiting, no darkness under the eyes to signal sickness. Usually the sickness was preceded by a boring day, or the announcement that Charlie and I had a social engagement the coming night. Then one or the other would feel "feverish" and "achy" and would take to her bed. Back in Massachusetts, in their three-female household, the ritual response to such claims was immediate attention and the dismissal of all other occupations of the day. Being sick in Massachusetts meant: you are special. You are now worth noticing. You are important. Being sick in Kansas City was not so much fun. I suppose I was a wicked stepmother; I didn't try to make being ill a special event, a wonderful thing. After a while the girls stopped getting sick at our house.

I never worried about Caroline and Cathy's schoolwork, either, although I read to them and gave them books and introduced them to ballet music and took them to concerts, and so on. I never worried about whether or not they had friends, or the right kind of friends, or any of the zillion little worries a mother has about her child's social life. Actually, when the girls were not with us, for more or less ten months of the year, I didn't worry about them much at all. Now it seems that I worry almost constantly about Adam and Lucy. Will it ruin Adam's life if he goes for these nine months without having any friends? Why won't he try to get himself dressed in the morning when Lucy, who is two years younger than he, zips right through it all, even puts on her snowsuit and boots? Will Lucy be pretty? I

159

can't tell, little funny girl with chicken feather hair sticking up all over. I think I'm liberated, but I still want Lucy to be pretty. Pretty people are so pleasant to look at. Will both children survive all the screaming and stomping and crying I do here? It has become terrible. I scream and stomp every day, and tears shoot out from my eyes like bullets from a gun, they are propelled by such an angry force. . . .

Today a letter arrived from the States from Ellen, Stephen's wife. All the news fit to print; gossip, Joe's teeth, Carrie's colds; how were we liking Finland?; she and Stephen had left the children with grandparents and spent a glorious few days swimming, horseback riding, and hiking in the New Hampshire woods; and Stephen had hired two new full-time people. Both women. One, an older woman with a Ph.D., who would teach Shakespeare and Renaissance lit; the other, a younger woman still working on her Ph.D. thesis, to join the freshman comp and lit staff. Fall was beautiful in New Hampshire, etc. They were carving lots of pumpkins; did they have Halloween in Finland?

I felt so sad at heart after I finished Ellen's letter that I wanted to weep. It was as if the leaden skies of Finland had finally dropped their heaviness down onto my shoulders. I couldn't bear the burden.

"I don't want to go to the Park Auntie's today," Adam whined. "I don't like it there. Just babies go there. I don't have anything to do there or anyone to talk to."

I had just finished reading Ellen's letter. But if

Adam doesn't go to the Park Auntie's today, I thought, I will not have a minute alone to think.

"Oh, sweetie"—first I tried the soft sell—"you always have fun once you're there. There are dump trucks, shovels, the sand—" It didn't work. "Adam, you *have* to go!"

"But I HATE it!" Adam wailed. "I never get to be alone with you. Lucy gets to be alone with you every afternoon while I'm at school."

"But Lucy naps usually, Adam, or has quiet time by herself in her room." So that I can sit at the kitchen table soaking in the silence, sorting out my thoughts, thinking through things. "I need the mornings to go get groceries. It's hard to get groceries with you around, honey, and it's boring for you. I want you to go to the Park Auntie's."

"Yaaaaaah! I don't want to go!" Adam swept his Legos onto the floor, and they scattered about like plastic fireworks, red, yellow, black, white, and blue pieces skittering across the floor.

Slap! I slapped his bottom and yelled, "Go to your room, you spoiled little monster!" Then I burst into tears. Lucy, watching it all, ran to Adam and threw her arms around him, trying to kiss and soothe him, but he pushed her away so hard she fell. And of course she cried, then, too.

I ran to my room and fell on my bed, on the ugly, grimy quilt that came with the bed in this rented apartment, and I cried. I hate myself when I spank Adam; I think it is an unnecessary thing to do. Yet I do it more and more, and right then, instead of remorse, I still felt anger. I had so many emotions colliding inside me that I couldn't sort them out. Was I so upset because Stephen had had a few romantic days and nights with Ellen? Did I miss pumpkins and crackling fires and football games and pumpkin pies so much? Or was it really that I felt *my* job had been taken from me at the university; Stephen had given it to another woman. Whatever it was, I needed time and space to think it all out. I felt pressured to the bursting point. Yet I realized that Adam's complaints were valid. Poor little boy: for two months he hadn't had one child to play with who spoke his own language and who would openly smile and relate to him. He sees children at his school, but they speak only Finnish and live far away. There are no children his age in the forty-eight apartments in our apartment house here. I know he is lonely. And he is so bright; I should read to him, help him write, paint, create, draw. His preschool is more pre than school, and because of the language problem he is not taught his words or letters. I *should* spend more time with him, hold him on my lap, gently say, "This is the way you write your last name," and so on. That would make him happy, I know. But what will make *me* happy? How do I get rid of this rage? I am overflowing with it, and I'm not sure why. Do I hate Finland so much? Do I love Stephen? Do I hate motherhood? Am I tired of following Charlie around everywhere?

Last night I dreamed a beautiful and erotic dream. I went into a house, and there was Count

Dracula, very aristocratic and handsome and mysterious. I fell in love with him and embraced him: merely embraced him, we did not kiss. I yearned to be with him, he was so tempting, and yet I knew everything about him was dangerous and wrong, and yet that only made him more attractive. I finally left his house, to walk in a garden, to think, to try to decide whether I would choose to live with him, really live with him, or not. There were heavy moral and religious questions involved, I knew. I had to do serious thinking, but underneath it all I was sexually stirred and excited as never before. And I was so happy, so exquisitely happy.

I wonder who Dracula is for me. Help, Freud.

I wonder if I can get through this gray day without screaming again or spanking one of my children.

I have never hit or screamed at Caroline and Cathy. It would almost undoubtedly have been better if I had; the noise and motion might have broken down some of the barrier that stood between us. In the later years, during the times I felt most bitter and angry, it would have made things much clearer if I had been able to scream at them, but by then the pattern had been too firmly set. And in the early years I felt resentful of them, or angry with them now and then, but I never felt the pure passionate wrath that my own children can call forth from my depths almost daily. A queer thing, this. A queer thing that I should feel so powerfully angry with my own children that I sometimes have to restrain myself from throwing them across the room. I never much yelled at Charlie, though once in a quarrel I threw my Betty Crocker cookbook at him and broke the book's spine. Yet it was only four days after Adam's birth that I wailed, "Oh, Adam, will you *please* shut up!" (Then in horror and remorse I grabbed him up and nursed him again.) But in the first year of both my children's lives anger was rare. It was the second year, and the third, and the fourth, that it really flourished. I was so sure that I would feel nothing but love for them that for a while, when I first felt the anger boiling up inside me, I thought I was going mad. What I didn't know was that mothers of small children need lobotomies. They need to be able to say, "Dear, would you please get your elbow out of your plate?" and, "Darling, no, you may *not* play with Mommy's lipstick, it is not a toy!" and, "Oh no, you wrote all over the wall with Mommy's new lipstick!" and, "Please don't climb up my leg and screech right now; this is a long-distance phone call," and other such phrases at least six thousand times a day. They must be able to say them sometimes simultaneously. They must be able to refrain from making love in the daytime and be prepared to interrupt lovemaking at any moment in the night if a sick child cries or coughs. They must be able to jump quickly at any given second. They must bend and stoop and lift and rock and wrestle, and sit with little feet pressing against their legs. Little feet pressing against Mommy's legs; how endearing it sounds. And they don't *mean* to hurt, they

164

simply can't keep from moving, and they like to keep in contact with Mommy. But bruises build up anyway, especially on the side of the thighs, where little feet press and push while little hands are sticking little forks up little noses during the process called mealtime. All that is endurable. One doesn't get really angry over having to say, "Adam, this is the fourth time I've asked you wipe your hands on your napkin instead of your clothes." One gets really angry on the rainy days, when one's husband is out of town for three days, lecturing in Copenhagen, and civilization and its beauties seem unimaginably distant to the mother stuck home with small children. Then one gets angry when both children want the star cookie cutter for their play dough, and they won't share and the phone rings, and when you come back they have mashed play dough into each other's hair. But mostly one gets angry, really angry, when the children get the parent trapped, so that there is no time in the day to think or read or even pee without a child crying or needing something. And as they get older, they become so disagreeable, they argue and fuss and demand and whine and say, "You're not my friend." And they don't care who you are or what you've done in life; they really don't care at all. They just want *more,* more of everything, pudding, toys, swinging, more of you. And these are good children, children you love, children who worry when you cry and who say from an airplane, "Oh, look at that big beautiful cloud, that must be God's cloud!" or when seeing a huge silver moon in

165

a play, "Mommy, how close that moon is. I could run up and put my arms around it and give it to you." Adam is, after all, the only one in my life who has literally offered to bring me the moon.

Of course the daily sweetnesses outweigh the daily nastiness. That is the other side of the story. Children are sweet and real and very, very beautiful. After baths, when Adam and Lucy run around naked, I love watching the way their plump legs and bums move, I love their perfect flesh. Sometimes I think I won't know how to endure it when I don't have all this voluptuous, creamy, smooth, silky, perfect flesh to wash and clothe and hold and kiss and smell and see. I think when my children are gone I'll have to raise horses, dogs, cats, flowers; I'll have to have beautiful fabrics to wear and sleep and sit on; I'll have to surround myself with cold beautiful artifacts to endure the sensual deprivation of my warm living babies.

Because I have friends with young children, I survive. My friends share their feelings, their angers and frustrations, and we dissolve much of our wrath in mutual helpless laughter. Because I have older friends, I know I will also survive the time when Adam and Lucy are grown and gone. In fact, if I can be like my older friends, then I will really flourish. I wanted my children, I want them now, even on the darkest days, but I want to teach, too, and so I watch my older friends like a teenager watching a movie star, and I store hints for the future in the back of my mind.

★ ★ ★

Part of my rage here, I suddenly realize, is because I am *here,* in Finland. It seems impolite and unsporting to criticize one's host country, but then I must say I don't feel that Finland is a *host* country. It wants my husband here, but it doesn't want me here. It is doing nothing to make my stay here pleasant. Part of it is of course due to what the Finnish travel books call "the Finn's innate shyness," which may be shyness to them but comes off as rudeness toward me. When I walk our children to the Park Auntie's, I feel more and more like a leper; no one smiles at me or says *"Paiva."* And the harder thing is that no one speaks to my children, except to tell them to go away. The other part of my difficulty in this country has to do with being a woman and a mother. Today, for example, professors are taking my husband to see Turku, an interesting Finnish town with an ancient castle and cathedral. I am left here in the apartment, alone with my children. My children and I are valueless here; we have no value; and no one will help us. When we arrived here in Helsinki, there was one orientation by the Fulbright people which I was unable to attend because I couldn't sit through the all-day lectures with my two small children, and since I had just arrived I had not yet been able to locate a baby-sitter. No one here helped me to find a baby-sitter. No one told me about the Park Auntie or helped me to find a school for Adam. It was as if I were set down in a cold foreign world and forced to fend for myself, to discover

167

everything for myself, without help, without anyone caring, without anyone even saying hello. They said hello to my husband, of course, formally, at the official Fulbright functions. My husband did not have to stay home with small children. He is a professor. His happiness matters. He matters. The children and I do not. The prejudice here is not against Americans or women as such, but against women with small children. And it is such a subtle prejudice: we are simply ignored, left frightened and alone to fight our trivial daily battles.

Only because I was lucky enough to have the washing machine in the bathroom break the first time I used it was I able to stay here at all. The machine broke the third day we were here. I called the *talonmies*—custodian—and a pleasant woman in her thirties came to the apartment. She smiled, she was warm, she spoke perfect English. I nearly wept simply to have her speak to me. She said it was a matter of a bad electric connection, and that her husband would fix it that night. During the few minutes she was in my apartment, she told me about the Park Auntie, and later called the Park Auntie to ask her to accept my children even though she officially had room for no more. She told me about baby-sitters and suggested preschools. She told me about the grocery store, the parks nearby, the library. And I have called her about once a week to ask where to get vitamin C tablets, or what a police form means, or which way to go to find the zoo. Thank God for this woman, whose name is Gunnel;

she has truly saved my life. Without this accidental, completely chance acquaintance I don't know how I could have survived here.

And yet it's more than all that, and different: it's me. If I were not so crazily ambitious, if I did not have this itch to teach, to work with words and people, I could be happy here. I could relax, enjoy myself, enjoy my husband, enjoy my children, enjoy the experience of a foreign country. It is not simply that I am a spoiled American woman who feels seriously deprived without all my electrical luxuries, although that is part of it; heaven knows how I miss Sesame Street. It is that I have managed to become competent in a certain field. It is that I want to work. That is part of who I am, who I have become. I can not imagine Charlie without his work; the thought is absolutely impossible, a contradiction in terms, Charlie *is* his work, and without it, without his books and working papers and felt-tip pens and lecture invitations and phone calls and students, without his work be simply would not be Charlie. He would not recognize his face in the mirror; I would not recognize his body in my bed. Charlie is a historian; that is as much a part of the man as his muscles or his breath. I am not so complete—and perhaps, because of the children, I can't be, for a while—but I still feel that my work is a part of me, an essential part, and without it I am weakened, disabled, blunted. I've lost my sense of humor, my sense of delight. Even if Finland were heaven, I would still be grousing because I could not work. It is unfair of me to be here, grumbling and unappreciative; it is doing no one any good. I don't see why I should stay here. I don't want to stay here—I won't.

I won't.

I will write the mathematician who is renting our farm to tell him that he must be out by January first. I'll tell him that for emergency health reasons (my mental health) I have to come home. I'll tell Charlie to stay or to come with us, but I won't be dissuaded from leaving here. Today I will begin to write letters to the universities and colleges within driving distance of the farm to see if they will hire me—but I know the chances are slim. If I don't get hired, if that particular miracle does not happen, I'll go home anyway, and put Adam and Lucy in a preschool and spend every afternoon working in a library on the research papers I've been longing to do, and perbaps they will get published and pave my way into a university position. I don't need to stay here sniveling, feeling sorry for myself and my children, hating Charlie for his success. I need to go home; I need to go to work. And I will.

I will.

Hooray! Hooray! Everyone was happy! It was July 1966, and Caroline and Cathy were coming to spend their second summer with us in Kansas City. They were so happy to be coming because this time their mother said she wanted them to come. And of course she did; why not? We were providing free baby-sitting service while she got married again.

170

Not that we thought of it in that way—well, perhaps I did, since I did the cooking and laundry and other dirty work, but Charlie didn't. He was simply overjoyed to be having his daughters with him again. He was glad the psychological counseling had paid off; Adelaide was okay, Adelaide had found someone else to love her; Adelaide was getting married. He was sure that she wouldn't call crying that summer.

This summer when Charlie wrote to ask about flying the girls out, he had received a pleasant letter telling him exactly what days to book both arriving and returning flights. "By the way," Adelaide had written, "as the girls will tell you, I am going to be married this summer, July 3, to a wonderful, wonderful man. He doesn't have much money and he is also divorced. And as he is good and moral enough to pay his wife alimony as well as child support, we won't have much money, so don't think you'll be able to get out of sending the child-support checks. Still we are buying a nice house and I'm hoping we'll be able to have another baby or two; I know Cathy and Caroline would like that. Please take good care of my little girls this summer."

"Everyone will be happy this summer!" Charlie said.

And that summer, everyone was. I had the brilliant idea of having a party at the house for the girls, and invited children from all over the neighborhood, and eventually Caroline and Cathy made friends. They were happier because they spent time with girls their own age, and I was happier because

171

I had more time to myself. Of course things were not perfect: once again I couldn't kiss or touch Charlie when they were around, and Cathy still occasionally sent little eye spits of hatred my way, but on the whole, it was a much better summer than the first had been. Charlie was busy completing a book in time for a contract deadline, so I took the summer off from my studies to play with and take care of the girls. With friends their own age around they were braver, and we went down to the farm and rode the horses and swam in the pond and took nature walks on the farm, and the girls slept out on the screened porch in sleeping bags. We made fires by the pond late at night and cooked hot dogs and marshmallows. When I had time during the day I read literary criticism and T. S. Eliot and e e cummings. In Kansas City we went to movies and swimming pools and parks and zoos again, and if I was slightly bored it was all right; everyone was happy. Adelaide called several times that summer, and cried a little bit, missing her daughters, but not quite so desperately. We even spent a few pleasant afternoons with June and Anthony Leyden. I thought we had all entered a season of peace and content. When Caroline and Cathy left at the end of August, they cried, and I felt genuinely, if minutely, sorry to see them go, and they both came to me and held their pretty faces up to be kissed good-bye.

It had been a good summer. It went by fast. In September what I considered "our" season—Charlie's-and-mine—began again. The blissful freedom of being alone to make love in the daylight in any room of the house, the uninterrupted moments spent reading together or discussing our separate days, the burden of extra cooking and laundry and cleaning and driving and organizing and caring and pleasing so completely removed—the girls had come and gone. Now there were fires in the fireplace and late pizza dinners and long hours in the library or with a pile of books and note cards at home. On weekends the farm and the horses, and kisses in the crisp fall air. And then it was Thanksgiving, and time to start buying Christmas gifts for Caroline and Cathy.

Christmas Day, 1966, Charlie called his daughters to wish them Merry Christmas and to see if they liked their presents.

Caroline answered the phone.

"Daddy?" she cried. "Oh, *Daddy,* I've been waiting and waiting for you to call. Daddy, *please,* I want to come live with you!"

I was upstairs on the extension phone, where Charlie had told me to be, my mouth open in readiness to yell, "Merry Christmas!" Instead, on hearing Caroline's words, I went speechless.

"Why, Caroline," said Charlie, "what's wrong?"

"Daddy, please, please, just let me come live with you. Cathy wants to, too. Please—" she cried, and then there were scuffling sounds and the next voice was Adelaide's.

"Charlie?" she snapped. "Is that you? What do you want?"

"I wanted to wish everyone Merry Christmas," Charlie said. "What's going on? What's wrong?"

"Nothing's wrong!" Adelaide shrieked, and the sound made my cars ring. "Stop prying into my private life!"

"Caroline said she wants to come live with me," Charlie said.

"Nonsense. She's just had a bad day."

"She's had a bad day on *Christmas Day?*"

"Oh, you always were the most sarcastic goddamned bastard!" Adelaide said. "Why don't you leave me alone!"

"Adelaide, I just want to say Merry Christmas to the girls. That's all. Okay?"

"NO! NO, it's NOT okay! Now STOP IT and LEAVE ME ALONE!"

There was a harsh click; she had hung up the phone.

"Merry Christmas," I said to Charlie over the hum of the disconnected line.

"Wow," said Charlie.

So that Christmas Day was spent with Charlie in his study, talking to the Ascrofts. It seemed that Adelaide's new marriage was having problems. The Ascrofts were vague, and they wanted to protect Adelaide as much as possible. They said they thought she was fine psychologically, just having a difficult time at a rocky spot in her marriage. The Ascrofts thought the reason Caroline and Cathy were upset was that they didn't get along with their new stepbrother when he came to visit. They thought there was some kind of rivalry, jealousy, there, but nothing to get excited about. They promised to keep an eye on things and to let Charlie know if there was anything he could or should do.

At the moment, there was nothing Charlie could do but worry. And he worried. That Caroline, quiet, restrained Caroline, had cried and asked to come live with him amazed him. He worried that if he called her back Adelaide would be furious with Caroline, but that if he didn't call her back Caroline would feel he had deserted her, that he didn't care.

I tried to reassure Charlie because that was what he needed, but secretly I felt sorry for the girls, too, and perhaps understood their problem more than he did. I had found stepping to be difficult and painful at best, and yet I was an adult: I had the power to change things, at least the freedom to leave the situation forever or to simply walk out of the house and down the street and away from an angry situation. But Caroline and Cathy were children, minors; they were trapped in the way that all children are trapped. Then, too, when they came to stay with us in the summer, we all knew it was a temporary arrangement, and there was a solace in that that made it all much more tolerable. We could temper our anger and secret resentments with the knowledge that it was not going to last forever, we would be free from each other soon. But Adelaide had remarried. That meant that Caroline and Cathy had to deal with a stepfather on a permanent, daily, and apparently eternal basis. They could not live for the end, or even rush off in a huff for one day. They must have felt panicked, as any helpless creature does when imprisoned in an unpleasant home.

Yet there was no way I could help them. I had no proof that they would be any happier living with their father and me than with their mother and a stepfather. The thought of the four of us living together on a permanent basis was something past the scope of my imagination. It seemed to me that the only likely result of such an arrangement would be that they would come to hate and resent me. I did not know what to say or do, what advice to offer Charlie. And selfishly, I worried about myself, about my work. I had only one semester left to finish my master's degree, defend my thesis, and take my orals. The coming spring would be the busiest time for me, with teaching and my studies. I really didn't want the girls to come then, with their problems and their mother's phone calls; I needed silence and peace around me; I knew I could not offer the care and attention that such a new situation would deserve. But I said nothing about all this to Charlie. They were his daughters; if they wanted to come, then this would be their home.

We spent a restless spring. Charlie wrote the girls and called them several times a month, but his letters were never answered and the phone conversations were unrevealing. Apparently the girls were happier, apparently some sort of peace had been achieved; at least that was all we could think given the information we had. Still, we worried; and felt helpless, because any attempt to help or understand would be seen only as an attempt to interfere and agitate.

In May, two nights before I was to have my oral examination to defend my thesis, Adelaide called. It was perhaps ten minutes till midnight. Charlie and I were in bed, asleep. I answered the phone.

"I want to talk to Charlie," Adelaide said. Her voice was clear, strong, calm, and grim.

I handed the phone to Charlie and sat in frightened silence as he talked.

Caroline was in the hospital. For several days she had been having severe stomach pains, and the physicians could provide neither diagnosis nor cure. Adelaide wanted Charlie to fly out the next day to see Caroline. She was worried, and she thought, quite rightly, that by God, Charlie ought to worry, too. Adelaide said that perhaps Caroline was having some kind of psychological problem because of the conflict of having two fathers. Charlie said that he would come as soon as he could. The conversation was short and quiet.

After he hung up the phone we sat up in bed among our wrinkled sheets, talking. We turned on the bedside lamp, as if seeing would help us hear each other better, and the warm circle of light seemed to create a magic small world that held only the two of us and our cozy bed, but the illusion was false. Other people were with us; too many others.

"I'll have Anthony take my class and I'll fly up tomorrow," Charlie said.

"Charlie, could you wait two days? Till after my

orals? I'd sort of like your support—"

"Oh, Zelda, Jesus, I'm so sorry. God, what timing! Listen, what can I do? What would you do in my place? My daughter's in the hospital, having severe stomach pains. If Adelaide thinks I can help—"

"I know. I know. You have to go. There's nothing else you can do. I hope she'll be okay, Charlie. I'm sure she will."

"Zelda, I'm really sorry about having to leave right now."

"I know. It's all right. Let's go to sleep; tomorrow will be busy."

We turned off the light and the warm enclosing circle disappeared in the darkness. We turned away from each other, Charlie to worry about Caroline, me to worry about my orals, and the great deep canyon suddenly there between us.

Charlie left the next day for Massachusetts, and the day after that I took my orals. They were held at three in the afternoon and went on until five-thirty. Afterward I was so weak-kneed and exhausted that I could scarcely walk. The head of the department, the notorious Catholic, woman-as-mother-lover, woman-as-intellectual-hater, had been unexpectedly nasty and petty and picky. He had led me astray, interrupted me, laughed at me, and in general looked down his nose at me until I wanted to rise from my chair and punch him in his nose. But I had kept my cool—he *was* the head of the department—and riding on the energy and sharpness that fear and anger provide, had done my best. I even

178

had room in the back of my mind to wonder as I spoke if male master degree candidates worried about the way their legs were crossed while they discussed Eliot's *Four Quartets*. And I wondered how much different the whole scene would have been if there had been just one woman professor on the committee instead of the five males. Would I have felt less threatened, one female facing a mixed group rather than one female facing five stern men?

When it was over, they asked me to wait in the outer office. I did. The secretary had gone home; everything was quiet. I stood next to a window, looking down at the grassy square and praying, "Please God, please God," over and over again.

Finally the door opened and my favorite professor came out and said, "Congratulations, Mrs. Campbell." My first thought was that I wanted to burst into tears from sheer exhaustion and relief, and then that I absolutely must not. The other men, including the department head, came out and shook my hand and offered their dry congratulations. We talked a bit of small talk, simply to prove that we were now all friends instead of adversaries, and then we all went home.

They went home and I went home, all by myself. It was spring, a warm May evening, a soft sexy evening, and I walked home alone. Everyone seemed to be outdoors, playing and laughing and being with everyone else, and when I saw my tiny pretty house I finally did begin to cry because it was so empty, because no one was in it to share my triumph. The windows reflected the sun and green trees and passing cars as if everything important were happening outside, as if there were nothing inside waiting for me. I didn't want to go in the house. But I couldn't simply stand outside and cry. I went in. The first thing I did was to take the phone off the hook. I didn't want Charlie to call and ask how it had gone and to hear my news, and then for it—my triumph, my success, my achievement—to be diluted by my having to ask, "And how is Caroline?" And he would say she was fine—he had called me the night before, and she was fine—and then we would have to discuss Caroline and Cathy and Adelaide, and my one bright golden moment would be muddied.

But, after all, things worked out, and perhaps in the long run worked out better than if Charlie had been there. For without him I had to take the first real, small steps from dependence on him to dependence on myself—and it is harder to be elated without the one you love than it is to be depressed; one can easily indulge in depression alone. I made myself a vodka tonic and sat down at the kitchen table, preparing to drink myself into a state of maudlin self-pity, accompanied only by the empty buzz of the telephone receiver as it hung by its cord to the floor. But my drink did not taste good; I did not want a vodka tonic, I wanted champagne. I had achieved something—I wanted to celebrate. I wanted to celebrate even if I had to do it without Charlie. I put the phone back on the hook, then picked it up again and dialed my mother and father, and then Alice, and then all the other friends I had, to tell them that I had finally, at last, done it: I had defended my thesis, I had won my master's degree. Finally, unsure of what reception I would get, I called Linda. She had dropped out of the M.A. program the past semester to have her baby, and I had sent her flowers and bought a small pink knit bunting for her new daughter, but she had been so wrapped up in the baby, and I had been so wrapped up in my books, that our conversation had kept sliding off into mutual disinterest. This night when I called her, however, she responded with the beautiful manic enthusiasm I had been so used to and invited me over to her house to celebrate. Her husband was out of town; her daughter was asleep. I stopped at the liquor store and bought a magnum of Champagne. The two of us drank it all. What a wonderful evening it was: we left the doors and windows open and let the sounds of the spring night drift in, and we sat in her messily luxurious living room eating cold roast, cheese, crackers, olives, nuts, anything we could find from her pantry, and drinking the champagne, and telling each other secrets, and laughing at the secrets until we both ended up rolling on the floor with laughter. We didn't get tired until three in the morning, and because it was so late and her husband was not home, I spent the night there. Before we staggered into our beds to sleep, we crept into the nursery, where little Dina, Linda's daughter, lay sleeping amid white and pink quilts in a small white cradle. How warm, how

181

moist, how sweetly aromatic that sleeping child was. I can remember it even now. The sight and scent of the little girl moved something inside me, like a small, pure, crystal chime just beginning to stir in a breeze. I hung above the baby, seeing her tiny white hand plump and relaxed among soft quilts, and felt a most delicate, exquisite, puzzling desire.

The next morning I had a hangover, but only a slight one. I drank black coffee and watched Linda give Dina first a bottle and then various globs of warm smooth food, and finally left for my own house. I brushed my furry teeth, took a long bubble bath, put on fresh clothes, and then fell asleep on the sofa. When I woke up, it was late afternoon and Charlie was home.

We kissed, and Charlie sat down next to me, and we talked about Caroline. She was out of the hospital and doing well. The physicians thought she had been chronically constipated, but they agreed something psychological was going on. Caroline had said only that she was perfectly happy and felt fine except for the stomach pains. Adelaide had admitted that she had never given the girls the letters Charlie had written—she thought they were too upsetting for Caroline and Cathy—but had agreed in the light of Caroline's strange illness to let them have the letters from now on as long as Charlie wrote only light happy things and never said he missed the girls or asked them to live with him. Adelaide had said that her marriage was fine, just fine. Cathy seemed content. Charlie was as satisfied as he could be in the situation.

Then we talked about me, about my small success. Charlie said he had not worried about me a bit, he had known I would do fine in my orals, but he still felt bad that he had not been there to support me or celebrate with me. I said what I had to say: nonsense, nonsense; he was not to feel bad that he had not been there; I had not minded; it hadn't mattered at all. Because of course I knew that he had done only what he had to do, being the good man that he was. And then I did not want him to know how really petty and selfish I was, that I had resented him and for a while even hated him, and his daughters, because I had childishly wanted for one day, one evening, to shine, to be the star, and had not been able to. It had been no one's fault; there was no one to blame. There was nothing to be done about it but to go on with goodwill. And Charlie did take me out to dinner at a marvelous restaurant that night, and he ordered a wonderful French champagne, and later he made love to me so beautifully that I would have eagerly forgiven him anything.

After I finished my master's I fell into a deep, deep slump. Part of it was because Charlie had agreed to be a visiting professor at a university in western Michigan the coming fall semester. A historian who taught there had arranged it; he and Charlie were working together on a book. In one way I was glad, because Alice, the woman I had fallen in love with at the symposium, lived there. And after the crush of work finishing my master's I wanted a break from my studies. But I was also eager to start work on my Ph.D., for I realized that that was the only way I'd be able to continue what I liked best (outside of making love and riding my horse): teaching English comp and lit to college kids.

That was the other part of the reason for my slump. I could no longer teach. I had somehow always blithely assumed that they would want me to teach part time at the university. I was so good, and I was so cheap. During the loose final days after I took my oral exam, I kept drifting back to campus even on the days I wasn't teaching. I wanted someone to ask me my plans; I wanted someone to say offhandedly as he passed me in the halls, "By the way, Zelda, we're planning on you for two introductory comp courses next year." But no one said it. No one really spoke to me at all. It was only by having coffee with some of the male graduate students that I found out who had and hadn't been chosen as part-time instructors for the following year. How damned mad I was as I sat there hearing the news from the other students. I got even madder because when I realized I hadn't been asked to teach tears came into my eyes and I wanted to blubber and wail. Instead I dug my fingernails into my fist, and smiled and acted nonchalant, and after a while we all got up to go our separate ways. I went to the office of my favorite prof, the one who had advised me on my thesis. He was in and not surprised to see me. Our session was short and not sweet: "Zelda, the way things are set up here we were able to give you a teaching assistantship while you were working on your master's. But we make Ph.D. students part-time instructors, and the pay scale goes up. It's handled differently. You've got a husband on the faculty. You're a woman. We've got to give these plusher jobs to the men who have families to support."

"But *Crawford?* You *know* I'm a better teacher than Crawford!"

"Yes, but he's a brilliant scholar and his wife is pregnant. We have to support him. Good Lord, we all know you're a great teacher; this is no reflection on your teaching abilities; don't take it personally."

"I'll work without pay. Just let me teach."

"Oh, Zelda. You can't. We couldn't even let you; it would blow all the fuses in the payroll computer. Come on. Be reasonable."

There was absolutely nothing I could do. Perhaps, back in 1967, if I had realized that women all across the country were reeling from the same shock from the same sort of words, I might have been able to do something—anything else. As it was, I just went home and cried. I felt defeated, I felt rejected. I felt that I had failed, that if I had only been *better* they would have had to hire me in spite of my being married to a faculty member, in spite of the English department head, who disliked women.

I began the summer of 1967 feeling dejected and defeated. For the first time in my life I was formally through with my studies; really through. I would go to Michigan with Charlie the next September instead of plunging into a new course of work, instead

185

of setting out for a new goal. The freedom and looseness and lack of responsibility were the most awesomely depressing things I had ever experienced. Of course I still had to play wife and housewife, still had to do the cooking and dishwashing and housecleaning each day, but all that did not really matter, did not really count. I did not take it seriously; it was of no importance to me. It did not even take up very much of my time. There were only the two of us, and we ate out many nights, or ate large lunches together at the university, then merely snacked at night at home, and the house did not get terribly dirty with both of us gone so much, and Charlie always helped me with the laundry, the dishes, the cleaning; there was not enough there to occupy my time or my mind. I could not think of it—being the keeper of Charlie's house and meals—as what I was about. What I was about was loving Charlie—but he was involved in teaching or working on his papers and books most of the day—and books and students and teaching, but I had been cut off from all that and could find no way back in. I felt lonesome, wasted, adrift.

I was accepted into the Ph.D. program, but I knew I wouldn't be able to attend classes until the second semester. Charlie suggested that I spend the summer and fall reading and relaxing. He thought I deserved a vacation. I didn't want a vacation. I was twenty-four, I had a master's degree and teaching experience. I wanted a job. But when I tried to explain it to Charlie, I succeeded only in making him feel bad. "I know you want to get started on your Ph.D. work," he said, "but this semester in Michigan is crucial to the new book. I've *got* to go. You could stay here, of course—"

But of course I couldn't stay. I had to be with Charlie. He would have his fortieth birthday that fall, and I wanted to make it a great big smashing occasion. Even without the birthday I never once thought seriously of staying apart from him that semester. It would have been like agreeing not to breathe for a few months.

And I must be honest: I didn't want him to stay home, either. The royalties from his first book were not large, but they were all the difference between scraping along on what was left from his salary after child support and doctor bills went out and living an enjoyable life. I liked having a little bit of money. I wanted him to write another book. I wanted him to go to Michigan, to write the book he and the other historian were planning. I wanted to be with him, always. I simply had to put my own life off track for a while. I knew I was making my own decisions. I had no one to blame for the direction I led my life.

Caroline and Cathy arrived in July for their third summer with us. Now they were nine and twelve; big girls. Each could make her own toast. The first few days they were abnormally quiet and jumpy and tense and nervous, but I was too wrapped up in my own gloom to care. I went about taking care of them with an automatic dutiful friendliness, and read Gothic romances when I had free time.

187

Luckily they had friends in the neighborhood to play with, and to spend the night with, and to generally fill their time with. I read lots of romances and mysteries and ate ice cream sundaes with the girls and gained weight and didn't care. It was a sloppy, superficial, easy sort of summer. It went by very fast. We were not friends yet, but we were no longer enemies. Caroline's stomach problems had disappeared, at least for a while.

One August evening the four of us went to see some idiotic horror show at a drive-in and had to leave early because of a sudden violent summer thunder- and rainstorm. We felt somehow cheated as we pulled away from the drive-in, and somehow saddened by the rain sweeping down over the cars and streets. The movie hadn't been good, but we felt grumpy being deprived of its ending. Charlie decided to stop at a pizza parlor on the way home, and we were all immediately cheered up. The pizza restaurant was as warm and cheery as a fireplace in autumn, with its padded booths and bright lights and spicy smells.

"Caroline," Charlie said, "I guess you are really all well. That's your fourth piece of pizza, and on top of popcorn, too."

Caroline grinned, her mouth full of pizza.

"It wasn't her stomach at all," Cathy volunteered. "It was her mind making her stomach sick; the doctors told us so. She didn't like calling Mommy's new husband Daddy, and it made her sick."

"Well, then why did she call him Daddy?"

188

Charlie asked.

"Cause Mommy told us to," Cathy said. "She said *he* was our real father from now on, not you. She said we were finally one big happy family again, and he was our real father. We had to call him Daddy. She spanked us and took our allowance away if we didn't."

"Wow," Charlie said.

"It wasn't like that," Caroline said in a sudden desperate tone. "Mommy wasn't trying to be bad, she just wanted us all to be close together and to love each other a lot and to be happy. She wanted us to be happy a lot—"

"I made a calendar for you for Christmas in Brownies," Cathy said. "It said, 'To My Father,' and it had my picture on it and I had decorated it, and Mommy made me give it to her new husband. His name was John, but Caroline and I called him Toilet secretly. You know—John—Toilet—"

The girls looked at each other and went into fits of guilty laughter.

"Mommy didn't make me sick," Caroline said when she stopped laughing. "She didn't, *really*. She was trying to make us all feel good. She wanted us to be a family."

"Yeah, but ol' Toilet was a real *stinker*," Cathy said, and again both girls cracked up. "He had hair in his ears! And he burped at the table!" Both girls began to giggle and fidget as if they were drunk.

"And he spanked Cathy once when she wouldn't eat her liver!" Caroline laughed.

"And he had these old cigars he smoked all the time and left lying in the ashtray like dog poop!" Cathy yelled, her giggling almost uncontrollable.

"Yeah," Caroline agreed, "we always said, 'Why, why is old Toilet leaving this poop around? He's a Toilet; why doesn't he just eat the poop?' "

The girls were laughing so hard that even Charlie and I had begun to laugh, helplessly, aware of our silliness. In the back of my mind a sudden thought occurred: What nickname do they have for *me*? What jokes do they tell about me?

"And Toilet had a little boy, and you know what his name was? PETER! Ha-ha-ha, and you know what we secretly called him? Pee! Hee-hee-hee-hee . . ."

"He was awful. He came only on weekends, but he got to have his own room in our house and Cathy and I had to share a room. And he always got more presents, Mommy said to make up for not being able to live with us."

"I never liked Pee; he stunk as much as Toilet!" Cathy said.

"Yeah, I'm glad they'll be gone when we get back," Caroline said.

"Gone?" Charlie asked.

"Yep, *gone*," Caroline said. "Really gone. Mom and Toilet are getting divorced this summer. Whoops, we weren't supposed to tell you that."

At the beginning of September that year Charlie had a conference in New York with his publisher. Since we were going to be up in Michigan anyway, we decided to drive to the East Coast. With what we saved on plane fares we spent a week in Kennebunkport with Caroline and Cathy. It was a good time, the best time the four of us had had together. We lay on the beach or swam all day and ate like crazy at night, then took long walks all over the little town. One night we walked along the beach in the moonlight and I was humming a song, and the girls were humming it, too, more softly, and then Charlie began a sort of rhythmical clopping counterpoint noise. No one else was near us on the beach, and somehow we all began doing a silly dance-march to the music there on the sand, the cold water racing down toward our toes.

"*La plume de ma tante,* BOOM BOOM!" I sang, and

"BOOM BOOM BOOM BOOM BOOM BOOM!" Cathy yelled, and

"*La plume de ma tante est sur le bureau de mon oncle!*" Caroline sang, and

"Clop-clop-clop-clop-clop-clop-clop-clop!" Charlie went, and we all marched, knees silly and high, funny gestures, loud singing, along the beach. It was the moonlight, and the hot sun still burning on our skins and the cool sand under our bare feet and the gay white line of surf chasing after our toes, it was a magic end of a summer night: the four of us all happy together. We were all slap-happily in love with one another, and wrapped arms around each other for warmth as we walked back toward the hotel.

We drove the girls to Massachusetts on Saturday.

We had spent the morning swimming, then cleaned up and checked out of the hotel at noon, and driven three or four hours back into the continent. We arrived in Hadley drowsy from the ride, stunned suddenly by the end of the summer.

Charlie found Adelaide's new house, the house she and her second husband had bought. It was a lovely old white frame colonial. It had a realtor's "For Sale" sign in front of it, stuck into the grass.

I said good-bye to the girls and gave them quick pecks on their cheeks, then got out of the car to help them get all their luggage. Charlie took the two biggest suitcases and walked with the girls up to the door. The three of them went inside.

I got back in the car and sat and waited. I couldn't believe it when I saw the clothes come flying out of the front door of the house.

"WET!" Adelaide seemed to be screaming, and then she appeared on the front porch of her house. She had a suitcase in her hand and was apparently trying to tell me something about it.

I got out of the car, puzzled and slightly curious.

"Wet!" Adelaide screamed, and flung more clothes from the suitcase to the grass. "You stupid little girl, don't you know any better than to put wet swimming suits in a suitcase? Now ALL THE CLOTHES ARE WET AND WRINKLED AND I HAVE ALL THIS IRONING TO DO!"

Those were the first direct words Adelaide had ever said to me. I was dumbfounded. I couldn't believe she was standing on the front porch of her house on a glorious sunny day with people bicycling and walking by, that she was standing there in shorts and halter top throwing clothes all over the grass. It seemed unreal.

Behind her I saw Charlie coming out the door, and I saw Cathy's and Caroline's anxious little faces.

"I'm sorry," I said, since it was obvious that I had to say something. "I wrapped the suits in towels—"

"Yes, and what do towels do, you ninny? They *absorb!*" More clothes flew about.

Well, you're right about that, I thought, it's just that I never thought about it before. I haven't thought about towels, absorption, wet suits; it never interested me before—"I'm sorry," I said. "I'm terribly sorry."

"Yes, you send home two suitcases full of wet dirty clothes—"

"I always wash and iron their clothes just before they come home," I said. "I've never sent home dirty clothes—" I couldn't believe our conversation. I was afraid people were staring. I was embarrassed. I also wanted to break out laughing, but knew it would be entirely the wrong thing to do.

"Yes, but this time you spent the last week at a *beach*. You can't wash and iron at a beach!"

"They wore only a few shorts and tops. Everything else is—"

"WET! *Everything else is wet!* Because of those damned swimming suits!"

"I'm sorry," I said again. I didn't know what else to say. I felt terribly bad about the whole thing. I felt I had ruined our whole summer by getting the clothes wet. And yet the comic aspect still made my mouth twitch.

Charlie came out of the house then and took Adelaide by the shoulders and pulled her into the house. Later he told me that he gave her twenty-five dollars to pay for a woman to wash and iron the clothes. Caroline and Cathy came outside and began to pick their clothes up off the grass. They didn't look my way or at each other, and they didn't talk. Then Charlie came out and kissed each girl and held them against him for a long moment. He came out to the car and we both waved and got in and drove off. We were on our way to Michigan.

That evening Charlie made a phone call from our motel room to the Ascrofts. He wanted to be assured that Adelaide and the girls were okay. The Ascrofts told him not to worry. They said that now that she had her girls back Adelaide would be fine. She had probably been in a bad mood that day—she had had such a terrible summer, the Ascrofts said. As if her second marriage breaking up hadn't been enough, the month her second husband had moved out Adelaide had found out that she was pregnant by him, and she had had an abortion in August.

FIVE

In the fall of 1967, Charlie was a visiting professor at a university in a small town in Michigan. He was Distinguished Visiting Professor; I was wife-in-limbo. I couldn't take courses or teach, I couldn't get my life to work for me. And then, that fall, when I was almost twenty-five, a strange thing happened to me. A shocking, totally unwanted and unexpected thing happened to me: I began to want to have a baby, a child of my own.

It was as if I had been strolling in the woods, innocently enjoying the peaceful day, and suddenly a huge and gloriously beautiful tiger pounced upon me, and dug his claws into me, and I was engaged in a furious struggle for survival, suddenly forced to claw and bite back, to fight him off.

Of course I was bored that semester, and dejected, and unsure of my future, and that was part of my ammunition against myself. You don't *really* want a child, I said to myself. You're just bored and dejected and unsure of yourself. Boy, you're a mess. You get away from a university routine for one semester and you go insane.

Part of it, too, I realized, was Alice, and Alice's friends. They were all such lovely women, and some were quite talented and some had professions, and some just played lots of tennis and golf, but they all had children. And even though they all had children, none of them was boring. It was amazing.

Charlie was busy all the time with his teaching or book writing, and I valiantly and dutifully kept to my reading list, preparing for my Ph.D. work, keeping notes, reading relevant criticism. But I couldn't read or study all the time, and Alice lived within walking distance of the house we were renting, and I wanted to take advantage of the few months I would have to live near her. So I visited her almost daily. Her home seemed like a storybook to me. All those children, each one so beautiful, and all their animals, dogs, cats, birds, turtles, gerbils, even a snake, and all the children's friends, and the babysitters who came sometimes just to chat—all that *life* was wonderful. Alice and her husband had a great huge Victorian house that twisted and rambled and had window seats and doors in the paneling of the front stairs and alcoves and lots of big wide halls. Everything was covered with hockey sticks or ballet slippers or sweaters and mittens or dog leashes or ice skates or dolls, except for the living room, which was majestically reserved for adults. Every evening from four till five-thirty Alice had a sitter come play with all six children in their big bright messy basement rec room while she and her husband read the paper and drank martinis and talked in the beautiful neat living room. Charlie and I often joined them and sometimes stayed for dinner, which was held in the big oak-paneled dining room with all the family. It seemed to me that Alice looked like a queen as she sat at the head of the huge oak table smiling down at her children. The four oldest children, who were twelve, eleven, nine and seven, had to help set the table and clear off. The two youngest ones had to sit up straight and eat as politely as they could or they were banished to a lonely meal in the kitchen. We never stayed after dinner; then Alice turned from queen into general and directed the table clearing, dish doing, floor sweeping, homework preparing, baths, storytime, and bed. She did it all so beautifully and elegantly that it never occurred to me to think that it could be hard work.

Alice was beautiful, her house was beautiful, and her children especially were beautiful. The oldest boy played the guitar and sang; the oldest girl was doing very well in ballet; the second son took piano and played as well as an adult and intended to go to conservatory; the second daughter could draw and paint. The two youngest children were simply very clever and very cute.

The youngest child, a girl named Vanessa, but called Nessie, was my favorite. She liked me because I always brought treats. She was just three, with great blue eyes and curly black hair. She wore her older sibling's cast-off clothes and looked like a charming Raggedy Ann doll. One stormy winter day I sat snuggled in a window seat off the kitchen, reading Nessie a story. She was curled up against me with her old soft blanket clutched in her hand; she was almost falling asleep. The doorbell rang and Alice went to answer it, and brought back into the kitchen a young woman who had just moved into a house across the street. Alice had asked her over for tea.

"This is a friend of mine, Zelda Campbell," Alice said, introducing us, "and that is Nessie."

"She's *beautiful*," the new neighbor said, looking at me, talking to me. "And she looks just like you."

"Why, she does, doesn't she!" Alice laughed. "Zelda, she *could* be yours. You've got the same curly black hair! But actually," she said, turning to the new woman, "Nessie's mine. My youngest."

The women laughed, and we went on talking and Nessie fell asleep. Alice came over and lifted Nessie out of my arms to take her up to nap in her bed. I wanted to cry out at the loss of the sweet warm weight of the little girl who looked like me. I thought: someone thinks I could have a child. I could have a child. I could have a little girl of my own. I *want* a little girl of my own! I was so agitated and excited and upset that I could scarcely keep my wits about me the rest of the afternoon. When I returned to our rented house, it seemed empty and lonely and dull.

The rest of the semester seemed like a war to me, and I was both sides and the battleground. I didn't tell Charlie about my feelings, I told no one. I was ashamed of wanting to have a child. It seemed an enormous weakness on my part, as if I were admitting that I wasn't enough for myself. I thought that every other woman in the world simply got pregnant by accident, that I was the only woman in the world wrestling with such a choice. I thought I was losing my mind, that my wanting to have a child was the same as admitting to be a failure as a professional person. I began to hate myself for wanting to have a child.

Christmas was the hardest time. We were invited to spend Christmas Eve with Alice and her family. The great Victorian house had been built for Christmastime, and the six children had decorated it in every corner. The Christmas tree was at least eleven feet high and almost hidden behind the sparkling lights and handmade decorations. We all sat around eating pastries and cookies and drinking laced eggnog, and the older children played Christmas carols on the guitar or piano, and then they all sang carols together in front of the fire—for Christmas Eve they were allowed in the living room. They opened the presents Charlie and I had given them, and said thank you, then were bustled off to bed.

"They'll be up at six to see what Santa brought," Alice grinned.

Charlie helped Alice's husband put a little bicycle together while Alice and I kept watch to be sure no children were sneaking back downstairs.

That night Charlie and I walked home in the snow, and I began to cry, and couldn't stop, and couldn't tell him why.

I felt as sad and relieved to leave Michigan at the end of the semester as a weight watcher leaving a pastry shop. Each day I was there I felt tempted toward something that I thought was intrinsically wrong and bad for me. I was glad to start my Ph.D. work back in Kansas City, and I was grateful that it was difficult and time-consuming. I told myself that I was going to be an interesting career woman, not a boring mother. I was afraid of becoming like Adelaide: dependent on children, feeling significant to the world because of them, void and helpless when they were gone. I did not want to be that way. I told myself repeatedly that I was crazy to think of it—of having a child of my own. But sometimes on spring evenings as I worked late in the library digging up my little clusters of obscure and useless facts, I wondered what I was doing with all that dusty dead stuff when what I wanted was life.

It all got even more confusing that summer, the fourth summer the girls came. Caroline was thirteen, and had braces, and Cathy was ten, and gawky and trying to act like her older sister, who had wondrously become a teen-ager. Both girls were interested in horror movies and clothes and rock music and competitive sports, and I was glad to drop my studies for a while in order to take them to horror movies and shopping and swimming and riding. Charlie was finishing up his book; that summer the girls spent more time with me than with him. The girls seemed to relax with me that summer, and we began to enjoy each other.

We began to share jokes.

CAROLINE: Do you know why the Dairy Queen got pregnant?

ZELDA: No. Why?

CAROLINE: Because the Burger King couldn't handle his Whopper.

ZELDA: Caroline! You're only thirteen!

Mad hysterical fits of laughter.

We began to share likes and dislikes.

CATHY: Which movie did you like best?

ZELDA: *The Claw of the Cat.*

CATHY: Me, too. It was scariest of all. I loved the part where they found the hand.

And we began to share memories. That was very nice, sharing memories.

CAROLINE: Is Liza getting old?

ZELDA: No, not really, she's only ten.

CAROLINE: Well, she *seems* old. It seems like I've been riding her forever. It's just like sitting on a big ol' comfortable grandmother's lap. I can really trust her. And I can remember that first summer, how scared I was of her, how afraid I was to ride.

ZELDA: Yes, I always felt bad about making you ride, because I knew you were afraid. But I wanted you to learn. I knew you'd like it when you had learned.

CAROLINE: Yeah, it was funny. I hated you when you made me get on the horse, but once I was up there I was glad you had made me. Sometimes I liked you for it while I hated you for it, you know?

ZELDA: Yeah, I know.

And we began to share hopes for the future.

CATHY: Zelda, we all aren't driving back to Maine this summer again, are we?

ZELDA: No, darn it, we're not. I wish we could, but Charlie's got to teach this summer, and he's got to get that damned book finished.

CATHY: Well, maybe we can go next summer. I'd love to go to the beach again. And we could all go eat at that neat lobster place!

It had happened. By the fourth summer I had been accepted, or assimilated, or something. I was part of their lives. We could share things. We could talk.

They were turning from children into pretty girls.

They were clever and bright and imaginative. Caroline showed me how to do simple macramé. Cathy, who was good at sports, began to beat me at swimming races. They were beginning to add things to my life. And when they left at the end of that fourth summer, I missed them. I missed them very much. They had told me about their friends, their projects, their fears, their desires. I found myself wanting to know how it all worked out: did Caroline get the good grade-7 teacher or the bad one? Was Cathy invited to rich Jennifer's birthday party? Suddenly the world was filled with things I wanted to share with the girls—movies, music, clothes, puzzles, jokes, games. I thought of them every day after they left. I remembered what rich pleasure it had been that summer, giving them things, how it had been as if I were giving myself presents because I enjoyed their pleasure so much. More and more my Ph.D. studies and professors seemed dry and dull and insignificant. I had to force myself to leave the summer, to enter the fall.

Charlie, on the other hand, was plunging deeper and deeper into his work. He had finished all his little projects, and the book he had coauthored with the other historian was now at the publishers. Charlie was starting another book—*his* book— which he had been collecting information and notes on for years. Everything other than The Book became a distraction for him. He taught and attended committees dutifully, then rushed back to his study at home. We had books and note cards all over the house, we read constantly, and spent less and less time at the farm, or eating out, or seeing friends. We worked. Charlie was past happiness; he was absorbed in his work. But I was lonely, and grew lonelier every day. I missed teaching very much. I often walked slowly by the classrooms, listening to other instructors explain metaphor or syllogisms, and I yearned to be there, in a classroom full of scratching, yawning, gum-chewing, note-taking kids. Instead I had the library, with its silent heavy books, or my house, decorated with piles of white note cards.

Adelaide had called several times that summer, but not so frantically, and once Charlie agreed to pay the bill for both Caroline's and Cathy's orthodontic work she stopped calling him completely. For once a fall passed without letters from her threatening to go to court. The girls had said very little about her that fourth summer, just that Adelaide was taking a vacation in Maine with a woman friend, and that she was taking a few craft classes, and that she wasn't dating at all. The girls were very happy that she wasn't dating. The three of them had moved into a small colonial house, and little by little were making it their home, and that made them all very happy, planning curtains and carpets and wallpaper and mirrors and such.

The first week in September that the girls were gone, I wrote them a letter. I almost couldn't help myself; I missed them. Still, I didn't say that; I didn't want anyone to get sad or mad. Two weeks later I was shocked to find a letter for me from Caroline. It was a long, newsy, silly, sweet letter; Caroline was warmer in correspondence than in person. I noticed that Adelaide had put the return address on and I smiled: so Adelaide had accepted me, too. To "Mrs. Zelda Campbell," from "Mrs. Adelaide Campbell." How funny. After that I wrote Caroline and Cathy about once a week, sending clippings from cartoons, jokes, and sometimes a tiny present, a dollar, or a little ring. I looked forward to Caroline's letters. She was a sensitive girl, I thought, always asking questions of herself or of me.

Whenever I listen to music, I'm happy. It's like being in a hot bathtub after a rainy day, I feel so warm and content. I love the Beatles, and I think I would die for them. I would give up all my possessions just to talk to John Lennon for one hour. Why do I feel this way? I think sometimes I love the Beatles more than I love Cathy or Mother or anybody. Isn't that strange? And I'm supposed to love God, but I think church is so boring. I feel closer to God listening to the Beatles than in church. I wonder why this is. Do you know? It's really embarrassing in a way, how warm and happy the Beatles make me feel. I think I must feel like adults do when they're drinking wine.

I always answered Caroline as well as I could, and I sent Cathy little letters each time I wrote Caroline. I didn't want to seem to like Caroline more, even though secretly of course I did. I kept reminding myself that Cathy was younger and not interested in writing letters yet, that she was a different person.

The fall semester passed slowly. The spring semester came. Nothing changed. The year clicked over; it was 1969. I wrote letters to Charlie's girls and waited for their letters, and wrote Alice and waited for her letters, and read books and wrote papers and waited for my professors' remarks. Charlie buried himself in his study, and when he came out it was to ask me to read and criticize the latest chapter of his book. The few friends I made at the university were graduate students, too, fighting the same battles I was fighting: when we talked, we talked about literature. My world seemed made of words. Printed words. All life seemed like chapters from books, overheard conversation seemed like dialogue. I couldn't look at a person without finding his twin in some literary work; I couldn't look at the countryside without trying to find the perfect words to describe it. When I slept at night I dreamed of my papers, of footnotes, bibliographies, indented quotes, words in rows. Sentences rearranged themselves in my head. I cooked absentmindedly, reading a book with one hand while stirring with the other, and it didn't matter, for we ate absentmindedly, uninterested in our food. Our Christmas vacation was spent on the farm, and our one escape from words was to ride the horses. But as soon as we entered the house, we saw the books and papers we had brought down with us, and we made a big fire and weak drinks and settled down to work again.

I was doing well. I was getting the best grades, the best remarks from my professors. I was doing what I had dreamed of doing all my life, and I was doing it well, and I was miserable beyond the reach of all those words at my command. A year had passed since I had seen Alice and her children, yet I thought of them every day. Alice and I wrote to each other often, and occasionally she included in her letters photos or a splashy bright painting made by one of her children for me. I would tape it to a mirror or the refrigerator door, and it would bring back to me vividly the laughter, the noise, the caressing and cuddling, the sheer good busyness of life which was a part of Alice's world and not a part of mine. I began to apply images of barrenness and sterility to myself. I would read Eliot's words, "ridiculous the waste sad time," and think of myself as a pale sad half-moon, curving emptily around nothing, drained instead of filled. When I saw pregnant women on the street I stared with envy and amazement: how could they have done it? Did they choose it? How did it feel to be so full, to carry another life? I would look away, ashamed. When I saw little babies in their mothers' baskets at the grocery store I would stare, dumbfounded at the size, wondering how it would feel to hold something so very small in my arms. When I visited Linda and saw little Dina, who walked and talked now, and cooed and babbled when she saw me, who was all soft pink flesh and immediacy, I felt nearly sick with longing. Sometimes, when I was very sad or tired, I would let myself indulge in the ultimate forbidden delight: I would imagine a child, a real child of mine and Charlie's, a child who would cuddle against me, a child who would hold my hand.

I did not understand what was going on. Had instinctual desire to reproduce suddenly risen within me like a yeast bread? If so, how base, how animalistic. I had to fight it off. I told myself that my feelings were temporary. I told myself that I would absolutely not give in to them. I took my birth control pill with fanatical regularity. I told no one, not even Charlie, of my feelings. I knew that what I wanted was ridiculous, unnecessary, senseless; I could not think of one good logical reason for having a child. Yet I wanted one with all my heart, every day.

I had my pride and the Pill as weapons against myself; I decided they weren't enough. I got a cat. A beautiful Siamese chocolate point. I named him Jami, after a Persian poet, and Charlie enjoyed Jami, too. He was an intelligent and a playful animal, and he entertained us and gave us a break from our work, and gave me something to love and to buy little treats for. I bought him a basket and wove blue ribbons in and around the wicker and tied a blue bow on top; he soon tore the bow to shreds. He slept on my lap when I read, he greeted me at the door when I came home. He rubbed against my ankles or arms when I cried, and when I looked into his face I only cried the more because he was a sweet cuddly creature but an animal, with whiskers and crossed eyes.

Finally the spring semester ended and the summer began. I was amazed at the joy I felt when the semester ended and at the relief I felt when I said, "No, I won't be taking courses this summer. Charlie's girls are coming again for two months. I've got to play stepmother. Charlie's almost through with The Book—he's got to work on it this summer."

I spent hours planning special events for the summer, hours looking at children's clothes which I eventually didn't buy, not knowing Caroline's and Cathy's sizes after a year's growth, hours looking at card games and toys. The night before Charlie's daughters arrived it finally hit me: boom. I was putting a huge stuffed teddy bear on each bed, a surprise for the girls. How happy they would be, I thought, when they saw the bright cuddly bears. I grinned in anticipation. I looked at the big stuffed bears. And knew—boom—what I was doing. I was acting as if Charlie's daughters were mine. I was making myself happy through them.

Jami wandered in and rubbed against my leg. I sat down on the bed and picked him up and stroked him.

"Is it a crime?" I asked him. "Is it, Jami? Whom am I hurting? What am I doing wrong?"

Sitting there, I remembered that whenever people used to ask me, "Do you have any children?" I had laughed and said, "Heavens, no, and I don't want any! I've got too many other things I want to do!" But now when someone asked I always said, "Not

208

yet, though I do have two stepdaughters."

"This is terrible, Jami, terrible," I said. "I think I'm going nuts. I'll take those damned bears back to the store and use the money to buy that set of critical essays I've been wanting." But I didn't.

I played with the girls all that summer of '69. They were suddenly perfect ages; fourteen and eleven; old enough to take care of themselves, dress themselves, enjoy the same museums and concerts and movies and jokes, yet young enough not to worry about being seen in public with adults. Charlie finished his book that summer and took us all to Colorado for two weeks. We rode horses and swam and hiked mountain trails and laughed in the exhilarating mountain air. Somehow, subtly, without announcing it, we had become two pairs: Charlie and Cathy; Caroline and me. Cathy at eleven was still gawky in the way a prize-winning show horse is gawky as a filly. Her lines and instincts were good. She adored Charlie and held his hand almost constantly. If he went to the garage to see about tires, she went. If he went to the post office to pick up a package, she went. She stayed up late at night, sitting by his side on the sofa, sitting in my former spot, curled against him, reading. Twice every half hour she would say, "Can I get you anything, Dad? Tea? A glass of water? Some cake? A brandy?" When the mail came, Cathy ran to get it from the box and brought it all to Charlie eagerly; if she'd been a dog, she would have wagged her tail and drooled. When the four of us played Parcheesi, she never captured or blockaded

Charlie, she tried to help him win. She was forever praising him, complimenting his clothes or hair or laughing at his slightest joke. Watching her, I felt both amused and saddened: she was acting just as I had acted when I first met and married Charlie, and I didn't act that way anymore. I couldn't—I had changed. I was so torn, so almost maddened, by my desire to have a child and my desire not to want one that I lived in a state of fury every day. Yet Charlie never guessed this; worse, he never did what I longed and longed for him to do: he never said, "Zelda, I can't stand it anymore. I want to have a baby with you. I want you to have my child." The fact that Charlie didn't long for the same thing I longed for, the fact that he didn't even guess at my raging sub-terranean desire, made me feel a real and sudden separation. We were not one person after all; we were two. We were separated from each other deeply. We were alone. It was frightening. I did not know then how in the course of a marriage, over a stretch of years and years, two people can ebb and flow to-gether, ebb and flow in closeness and then in isola-tion, yet never really part. I knew I loved Charlie; I knew he loved me. We were still happy with each other in our daily lives. Yet I was lonely. There was something I wanted him to know, something he did not guess and I could not bring myself to say.

So I played elaborate card games with Caroline, and Caroline and I read biographies of famous people and discussed them. We sat reading in silence while Cathy chattered to Charlie. On the farm

Charlie drove the tractor with Cathy standing on next to him; Caroline took Charlie's horse and went off riding with me.

That summer I knew I loved Caroline. With her braces and her skinny angular height—she was now as tall as I—and her philosophical curiosities, she seemed marvelously dear and precious to me. It was already obvious that when boys flirted, they flirted with Cathy, not with Caroline; Caroline did not have that winsome instinctive way of charming boys that Cathy had. She tripped when she was near boys her age, or dove into four feet of water and hit her head on the pool bottom, or spilled her Coke, or if she did nothing wrong she still didn't manage to look up at the boys the way Cathy did, like an ingénue vamp, raising the eyelashes so slowly, letting a slight smile slip out so tantalizingly. Even when Cathy was eleven, boys gave her things; they always would. They couldn't help themselves. But they barely looked at Caroline back then, and Caroline seemed to shrink inside her clothes when she came near a boy. I wanted to protect her. She was so bright, so sensitive—and in a few years, I knew, and she could not believe, she would be beautiful.

The night before the girls left that summer, Caroline and I sat up late, talking. Or rather, Caroline talked. She told me about her friends in Massachusetts, and her clothes, and all the items in her room, and her records, and the plots of all the books she'd read, and all the movies she'd ever seen. She didn't want to go to bed because then she would wake up,

211

and leave, but she couldn't say that to me, and I doubt that she could say it even to herself.

There was a tension in the air between us, a feeling of longing and need, of things left unsaid. Caroline was not the kind of girl who could say the simple basic phrases; she was saying everything else that came into her head.

"Caroline"—I finally interrupted her—"I'm going to miss you so much. Do you think you would ever want to come live with me and Charlie?"

"Me and Charlie," instead of "Your father and me." It was an impulsive question.

"Oh, gosh, oh, uh," Caroline said. "Yeah, of course, but you know—my mother—"

"How's your mother doing? She hasn't called much this summer."

"Well, she's good, you know, really good. She's taking a course in sailing this summer at the Cape with Irene; that's her best friend. And she's really happy with her job. She's the assistant to the Registrar now; good job, good money, big deal, you know. I mean she's pretty happy usually. She's calmer. But I don't know about leaving her. I mean are you serious you'd want me to come live here? And Dad wants me, too? This is a real invitation?"

"Oh, Caroline, you know you and Cathy have always been welcome to live here with us, always, at any time." As I spoke, I remembered the early years, when I would have been absolutely dismayed at the idea of the girls living with us. No, they had not always been welcome, not by me. Perhaps they had known that, had sensed that, as children do sense the unsaid things. But things were different now, had been different for some time, and I wanted to announce the change, to make things clear. I wanted to say the words aloud. "We love you, Caroline. You don't need an invitation to live here. We want you to be with us. But we don't want to upset—things—or to interfere or cause trouble. I feel bad even now asking you because I know your mother wouldn't be overjoyed, and I don't want to cause your mother problems. But I love you so much and enjoy you so much and miss you so much when you're gone, and I know Charlie does, too— Caroline, don't cry. I didn't mean to make you cry. I wish I hadn't said anything—"

"I wish I could live here. I'd like that a lot, I think. But it would kill Mom. And I'd miss Cathy too much. She would love to live with Dad, you know. But we can't leave Mom. I mean we want to live with her, too. She's our *mother*."

"Caroline, don't cry. Really. I'm so sorry I mentioned it. Listen, let's go make some popcorn and watch the late movie and then go to bed."

We made popcorn and ate it as we watched some old black and white movies and we went to bed about two-thirty in the morning. At four, Cathy came into our room.

"Daddy? Can you wake up? Caroline's got those stomach pains."

Caroline was lying in her bed, twisting and moaning, her hands pressed over her stomach just

213

below her chest. Tiny lumps of breasts stuck up under her summer pajamas. Tears were running down her face. Her pillow was wet.

"It's those goddamned stomach pains again," she said.

"We'll get you a doctor," Charlie said.

"A doctor won't help. Nothing helps these bastards. You guys go on. I didn't mean to wake you up. They'll stop pretty soon, they always do stop after a while. Go back to sleep."

"We ate popcorn about midnight—" I said to Charlie. I wasn't brave enough to tell him I'd asked Caroline to live with us.

"It's not popcorn," Charlie said. "Cathy, you go get in bed with Zelda. I'll sit here and hold Caroline. Come on, honey, I haven't held you for a long time. I'll rub your back; maybe that will help."

So we ended the summer strangely. Charlie sat up into the morning, holding poor big Caroline, who finally slept, and Cathy sprawled peacefully in the double bed beside me. And I lay awake on my half of the double bed, feeling guilty and bad and sick at heart. I vowed never to ask Caroline to live with us again, never to put her in such an emotional bind.

The next day Caroline was all right and the girls left on schedule. When they left I didn't cry, not at the airport. But later that night, in the privacy of the bathroom, running bath water to hide my noise, I sat in the tub and bawled. Caroline wasn't my child, she could never be my child, She was Charlie's child, and Adelaide's child, and she belonged to

214

them. My position was less intimate less important: I would forever be something perhaps a bit more valuable than a favorite aunt. Caroline had a mother and a home, and it had been cruel and selfish of me to suggest she leave it. I had been confused and wrong to think she could live with us. And, in a way, I had been immoral and opportunistic. I had wanted to use Caroline to fill a need in me. It was true that I loved her, true that I would have loved having her live with us. But I had let that clean, clear love become entwined with my own physiological greed. I will never know if having a stepchild live with me would have stopped my raving desire for a child of my own, but I think I still would not have been satisfied. I think that seeing Caroline every day would have made me long even more for a daughter of my own.

I wanted a daughter of my own. I wanted to watch my own child grow and develop, to become pretty, sensitive, interesting. I wanted to guide my own child, to be indispensable. I wanted someone to say of me, with that total unfathomable security and significance, "She's my *mother*."

I didn't want to be only a stepmother.

I wanted to be a mother. I wanted to have a child.

Instead I had my Ph.D. work. It was fall again, I had courses to take again, and it all meant nothing to me. I hated it. I hated my books, my papers, my schedule. Charlie had finally finished his book and was feeling gay and light. He wanted to go dancing and drinking and driving in the autumn to see the colors of the leaves. He couldn't understand why I was acting so dull, so leaden, so confused.

One day he said to me over breakfast, "Zelda. You've changed."

I said, "I know. I feel so—heavy. Boring. Bored. I want—" I was afraid to say it outright. "I want some *life* in my life. I thought that at last Charlie would miraculously understand and say, "Oh yes, Zelda, I know what you mean. We should have a child."

Instead he said, "You're tired of the work, I know. All Ph.D. students go through this. I remember—"

"Charlie"—I interrupted him, I could hold back no longer, I nearly yelled it—"I want to have a baby."

Charlie could only stare at me, his knife and fork raised in the air beside him in surprise. Then, "What in the world?" he said. "Where did you ever get *that* idea?"

"It's not an *idea* that I *got!*" I said. "It's a feeling inside me that I can't push away. It's—it's like a passion, like falling in love."

"Oh, Zelda darling; oh, Zelda. You don't know what you're saying. A baby—I'm forty-one. I can't spend the rest of my life raising children. Honey, you don't know. Babies aren't just sweet cuddly things. They ruin your body and screw up your sex life and change your whole life forever. Nothing is ever the same again. You're *bright*, Zelda, you've got a future. You don't want to waste it. If you drop out after all this work—"

"I won't have to stop. I can do it all. One little

baby wouldn't be much work. Babies sleep a lot. I could have babysitters. I—"

"Zelda, you just don't know. You'd have one baby, and then you'd decide that an only child would be too lonely and you'd have another. And little babies do not sleep all the time. They would be sick the night before an exam. They would get hurt the day you have to turn in a paper. Babies demand everything of you, everything. There would be nothing left for your work; nothing left for you and me."

"I would *make* space for you and my work. I'd have a babysitter."

"Baby-sitters cost money."

"Well, then, I'd *work*."

"You'd work and take courses for your Ph.D. and write your thesis and take care of a baby and run this house and be with me?"

"*You* weren't with *me* very much this past year. You were always with your book."

"But that's over now. I'm with you now. It took just one year. A baby would take up the rest of our lives. Years without any letup. Zelda, I don't want any children. I just want you."

"But you can say that only because you already have children. I don't."

"Caroline and Cathy spend as much time with you as they do with me."

"Yes, but it doesn't *mean* the same. You are their *father*. You are connected to them. I'm not. You *matter*. I don't. They look like you. They're a part of you. I want a child to look like me, to be a part of me. I want to nurse a baby and guide a child and teach her about flowers and horses and poetry. I want to sew mother-daughter dresses, God dammit. I want to have someone special in this world. I want to do the normal, traditional, conventional thing. I want to be a mother."

"I never thought I'd hear you talk like this, Zelda."

"I never thought I'd *feel* like this. It's worse than wanting to fall madly in love when you're only twelve. I'm really longing for a child of my own."

"Look, let's do this, just finish your Ph.D. and try teaching one year. You are so close. You've wanted it so much. When we were first married, that was all you wanted—your Ph.D., your teaching, and me. It will take you just a while longer to finish it. Finish it. Then see how you feel about having a baby. You're young, after all. You've already come so far. And you know how you love teaching, how you miss it now. Think of how you would miss it if you had to give it up entirely."

I knew rationally that Charlie was right, although underneath it all I was sobbing and tearing my hair. I agreed to finish my Ph.D. first. I continued to faithfully, furiously take my Pill, but I prayed every night that it wouldn't work.

For nine more months I worked on my Ph.D.; I wished I were using those nine months to grow a baby. All that long fall and winter and spring I wandered about the university feeling lonely and bored, calculating just how many semesters, days, hours, it would be before I could get my Ph.D. and then get pregnant. Suddenly, insanely, my Ph.D. seemed only an obstacle in the way of what I really wanted. I appreciated the ridiculous irony of it all, but I couldn't help myself. My body had taken over with its deep, fierce craving, and it seemed that I spent my days wrestling myself through the world. I became nervous and jumpy and absentminded and sensitive. I longed for magic.

I finished my fifth semester of Ph.D. work and most of the sixth year of my marriage in the spring of 1970. I was twenty-seven. I felt old. I felt stale. I felt bored. I felt like a princess who wanted to become a frog. By the end of May, I had managed to totally bind my ability to make decisions in irrational ribbons of desire and despair. I should have known it was a classic intellectual disease: too much thinking, not enough sheer pure acts. I wanted a baby, but I was unable to make the choice to have one. One late spring night I approached Charlie about it again. I was timid, irritable. I wanted him to read my mind, to make the decision for me.

"Charlie," I said, rolling a pebble from our patio in my hands, "I have to talk to you. I think I'm going crazy. I can't continue my Ph.D. work. It means nothing to me anymore. Surely you've noticed how I've changed; this last semester was awful for me. My mind is tired—"

"Zelda," Charlie said, "I know. Listen, I have some news. I didn't want to tell you until I had it all arranged and confirmed. I didn't want to raise your hopes and then disappoint you. But the official letter came today. Did you see the champagne I bought? We'll celebrate tonight. Zelda, you can take a year off and rest your poor sweet tired mind. My love, we're going to France. I've been asked to be visiting professor next year at the Sorbonne."

The Sorbonne. Paris. France. Europe. Magic words. I had longed to live in Paris, and now Charlie was giving me the opportunity. I squashed my desire into as small a package as I could make and carried them to France with me, like an invisible, unwieldy, extra set of luggage, like a pair of kittens pushing at the sides of a soft basket, mewing to get out, always there, bouncing and bumping at my side. But I went. We spent a blurred, scurried summer entertaining Charlie's girls, interviewing people to rent our house, talking with travel bureaus and other friends who had lived in Europe and wanted to give us necessary advice, buying clothes and prescription drugs, practicing our French.

For once the girls were not the stars of our summertime, and this bothered them; when we told them we needed to send them back to Massachusetts early so that we could pack and get the house cleaned, they seemed relieved. We had asked them if they wanted to come to France, for any length of time at all, and they said that they very much did want to come. But Adelaide quickly ruled out any possibility of that: she said that if Charlie had enough money to buy them plane fare to and from Europe, he certainly had enough money to pay off their orthodonist bill immediately, or to give her some extra money for improvements on their house, which after all would do the girls more long-lasting good than a short trip. . . . We let the idea drop. We packed our bags, our boxes of books and note cards, and went with all our luggage, real and psychological, to France.

Many things might make one forget the desire for babies, but a year in France is not one of them. Charlie and I found a small cheap apartment on rue de la Rochefoucauld, and we bought a small white Fiat 850, and when Charlie wasn't teaching we were in the Fiat, driving to Switzerland or Germany or different parts of France. When he was teaching, I made trips to museums and cathedrals and learned how to cook rabbit and sat in cafés, drinking and talking with friends. I drank an awful lot of wine, and read Balzac and Stendhal in French, thinking I was improving my mind, and memorized unnecessary facts about de Gaulle and Fouquet, and sat in les Jardins de Luxembourg, feeding pigeons, and wrote lots of letters and sent lots of presents back to Caroline and Cathy. I bought Christian Dior underwear for myself, and all sorts of expensive perfume, and several thousand postcards. And every day when Charlie was teaching, I lay on my bed sobbing and digging my fingernails into my arms. I hated myself for it, but France in all its beauty was not what I wanted; it was not sufficient. While walking through the great gardens of Versailles, I would think, Yes, yes, it's beautiful, but all these statues are dead and I'm alive. I can create something beautiful, and alive, too. I began to resent Charlie for denying me what I wanted most—his child.

Paris became a blur. I was either drunk or crying. All the beauty and excess of the place stirred me up, but perhaps anything would have then. In March a graduate student sent me a list of critical books he thought I should be reading so that I could keep up with my work. I went to the William Smith bookstore, near the Place de la Concorde, and found a few of the books and went back to my apartment to settle down to work. For some reason bells were ringing that day, and their sounds moved through me as though I were made of air. Charlie was teaching and I was alone in our *troisième étage* flat. Something was simmering in wine on the stove, and I had a glass of wine at the little table I used for a desk. I felt lonely and incompetent and useless and drunkenly morose. The essays I was trying to read were stuffy and petty, and I suddenly knew with the wisdom that wine drunk in the afternoon brings that I couldn't stand to read another essay. I felt I had to do something drastic and dramatic to clench my decision, so I went out on our tiny balcony and began tearing out the pages from the book of essays. I let them float and fly, one by one, down to the street below. After a while people began to look up at me, after a while the pages were badly littering the street, but I didn't care. I didn't stop until all the nice new pages of the books were torn out and set free. Then I went back into the apartment and fell onto the bed and slept. When I woke up I remembered that I had been drunk and wasted money and acted foolishly, but I also remembered my decision, and I knew I would not change my mind. When Charlie came home that night, I told him that I had to have a baby or I would leave him and find a new husband/father. Charlie said all right, since those were his choices, we would have a baby, although he was afraid it would ruin everything between us.

And after all, perhaps it has. After all. Now, early in November, here in Helsinki, Charlie's been gone almost a week to lecture at various universities in Germany. Before Adam and Lucy, I would have gone with him. We would have enjoyed seeing a new town together, tasting new food, making love in new rooms and beds. But now, with four of us, it is too expensive and I really couldn't enjoy it anyway, dragging my two little ones from railway station to small hotel in the cold November rain. I wouldn't be able to go dining and drinking with Charlie and his friends; the children are too young to be left with a strange baby-sitter every night, and they don't go to sleep before nine, so I wouldn't be able to slip off down to the bar or restaurant, as I did when Adam was just a baby. They are too young to appreciate Germany, and the hotel rooms would have nothing to occupy them. And there would be all the paraphernalia, diapers and diaper liners, bottles and nipples and caps, clothes and love blankets and toys. No. I could not go this time.

My baby-sitter has just called to say she cannot

come to baby-sit tomorrow, after all, so I will not be able to go out to meet Charlie's plane when he returns. Before the children I met every plane that Charlie returned on. I would laugh and cry with joy to see him so big and real again, and we would come home and throw off our clothes and make love, and then eat and drink and discuss his trip and my week, and then we would make love again. Now I won't be able to meet his plane—and we won't be able to make love when he gets here. We won't be able to eat and drink and relax and talk. Adam and Lucy will be mad with delight to see him again, and they'll climb all over him and insist on sitting on his lap and climbing up his leg and having pony rides and showing him all seven million pictures they painted and drew this gloomy wet week. If Charlie and I try to talk for a long time, they'll become jealous and feel ignored and go crazy. I don't hate them for this, my children. I understand how they feel. They are in a strange country, away from friends and toys and Sesame Street and the comfort of their cozy rooms. They can't remember the past or dream of the future to help them make it through the present. *Now* to them is a cold gray linoleum floor and a big window full of cold gray sky and electrical power lines and construction cranes hanging deadly in the air. Now is a season of harsh weather and frozen sand and the swings removed from the playground so that their hands won't stick to the icy metal rungs. Now is having no little friends to giggle with and no safe secret place to hide and no granola bars. They need the comfort of my smile and touch and lap. I cannot bear for them to be unhappy for long. For a few minutes, yes, but not for hours, not for days.

When I gave birth to Adam and Lucy, I changed. It was as if when they were inside my body they had reached up and literally torn off a piece of my heart and my stomach and swallowed them, so that they now carry a part of me everywhere with them. I am linked to them by something more physically real and less scientifically observable than laser beams or remote control. They are small creatures, but I love them hugely, more than I love the earth or myself. More than I love Charlie. There it is. My children have become my lovers. I am finally unfaithful to my husband. Their smooth, fresh, rounded plump limbs are juicier and more delicious than Charlie's. I fondle them more. Their eyes are brighter, their breath sweeter. They gave me an understanding of life at their birth that Charlie had never been able to reveal to me; they connected me up to something deep and wide and wild and good in this world. Their births gave me the shocking great knowledge that I could eat grass, dance in trees, fall from roofs, and dissolve into shimmering molecules of sparkling snow. Their births made me know that I was grabbing death and tearing it in half and washing it away with my warm proud blood. When I took their naked perfect bodies in my arms, I felt ecstasy and content. Now, four and two years later, that hot exhausted joy is over, but the strength of feeling re-

225

mains. I press their bodies against mine and kiss them and stroke them more than I do Charlie. They surprise me more than Charlie does; they are more extravagant and lustful and ferocious in their love. After we have known each other for thirteen years, I am sure my children and I will be less hot and vivid in our relations with each other. Undoubtedly I will be more rational. But until then, at least for a few more years, I will continue to wade through this life with my little children as if I were wading through a vat of hot, sticky, sweet chocolate: the chocolate impedes me, slows me down, often irritates me, but I still stay here, happy in the hot thick gooey mess, licking sweetness off my fingers and arms and belly.

Charlie needs only what he has always needed: me as a companion and lover and live-in friend. I need more. I need my children, and I need a lover and live-in friend, and now I know I need to teach. Charlie wants only one thing, or perhaps two, counting his work; he does always want his work. But I want three things: him, my children, and my work. I want three things. Suppose I can have only two? I realize more and more, as I live out my time here in Helsinki, that as a woman, an *American* woman, I am spoiled. I have many luxuries, many electrical conveniences and psychological freedoms. And yes, when I think of it, I feel guilty, and yes, I would change it if I could. I would like for the whole world to be in a better balance. I know I do want *everything*—husband, children, work, harmonious complications. I seem to myself a bit greedy. Or is that old-fashioned thinking; am I trying to protect myself from the responsibility of a decision? After all, I must go home sometime, and I really don't see how my not teaching can help anyone else. How tangled my thinking is, yet certain lights are beginning to shine through.

But after all, I didn't make the decision in Paris. That day in the spring of 1971 when I got drunk and threw the essays out of the window and told Charlie I would leave him if I couldn't have a child passed. The next day I received a letter in the mail and ran to Charlie, crying, "Cancel yesterday! Forget everything I said!"

A former professor of mine had just become the new head of the English department at a small junior college. He was writing to ask if I would be interested in teaching freshman English and literature full time the coming year. He had always been impressed with my teaching, he wrote, and hoped I could join his department. He didn't care whether or not I had finished my Ph.D.

I went mad with joy. Charlie was pleased. I accepted.

That summer when we returned from France was a totally happy one. Charlie and I scarcely had time to unpack before his daughters arrived. Caroline was sixteen now and a serious reader; Cathy was thirteen and a teen-ager. Cathy had braces now, too, and both girls glittered and flashed when they smiled, if they didn't remember to hide their mouths with their hands like timid Japanese. Charlie was working on a paper, but it didn't consume all his time. I was busy getting together my stuff for the fall. I was so excited by the prospect of teaching again after three years away from it that I prepared more lesson plans, diagrams, exercises, jokes, quizzes, and reading material than I could possibly have used. I read and reread the grammar book and the anthology of literature. While driving to the grocery store or dentist I would imagine my first day in class, and my second and my third. What would I say? How could I inspire them? How could I make them *love* the language?

I asked Caroline a thousand times for her opinion. She was very bright and helpful. She read some of the short stories and discussed them with me. We spent a lot of time in the backyard in our shorts and halter tops, with our bare feet in the water of the little lily pond and books in our hands and a pad of paper next to me and a pencil behind my ear. How beautiful Caroline was then, even with her braces and the short chopped hair she had appeared with that summer. She was slender to the point of skinniness, all ribs and elbows, but her hair was the thick silver-lighted gold that Charlie had; it gleamed when she turned her head. She looked, in fact, as Charlie would have if he had been a girl. She was still shy, still reserved, she still could not easily touch anyone. She always kept a space between herself and others, as if contact might cause pain. Except for that one characteristic she was a normal, happy girl, and to me, a friend.

Cathy still adored her father, still followed him everywhere. When he was working and Caroline and I were reading, she did elaborate jigsaw puzzles or macrame, or she sewed. Usually, if we weren't at the farm, or swimming, she was off with her girl friend Nicole. Caroline had let her neighborhood friendships lapse and seemed to prefer staying with me, but Cathy flew out of the house every morning after breakfast to go to Nicole's house. They preferred Nicole's house to ours because Nicole had older brothers and their house was full of current rock records going full blast and fifteen- and sixteen-year-old boys. Charlie thought Nicole was rather dumb and dippy, too silly and boy-crazy for thirteen, but he didn't interfere with Cathy. Instead he spent more time with her, trying to get her interested in other things: art, classical music, history, watercolor painting. Still, that summer Cathy seemed to be nothing more than a giggler, flashing out the door, letting it slam behind her.

One week it rained, and Nicole and her family were away on a trip, and Charlie had meetings and the week seemed stuck in mud. It was a dirty, dull week, it wouldn't move. After three boring days we came up with the deliciously foolish idea of writing and presenting a play. The girls—and I—were still enamored of monsters and werewolves and ghouls, and that week the setting seemed perfect for horror, what with the windows darkened by the perpetual rain and clouds and the sky dramatically shaking with thunder. I popped popcorn and the three of us sat around cross-legged on the floor, writing a play for three parts: the heroine, the vampire, and the hero. I was certain the girls would cast me as the villain, but they didn't. It was after all the best part. They had to toss a coin to see who got the villain's role—Cathy—and Caroline became the heroine. I had to be the hero. It was awful, being the hero, I only got to run in during the last two minutes of the play to stab the vampire through the heart. The vampire got to die a writhing and melodramatic death. Caroline swooned and said, "My hero!" and I got to say my lines: "There! He'll never bother you or anyone else again! Once more goodness triumphs!"

Since I had such a short part, I was also made into general stagehand, director, and wardrobe maker. Caroline had to wear something appropriately heroinical and flowing, so I took her to my room to try on my long dresses. She was now at sixteen a good inch taller than I, and when she put on one of my dresses tears jumped into my eyes. Suddenly she seemed grown-up. Mature. After that summer I thought of her as a grown-up, and that was a mistake. She was still a child, needing what children need. Cathy wore her best slacks and a white shirt of mine and a bow tie of her father's, but we had to buy black material for a cape. It was cheap shiny material and it made a great cape: in the dim rainy light it glistened elegantly, voluptuously, sleekly. I wore some slacks and a tailored shirt and Charlie's suede jacket and cowboy hat, both of which were far too big for me. Still, without a hat I didn't look male enough to be a proper hero.

Our play seemed so good that we invited all the neighborhood children. About fifteen of them came and squashed themselves into our dining room; our stage was the living room, and we entered from the hall closet. We had draped the furniture with dark quilts and turned down the lights and hung construction paper bats and spiders all about. No one forgot her lines. We were a splendid success. I sat in the coat closet waiting for the end of the play and my three lines, and smiled as I watched Caroline and Cathy through a crack in the closet door, and thought that we were now really all friends—*comrades*. I thought we would always be close and good friends.

I was sad when they left that summer, but not too sad: I was eager for the fall, and for my teaching.

That fall Anthony Leyden came to our house to tell us that June was divorcing him. She had been having an affair with her children's piano teacher, and she wanted to marry him. I laughed out loud and couldn't stop for several minutes when Anthony told us the news. June, proper, prissy June! Had fallen in love with her children's piano teacher! And wanted to leave her children's father! I loved it; it was wonderful. I hoped that someone somewhere would righteously snub her as much as she had snubbed me, but I also wished her well. I thought she was doing a splendid and valiant thing, giving

231

up her respectable home and its superficial tidiness for the messy depths of sexual love.

Part of the problem, Anthony said, was that she didn't want the children. She was fixed on the idea that she and her pianist would go to the Caribbean for a year of sun and love. He would support them by playing at a piano bar in a tourist hotel. She would wait tables at night, if necessary. This set me off into laughter again, the thought of June Leyden in a little cocktail waitress uniform, with black lace stockings and flounces around her prim little butt. Anthony said he thought it was humorous, too, and that didn't really bother him, June leaving him that way. What bothered him was that she wanted him to keep the children. Dickie and Dierdre were now sixteen and thirteen, not babies but not old enough to be on their own. And Anthony, handsome Anthony, didn't want them around. He had a lover himself, a young girl who had been a student of his. He didn't plan to marry the girl, but he did want to live with her awhile. He wanted some romance and freedom, too, and he couldn't have that with two teenagers in the house. He thought that June should keep them without question; she was after all their mother. He would give them lots of money to live on, he said; he just wanted his own apartment and his own life, without two hulking teenagers trailing through it, dropping clothes and knocking on closed bedroom doors.

Charlie gave Anthony the name and address of his lawyer. I sat and laughed. I felt glad for them all, even the children. Dickie and Dierdre had become

232

spoiled, coddled, snotty teenage kids, and I didn't like them. Caroline and Cathy didn't like them, either, and always tried to see as little of them as possible. I thought that perhaps this change would be good for the Leyden children, would toss them out of their complacency, would reveal to them the turmoil of emotions hiding beneath ironed sheets and behind polished windows.

I would have given a lot to read the letters that passed between Adelaide and June. I wondered: If Adelaide condoned June's mad amorous actions, could she still hate Charlie for his? Would she think it acceptable for a woman to leave a man because she loved another man but still not acceptable for a man to leave a woman he had stopped loving?

We hadn't heard much from Adelaide that summer. When the girls were asked about her, they said that she was happy, more or less, and settled. She didn't date, they said, she was very bitter toward all men. She thought men were a rather shabby lot compared to the noble species of women.

"And how do you feel about men?" Charlie asked Caroline that summer.

Caroline went pale, as she always did when the talk got serious.

"I don't know," she said. "I guess I don't hate them, like Mother does, but I know I'll never be able to trust them."

"Not even me?" Charlie asked.

"Most of all, not you," Caroline said. "You left us. I mean I don't hate you; I love you. But you left us.

I guess you thought you were taking just yourself away, but you took everything, it seems, everything. You took yourself, and our home. And in a way you took our mother. She changed. She couldn't be just for us. She wasn't home when we came home from school; she was at the university, working. She didn't spend lots of time with us, she had to see her friends and boyfriends and psychiatrists and such. I know you think you did the best thing for us. But still *you left us,* so how could I trust you completely?"

"That's too bad," Charlie said. "I'm really sorry, Caroline. Please don't hold my faults against all men. I—I did do it the only way I thought best for all of us." He was quiet a moment, thinking.

"*I* like men!" Cathy volunteered. "I have lots of boyfriends. And even though Mother hates you, Dad, don't worry, cause I love you anyway. I can see why Mother hates you, but I love you, and I always will."

I sat silently through the conversation. It was a rare one, for the girls seldom discussed love and hate face to face. I kept hoping that Caroline or Cathy might say, "And we're glad you married Zelda. It's been neat knowing her." But no one mentioned me at all. I felt like what I was: an interchangeable part.

I still longed for a child of my own. I was still determined to have one. But that summer the desire was subdued. I was excited about teaching again. And I told myself that I was only twenty-eight; I still had a lot of time left, I could really establish myself at the junior college, become a part of it, and then have a baby. For once it seemed that I had my life in control, that I was doing what I wanted to do, that I was going where I wanted to go. I was happy.

SIX

"No! No, I won't be 'reasonable'! *You* be *reasonable!* What you're asking me to do is to give up *everything* in order to have *nothing!*"

It was April 1972, and I was yelling. I was yelling at Charlie. In February he had been offered a prestigious chair at a university in New Hampshire. Now the time had come to let them know his decision. He wanted to move, of course. I didn't. I didn't want to move at all.

"I didn't know that you thought of your relationship with me as *nothing*," Charlie said.

"Oh, Charlie, that's not fair. I don't think of our relationship as nothing. I love you. *I love you.* But I love my work, too. You can have me and your work. Why can't I have you and my work?"

"You could finish your Ph.D. at the university there. They've got a good English department."

"I don't want to finish my Ph.D. I want to teach."

"You could probably teach there, somewhere. There are surely junior colleges and small colleges in the area."

"Charlie, you know how it is these days. A thousand English majors are wandering the continent, looking for work. There are no jobs. You have to *know* people. I don't know anyone in New Hampshire. And I want to stay here. I like it here. Wilbur likes my work; he's going to give me tenure. *Me. Tenure.* I could stay here forever and teach and help develop the department, even influence the development of the college. I love it. It's my work. How can you ask me to give it up?"

"How can you ask me to turn down the Wallace Chair? It's one of the greatest honors a historian can have. And I'm tired of the department here. I've outgrown it—"

"Oh, Charlie, I know. I know. But—"

"And there's the matter of money. The Wallace Chair would give us more income than both of our salaries here."

"But I don't care about the money. My life doesn't revolve around money. Besides, I want to be making *my own* money. It may not be much, but it's very important to me to make my own money."

"Look, Zelda, be realistic. We're just making it now, even with your money. In another year Caroline will start college. And then Cathy. The only way I can send them to college is to make more money."

"You could write more books—"

"Oh, darling, you know how little my books bring in. And my work is growing more and more philosophical and difficult; only a few will be interested in it. I've got a reputation, and my writing will secure that. But it won't send the girls to college."

"So. We send your daughters to college and you get a prestigious position and I get nothing."

"There are other things in the world besides teaching. You could work in some other field. You could—"

"Oh, Charlie, stop it. You've won. You've beaten me down. We'll move. But Jesus Christ, I hate it."

"Zelda, don't cry. Zelda, don't. Zelda, believe me. I don't want you to be so unhappy. Zelda, I love you. I want you to be happy. Zelda, listen. You could have a baby."

During the first weeks of June, Charlie and I and a moving company moved us to New England. Once Charlie had said the magic words, everything seemed to fall into place. We sold our Crestwood house and the Ozark farm and spent Easter vacation in New Hampshire, looking for a new home. We found what seemed to us a small paradise: thirty acres of land with a rushing brook, an old apple orchard, two fairly usable barns, and a lovely old colonial house. The house was red brick with green shutters and slate walks. It had four fireplaces and four bedrooms. Charlie and I would share the largest room; I thought I would fill the remaining bedrooms with children. I would have at least three, I thought, and perhaps, since there was room, six. I would grow our own vegetables, make our own applesauce, and raise healthy, laughing children.

In April, after our decision to move to New England, Charlie received an invitation to teach at a university in Amsterdam. We decided that we wanted to go; we had enjoyed Paris, and we agreed that it wouldn't be so easy to travel once we had children. Charlie's department in New Hampshire was willing to let him have the fall semester off so that he could go to Amsterdam; he would start his teaching duties in January. It all worked out, so easily. We felt certain that we were doing exactly the right things.

I planned to become pregnant sometime while in Amsterdam, perhaps in December, so that I would have time to work on the inside of our house in the spring, and to plant and harvest my first real garden. Instead, to my amazement, I found that I was pregnant in June, one month after I had stopped taking the Pill. I almost couldn't imagine how it had happened. I had been having intercourse for so many years without any noticeable result that I thought getting pregnant would be a more momentous event than it was. I didn't know when I conceived; there was no heart-stopping, heart-starting moment. By the time I was aware of it in early June, it had already happened. I sat for hours staring at my flat tummy, talking to it as if it were a stranger with a secret and willful life of its own, which after all it was.

It was as if I were the first woman ever to become pregnant. The world spread out in lovely waves from my stomach. I wouldn't have traded places with kings. I missed teaching, my students, my colleagues, my office and papers and books, the thought of a settled future of teaching, but all this didn't matter quite so much anymore. I listened to my stomach, noted each slight change, and began to read books on natural childbirth. I had gotten pregnant so easily that it seemed, along with everything else, to confirm my feelings that Charlie and I were doing everything right, going in the right direction.

Caroline and Cathy came to the farm in the last days of June. They were now seventeen and fourteen. Teen-age girls. Caroline had her braces off and her smile was stunning. Such perfect, even, white teeth. Her blonde hair had grown to her shoulders, and she now stood a good three inches taller than I. Walking along beside her, I felt like a dark little peasant escorting an Amazon princess. Cathy still had her braces, but she was pretty, and she was seriously interested in boys, even more than Caroline. Both girls oohed and aaahed when they saw the big old house, the apple orchard, the rolling green pasture. But it was obvious that farm life was going to be a little too quiet for them. Our neighbors lived far away, and were older people who kept to themselves. The little town where we got groceries was scenic, but dull. There was nothing exciting to interest a teen-age girl. They were too old to spend their days making up silly plays and too young to go off on their own to the bigger town, where the university was, twenty miles away. Even the first day Charlie and I could tell they were bored and restless. Physiology was taking over their lives just as it had taken over mine.

We didn't tell the girls that I was pregnant simply because I was superstitious about it until I was four or five months along, as if speaking of the baby would cause it to disappear.

"Look, girls," Charlie said the fourth day they were there, "this can't be much fun for you. All Zelda and I will be doing this summer is painting and scraping off old paint and fixing fences and unpacking. If you want to stay and help, I'll pay you for the work you do. But I've got a better idea. Why don't you go back and spend the summer with your mother and your friends, and then come spend the semester with us in Amsterdam?"

The girls stared first at Charlie and then at each other, surprise and hope and fear spreading across their faces.

At last, almost whispering, Cathy spoke first. "We'd have to be home for Christmas. Mother made us promise that no matter what we'll always spend Christmas with her."

"Of course you can go home for Christmas," Charlie said. "Look, why don't I call Adelaide right now and see what she thinks?"

What Adelaide thought, after an hour's polite persistence on Charlie's part, was that yes, that would be all right. She could hardly refuse a European experience twice for her girls, especially since the orthodontist bills were paid and Charlie promised to keep the child-support checks going to her even when the girls were with us in Amsterdam. And she was happy at the thought of having the girls with her once for the entire summer. She was not pleasant on the phone with Charlie, but she wasn't hysterically raging, either; it was as if she had worked a few things out, had reached if not a beautiful at least a calm resting place. The next day the girls went back down to Massachusetts—their home was now only a three-hour drive from our home—and we didn't see them again until September, when we all flew to Amsterdam.

Charlie and I flew to Amsterdam first and got settled in our apartment. We had a beautiful apartment right on the Prinsengracht and the Leidsestraat, looking over the prince's canal and the gay street where trams ran and calliopes played. In September the trees were still green, and they arched over the canal as perfectly as if drawn there by an artist, and ducks swam in the water and gulls dipped in the air. Amsterdam was full of museums and concerts and ballets and great shops and things to see. I knew we would all be happy.

And we all were happy, but not at first. At first we were all miserable, for a while.

When we arrived in Amsterdam, I was four months' pregnant and wearing maternity clothes simply because my regular clothes were too, tight and I knew I'd eventually be in maternity clothes and didn't want to have to pack two, sets of things. By then the baby was kicking and I was through having morning sickness, and was feeling totally rosy and fine. I was so happy to be pregnant that I was gay and sexy and silly all the time, and of course Charlie enjoyed that. Somehow we forgot that he had never told Caroline and Catherine about my being pregnant, and I was so used to being pregnant, to looking pregnant, that I didn't stop to think that I would look different to Caroline and Cathy than I had a few short months before.

Charlie met his daughters at Schipol airport and brought them back to the apartment, where I was waiting. I had been fixing their room up, as I always did, putting little Dutch presents on the beds and planning what sight-seeing we would do first. When the door opened and the three of them walked in, I rose from the sofa, where I had been sitting sorting travel brochures, and went to kiss them. At first they smiled at me, and then their faces changed: they blanched, stopped, looked confused and hurt. Then they turned and looked at each other with that secret resigned put-upon look that they so often in their teen-age years had shared. When I kissed them, they turned their cheeks away, and their hello was cool. That is, Caroline's was cool; Cathy's was nonexistent. She burst into tears and pushed me away and said, "I want to go home!"

"What?" I said.

"What on earth?" Charlie said. He tried to take Cathy in his arms, but she pushed him away. "Cathy, what on earth is the matter?"

"*Nothing's* the matter," Cathy said. "Just let me go home."

"Look," Charlie said, "you can't possibly go home right now. You've been flying for hours, you're exhausted. Let me take you to your bedroom, and you lie down and rest a bit. Then if you still want to go home, you can."

Caroline put her arms around Cathy. "Come on,

242

Cath'," she whispered. "Let's go to our room for a minute. Come on."

"Look," I said, "please tell us what's wrong. You walk in the door with smiles and suddenly you want to go home. Can't you please tell us?"

But the girls drew together, pulled away from me, actually shrank from my touch.

"I want to go home. I want to be alone," Cathy cried, and her cries turned into real wracking sobs.

Charlie led her and Caroline into their little bedroom. I didn't follow. I heard him shut the door; I heard him put the suitcases down. It was at times like this that I wished I smoked; I longed for something to do to keep my hands busy. Instead I was simply left standing there, the space around me vacant and disturbed. I could hear low voices coming from the girls' room and I felt crazy with desire to know what they could possibly be saying. Too curious to restrain myself, I crossed to the wall that separated their bedroom from the living room, and pressed my ear against the wall, and listened.

"Yes, she is going to have a baby," Charlie was saying. "But that won't affect our love for you at all."

"But I don't want you to have a baby," Cathy was sobbing. "It's not fair. We never had all of you, and now we'll get even less. You'll give all your time and love to her baby."

"That's not true," Charlie said. "I love both of you girls with all my heart. I couldn't possibly love any other child more. You two are my first children, remember that, I've loved you first."

243

"It's just not *fair*," Cathy wailed. "Oh, I want to go home. I don't want to stay here. I don't want to see you ever again."

"Cathy, baby, please—"

"Don't call me baby! I was your baby once, but I'm not anymore. You've got yourself a new baby now. A nice new baby who can live in your house and be yours all the time."

"Caroline," Charlie said after a while, "is this the way you feel, too?"

There was a long silence. I could imagine Caroline sitting on the bed, staring down at the floor, her hands twisting in her lap. "I don't know," she said at last. "It doesn't really matter. I don't care."

"I'm sorry," Charlie said. "It's my fault. I mean we shouldn't have surprised you with it like this. I should have told you before. But I actually sort of forgot it until now. Zelda sure looks fat and funny, doesn't she?" That brought a slight, grim, satisfied chuckle from one of the girls. "Zelda's been wanting to have a baby for a long time—you girls know you both want children when you grow up, I've heard you say it a thousand times. Well, Zelda wants children, too. But she loves you, and I love you, and no new child will change that. I was hoping that you would enjoy having a little brother or sister around. I thought it might even be fun for you."

"Zelda's baby will never be *my* brother or sister." It was Caroline speaking, and her voice was so hard and cold and sure that it cut me like a knife.

There was more silence. I leaned against the wall

244

praying for Charlie to say something, to somehow find the right, the perfect words. But after a long while all he said was, "Well, then, I don't know what more I can say. I'm sorry you both feel this way. I love you both. You know that. I'll always love you. Zelda loves you. We were planning to have an exciting time here in Amsterdam—the baby isn't due until the end of February. We were planning to go down to Paris in November, and—well, we had a lot of things planned that we thought you'd enjoy. I think it would be too bad if you deprived yourselves of an experience like this simply because Zelda happens to be pregnant. The baby isn't even born yet. Why don't you wait till then to worry?"

"You'll never understand," Cathy said.

"Perhaps I won't. Perhaps I can't. Look, why don't you both lie down and rest? You've been traveling for a long time. You're exhausted. Just do this for me, lie down and rest, and if you want something to eat or drink, let me know. Then if you still want to go home, you can."

I left the wall and walked over to the tiny kitchen area and was busily making tea when Charlie came out of the room. I felt like crying myself; I hadn't thought at all about how the girls would react to my pregnancy, but this certainly wasn't the way I would have chosen. I felt sorry for them, and yet already strangely defensive for the unborn child inside me. I didn't want him or her exposed to the hate of the girls. And I felt really, deeply hurt: if the girls loved me, I reasoned, they should love my child.

It occurred to me as Charlie crossed the room that I should still not know what the trouble was. I didn't want Charlie to know that I had been curious enough and devious enough to listen at the bedroom wall. I was afraid my face would show something, everything. I turned my back and looked for teacups.

"They're jealous of the baby," Charlie said, and put his hands on my shoulder and leaned against me. "It's too bad. I didn't think, hell, I didn't give it a thought how they'd react to the baby."

"But they're fourteen and seventeen!" I whispered. "How can they be jealous of a baby? I'd understand it if they were small, but they're not. They're almost grown."

"Jealousy never does have to make sense," Charlie said. "I should have told them; it was bad to surprise them that way. Well, they're resting, maybe they'll sleep. Maybe they'll feel better after they sleep."

And they did. They woke up in the early evening and came out to ask where the bathroom was, and if they could have something to eat, and then Charlie took them out for a walk around the city, which sparkled with its bright lights and its still warm air and its streets full of young people playing guitars and singing. The girls decided to stay for another day, and after that day, for another, until at last they unpacked their suitcases and hung up their clothes and said they wanted to stay for the semester. It was awkward at first, it was difficult. Everyone knew what the problem was, but no one would discuss it; it was as if talking about it made it

246

real but ignoring it made it nonexistent. And so we lived our lives there, and my stomach grew larger, and the word "baby" was never said. It was as if I were having a surreptitious pregnancy, as if we were all pretending that the offensive part of my body wasn't really there. It was a strange way to live. I was already head over heels in love with my child, and I longed to call out, "Oh, look! Can you see how he's kicking? Isn't he strong? Come feel!" But I knew no one there would share my joy. And that made me feel slightly bitter, slightly angry, slightly sad.

Our days fell into a pleasant routine. The principal at Caroline and Cathy's Massachusetts school had agreed to a strange proposition that Charlie, in desperation, had come up with when asked about the girls' schooling. I was to be their tutor. I was to see that they studied, and to pace their reading, and to compose and give them tests. Whatever grade I gave them at the end of the semester would go on their transcripts. In some states it is true that if the parents are teachers the children do not have to attend school; this was some variation on that theme. So our schedule was set up: every weekday morning I tutored the girls in history, French, English grammar and composition, literature, and science. We hired a special tutor for Caroline's trigonometry; he was a thin young Dutch man named Martyn who spoke excellent English and came once a week, in the evening, to sit at our dining room table to talk in a low accented voice to Caroline. We used the school's textbooks, and I typed up tests on Charlie's typewriter so that they looked appropriately official, and the girls studied well, and did well.

In the afternoons we went out. Early in the semester, when the sun was still warm, we rented bikes and rode over to Vondel Park and had picnics in the grass. We must have been a strange-looking bunch on our rented bikes: big blond Charlie and his two big blonde daughters, and then dark little me with my fat tummy, pedaling along behind them, wobbling along unsteadily, happy and puffing and out of breath. Or we walked, all over Amsterdam, to Dam Square, to tours of the Heineken Brewery, where the international hippies congregated for free beer and cheese, to interesting shops, all about the lovely canals and streets. Our favorite discovery was the Moses and Adam Church, which was a baroque, rococo, almost hideously ornamented once Catholic church which was now used by hippies as a teahouse and meditation center; the place seemed to perfectly represent the religious tolerance of Amsterdam. Later, as the weather grew colder and darker and rainier, we spent more time inside museums, the Stedelijk and the Rijksmuseum, the smaller individual houses, Rembrantshuis, Anne Frank's house, the Weigh House . . . There was an endless supply of places to visit and learn from.

On weekends and long holidays when Charlie didn't have to teach, we took trips. Sometimes they were short trips to surrounding areas, to Den Haag to see the Maritshuis, or to Haarjuilens to see the fairy-tale castel de Haar, or to the somber and authentic castle at Muiden. Friends drove us to Edam and Volendam and Markam, where people still wore wooden shoes and long dresses and baggy black pants. Once we took a long train trip to Germany to visit friends in Lübeck and Hamburg and Kiel and to walk on the fresh sandy shores of the island of Sylt. Another time we rented a little Fiat and drove south to France and spent days being tourists in Paris, showing the girls the Louvre and Sacré Coeur, getting drunk with old friends at La Coupole. We strolled along the rue de la Rochefoucauld, showing the girls where we had once lived. I smiled to myself as I looked up at the balcony where I had once stood ripping essays from a book, daring to make a decision. Being Americans in foreign countries made us draw closer together, made us laugh at things—the harsh German toilet paper, our dreadful French and German accents, the trivialities we missed from home.

We were the closest, Caroline and Cathy and I, on Thursday evenings. That was when an hour-long American show came on television, with the words spoken in English. We would prepare for the show by going to Dyker and Thies, a specialty import store just across the street from our apartment, and buying an expensive can of S&W popcorn. Then we would all sit, grinning and munching popcorn for one happy American hour, watching a droop-eyed detective in a sloppy raincoat. We would complain about feeling homesick then, but not for long. There was too much else to do; we never had time to sit and sigh. We met people, and were invited to homes, and had friends in, and Caroline flirted with boys on the street and sometimes went off with them to a movie or Orange Julius while Charlie lectured or wrote and Cathy and I stayed home and played cards. So our days were neatly patterned, and filled with an endless variety of pleasures and delights.

The best time of all—for me, just for me—was Tuesday afternoon. That was when I took the tram by myself to Schubertsstraat to take Lamaze courses from an elegant sexagenarian named Madame Rouva-Carmen. It was the only time I was able to feel openly, happily pregnant. I hated to leave when the hour was over, I wanted to linger with all the other mothers, to hear them talk about childbirth and breathing and nursing and such. I was so grateful for any chance remarks—"You're carrying your baby low, that means you'll have a boy!"; "You've gained weight on your body but not on your face, that means you'll have a girl!"; "I'm starting to have awful cramps in my feet, do you get them, too?"—that I nearly cried when spoken to. It was so good to have my pregnancy spoken of as a normal, natural, acceptable thing. I was proud of my stomach, I adored it. But in our apartment on the Prinsengracht everyone simply pretended that it wasn't really there. I felt that pregnancy was some-thing that I was actively doing; it was a part, a joyful part, of my life, and I hated pretending otherwise. I began to long for my parents, for my American friends, for Alice, for anyone, to say, "How are you feeling this morning? Are you keeping your weight gain down? Have you thought of a name yet? Do you want a boy or a girl?" Sometimes in the privacy of our bed I would talk to Charlie about "it"—the baby—or about myself. And Charlie was kind, but not really interested, not full of passion and hope, as I was. And I suppose it was then that I felt again the rift between us: not a great sudden overwhelming chasm, as in times of crisis with the girls or Adelaide. Not that. This new division was more like the flat bare stretch of sand between the shoreline and the water when the tide has ebbed; we know the rush of ocean will return, but the long empty space caused by its absence brings an uneasiness, a pang.

December was the best month. In Amsterdam the custom is for St. Nicholas to come from Spain by boat with a Moorish helper, Swart Piet, to give small gifts and ginger-flavored cookies to very young children. There are parades by boat and by horseback throughout the city on various days, and from the first of December small children wake up every morning expecting a small treat from St. Nicholas. The custom was too charming to be ignored, even if Caroline and Cathy were no longer little; we bought and hid little gifts each night: small blue and white porcelain Dutch shoes, fingernail polish, fancy chocolates, souvenirs. Charlie and I had as much fun finding and choosing and secreting the presents as Caroline and Cathy did in discovering them each morning. And on December fifteenth, the day before the girls left to go back to the States, Charlie and I awoke to find little gifts for us placed next to the door of our bedroom. Chocolates for us both, a necklace for me, a book for him. I cried that morning because, for the first time in all the Christmases we had known each other, Caroline and Cathy had given me a present. I had not minded before, all those Christmases when I did not receive a gift from the girls; I knew that present-giving in our situation was fraught with tense significances. When Charlie and I chose Christmas presents for Caroline and Cathy, we had to walk a dangerously thin line: if we didn't send enough, it was a sign that we did not love them; we were selfish. But if we sent too much, we were either trying to make up for our lack of love by tangible items bought with money or we were trying to show them how wealthy we were, how much we could give, and thus were trying to lure them away from their mother. There were always so many clever ways to interpret and warp and ruin the simplest act. I could imagine the difficulties that Caroline or Cathy might have had if they, with their very limited amounts of money, saved allowances, had wanted to send me a present. If they had, for instance, ten dollars to spend on Christmas gifts, just how much of that could they spend on me without hurting their mother's feelings? How much should they take from their mother's gift to spend on me? No, it was too complicated, too complex for them to handle. So I was pleased and touched when Caroline and Cathy gave me a present that year in

Amsterdam—although the necklace, charming as it was, was not the present I would have chosen for them to give me. If I could have chosen a present, it would have been for them to say, just once, "Gee, Zelda, you are sure getting big; look how tight that maternity top is. I'll bet you can't wait to have your baby." Perhaps the girls felt that way now and then. They certainly had to notice; we lived together, months passed, my baby grew. There were times when I was tutoring the girls when I would lean over Caroline's shoulder to point out a mistake or an interesting phrase and my fat stomach would accidentally press against her shoulder, my baby touching my skin, my skin touching Caroline. The kitchen we had was so tiny in its quaint European way that after a while no one else could come into it when I was in there. If Caroline came in to get the silverware to set the table while I was draining the spaghetti, she simply had to brush against my belly; there was no other way.

But all that time, after that first surprising day, no word was ever said about my pregnancy or the coming child. It was as if we had made a pact, as if, without words or gestures, we had all made a secret, irreversible agreement not to mention the new child. Perhaps Caroline and Cathy thought that if we didn't speak of it, if we pretended it was not there, it would not be there, it would go away. Probably Charlie felt as I did, that in keeping quiet about the baby we were keeping a peace and making the girls feel important. If words were what was measured, the girls must have felt very important, and the baby should have felt of no significance whatsoever. And I suppose I understood. I understood that although Caroline was seventeen and taller than I, that even though she could solve mathematical problems that boggled my mind, that even though she threw around words like "self-aggrandizement" and "global love," she still was a child. Charlie's child. Charlie's first child. And even though Cathy was fourteen and wore pierced earrings and eye shadow and lipstick and blush-on and ankle bracelets and received letters in the daily mail from three different boyfriends, she was still a child. Charlie's child. Perhaps his favorite child. And my child, the new child, was not welcome.

We had gone back, I suppose, in a way, to square one, to the early years, when things were confused. The complication now was that not only did the girls love Charlie and because of that not want to hurt him or make him angry, they also cared for me. I will not say they loved me. If they loved me, if they ever loved me, they never told me, they never made it clear; it would have been only a vain and optimistic and probably erroneous guess on my part. But I do think that they cared for me by then, after seven years of knowing me, and in their way they probably felt as they had when they first met me. They wanted me to be happy because they liked me. But they didn't want me to be happy in the way that I was happy, by being pregnant.

It was the worst of our times together. I was miserable and lonely, I felt unloved, slighted, unappreciated, mistreated. I knew, because I had friends with teen-agers, that teen-agers, no matter how sweet and willing they might have been a few short years or even months before, eventually become surly and unwilling to help with household chores. This was the first time we all had lived together for any length of time, and it was the first time that I actually wanted and needed help. Domestic tasks in small European apartments are time-consuming and difficult. I had to go every day to the butcher and the greengrocer and the baker because our refrigerator and kitchen were so small. We had no washing machine, and I had to carry piles of sheets and jeans and towels several blocks to the laundry, and back again. There were four of us living together, four large people, and that required lots of cooking and dishwashing and cleaning. I at first blithely assumed that Caroline and Cathy would gladly help with all of this, simply out of their own sweet natures. And at first, for the first two or three days, they did. But then, to my amazement, a simple task such as drying the dishes that I was washing became the cause of a major fight. Caroline would hiss at Cathy that it was her turn, and Cathy would hiss back that she had done them two nights in a row, and quite often I would end up doing it all rather than asking for help and starting a quarrel. It was even worse when I needed help to do the things that were awkward for me to do because of my pregnancy. It was difficult for me to carry a large basket full of laundry; my arms simply would not reach out in front of both my stomach and the basket, and if I tried to carry it on one side or the other I felt unbalanced and uncomfortable. When Charlie was around, he would of course help, but when he was gone, I did everything myself. If I asked for help, both girls responded with such weary, superior, put-upon expressions that I felt a balloon of rage well up and explode inside me. It was easier to carry the laundry than to cope with the rage. I had heard, everyone had told me, I knew when I was being sensible, that this was the way that teen-agers were; still it hurt me that the girls acted this way when I needed help. Everything logical seemed on my side: I was doing so much for them, not just buying food and cooking for them, but spending so much time tutoring them and making up tests for them and taking them around cities, trying to point out things of interest, playing cards with them when they were bored and I would rather have been reading a book. Even if I hadn't been pregnant, I should have had more help from them, I thought. But they had become creatures that I didn't really know, creatures I wasn't totally comfortable with anymore. On one day we might all discuss an interesting idea from a textbook, and laugh at the gulls as we leaned over a stony bridge throwing bread crumbs, and sit in a movie together, and yet if I asked for help with the dishes so that we could go to the movie on time, I was treated to looks of great disdain and what seemed to be even hatred. It was startling. It was disconcerting. I had thought that I loved them, certainly that I had loved Caroline. Now I was not so sure. It is hard to love into the face of hate.

Yet it was also in a way the best of our times together. Because they were teen-agers, they could now discuss and understand things that I was interested in; we could share many things. And Amsterdam was such a happy city, so full of music and life, that one had only to go out onto the streets to feel one's spirits lift. There were parades of all kinds, and Jesus freaks who ran down the streets at night playing guitars and singing happy loud songs about God and Love, and there were the organ grinders with their marvelous ornate oompah-pah calliopes all gilt and gay, and there were the Hare Krishnas who moved along the streets with their long back braids and their robes, chanting melodiously, and there were men standing on the street corners playing violins while their dogs waited nearby. The young women were wonderfully bright, with orange hair and black fingernail polish and green boots and purple coats; they mingled on the streets with the very many handsome gay young men who walked along in matching silk suits and high boots and leather purses holding hands and hugging. Everyone laughed and kissed on trams and buses and smiled at us as we passed by, and quickly offered help if we were lost. Nothing was too far away or difficult to get to, we could walk or tram everywhere, and yet everything was there, the marvelous ballets and concerts at the Concertgebouw or the

Operahouse, the newest American movies, Spanish or Russian or Filipino dance troupes, restaurants of any nationality serving excellent food in exquisitely diverse and luxurious settings, and of course the Rijksmuseum. It was simply impossible not to be happy in Amsterdam. We were happy in Amsterdam, all of us, together; we were a sort of family, that is a group of people connected to each other, sharing life.

I was happy in Paris, more or less, and I was happy in Amsterdam, more or less. Why am I so unhappy in Helsinki now, when I have more of what I thought I wanted? Why was I so euphoric and hopeful and optimistic and cheerful when I was pregnant, why am I so depressed and pessimistic and strung-out now that my children are here, alive and walking around? It is not just Helsinki. Helsinki also has great concerts, museums, ballets, movies, and restaurants. The Esplanade is beautiful now, all covered with snow, and the marketplace on the harbor is bright with its orange tents full of vegetables and fruits and fish and fresh flowers. It is not the outside world which troubles me, or rather it is only partly the outside world, for with children my outside world is limited mostly to our small gray apartment and their small constant needs. I am the cause of my trouble, and I know it. I'm floundering around this way because for once I have to make, all by myself, a crucially important decision. It seems that the only other major decisions I've made in my

258

life were to fall in love with Charlie and then to have children. But then they were not really decisions; they were wild, irresistible desires, birds that grew out of my belly and carried me high and far away. But now I am thirty-four, a mother and a wife and a grown, intelligent woman. Surely now at this point in my life I should be able to take charge of my life, to get it in control. Surely now I'll be able to take each decision in my hands as if it were a puzzle, and I'll be able to ponder all the pieces and work them out so that they fit together perfectly, so that the puzzle comes out just the right way. A nice metaphor that, one that comes easily to me, because I am always doing small wooden puzzles made in China which I bought here for my daughter. Each little puzzle is thick and solid and brightly painted, each has nine pieces, each one is a picture of an animal playing a musical instrument: a dog playing a banjo, a rooster blowing a horn, a bunny playing the drums. My daughter's hands have dimples in them, and because she is chubby and young it takes her sweet fat hands a long time to put the pieces together. It is difficult for her, yet she eventually does it, gets all the pieces to fit together the right way, making the right bright cheerful pretty picture. We clap and say "Hooray" and celebrate each time she finishes a puzzle. It is nice to have that accomplished, to make something whole and good out of pieces. Yet the pieces were made that way, were meant that way. I do not think that life is so concrete and easy; I see no signs that indicate a pleasant, pretty, sensible whole.

For example, in three more days Stephen is supposed to arrive here in Helsinki. BEA 270, November 29, 11:30. That is one piece of the puzzle. Incredibly, unbelievably, Charlie is leaving tomorrow to lecture for five days in Sweden. Is that another piece of the puzzle? Has fate arranged for my husband to be gone so that I can easily be with my lover? (Is Stephen my lover if we haven't actually made love yet? I'm not sure of the details. Perhaps he is my lover simply because he loves me, but then I'm not sure he really loves me, either. What shall I call him then?) Since fate has arranged for Charlie to be gone, does it mean that it is *right* for me to be with Stephen? Am I supposed to choose Stephen? What am I supposed to do? Do I want Stephen? What do I want?

I want to teach. I want to teach, I have always wanted to teach, and I'm trying my best now to find a job. I have written the colleges within driving distance of our New Hampshire farm, but mail, even air mail, from Finland to the States, can take a long time, can often be irregular, and I have not as yet received any reply. It occurs to me that I could try to make a deal with Stephen: *Give me a job, and I'll sleep with you.* But no, no, I could not live with that; that is one thing I know I will not do.

It must mean something, though, that I can't think of Stephen apart from his position as holder of jobs that I crave. How funny it is that now when I have a handsome man who wants to be my lover coming to see me I don't think about sex or love. How funny it is that now when all my friends are writing me letters about their new lovers and new love affairs, or their husbands' lovers and love affairs, that while they dream of rendezvous with passionate men I dream only of a nice clean office with my own desk and a great big classroom full of eighteen-year-old kids who don't know how to use the subjunctive. Am I crazy? What do I want? How do I decide whether or not to sleep with Stephen?

Let me think now, let me turn the puzzle pieces in my hands and think. It is after midnight now, and Charlie and the children are asleep, and I have gotten out of bed because no matter how I closed my eyes, no matter how many times I reminded myself that I will be exhausted and bitchy tomorrow, I still could not get sleep to come to me. I've come into this little kitchen and shut the door so that my noises won't disturb anyone else. It is strange how the kitchen which seems so dark and dull in the day suddenly seems bright and somehow mysteriously gay at night. It is because it is snowing outside now, and the streetlights look like golden globes, and out on the highways the cars pass with bright lights under the bright highway lamps. I've fixed myself a scotch and water, a strong one, to make me sleep, and I'm sitting at the good old rocky kitchen table, drinking and looking out the window at the snow and the street and the apartments full of sleeping people. No one is walking outside. It is very quiet. Surely now in all this silence I will be able to think and to come to an intelligent, sensible decision.

Should I meet Stephen? Should I make love with him? I promised him I would. And he is handsome and sexually exciting; I would probably enjoy making love with him. Should I tell him I'll marry him? Ouch—why does that thought hurt so much? Marriage. It's the thought of marriage, for heaven's sake.

Marriage. I am already married to Charlie, I am already involved in a marriage. We've been collaborating in this marriage for thirteen years. And what does it mean? When I first met Charlie, and in those first early years, I desired him, I lusted after him, more than I ever have for anything else in this world. Thirteen years of having him has calmed me down considerably. Yet I have never desired Stephen, or anyone, as I once desired Charlie. Sex. Sex was not all of it, and isn't now. I did not desire only to screw Charlie, I wanted something more, and I must say I feel I've gotten it. On that score I am satisfied. I am satisfied with my marriage.

So then why am I even considering sleeping with Stephen? Or, for heaven's sake, marrying him? Those first insane sharp sexy moments, that first surge of desire, those first kisses, are awfully sweet, it is true. And after thirteen years of following Charlie around, it's fantastic to have someone following me. But I'm not sure I want to go any further. I really don't think I want anything more. It's as if Charlie and I have built a bridge together, a great strong stony bridge that arches and supports us both over the eerie chasm of death and loneliness and meaninglessness.

It is something real and good and special, that great bridge. It supports Adam and Lucy, too, it is a place where they can stand safely until they can build their own lives. I don't want to break off my part of that bridge, or pull it down with me in one resounding crash, simply to grasp a butterfly.

Butterflies, bridges, what am I talking about? There are bread crumbs under this kitchen table, and the scotch has hit me in the head. No, I can't put a decision together like a puzzle. At least not tonight. But deep down inside I feel things moving together. I suppose I will have to surprise myself once again.

On February 5, 1973, there was a blizzard in New Hampshire. It was frightening how the wind howled and blew at the walls and windows of our house, frightening to see the snow pile up in barriers across the road, frightening to hear great tree limbs crack and break and fall. Charlie was in bed, asleep, but at midnight I was downstairs in the kitchen, looking out the windows and crying. I hadn't slept well for oh, how many nights, so many nights, each night waking up to pee and then being unable to go back to sleep because of the discomfort of my body and the discomfort of my thoughts. I was irrational, and as I stood in the dark kitchen, my bare feet cold and my robe too small to wrap around my great belly, I cried and whispered to the howling wind. I wanted to make a deal. I wanted to, make a deal with *someone*, with *something*, and the howling wind seemed to represent whatever it was that was in charge of my life. It had come over me that in having a baby, in giving a new person life, I was stealing years of life from my husband. He was now forty-five, and suddenly forty-five seemed very old to me. I felt horrified at my audacity in becoming pregnant. Who did I think I was? What in the world did I think I was doing? It was Charlie I loved, it was Charlie I wanted to give my love to, all my love. By bringing a new person into our lives I was taking love and care and concern away from Charlie. It wasn't fair. It wasn't right. I leaned against the window, the cold panes sending chills through me, and I whispered out at the storm, "Let this baby miscarry, let this baby die, and let the years of its life be added on to Charlie's life. Let Charlie live forever and forever, or at least as long as I do. Give Charlie the life, the years, and if it means depriving our child of life and years, so be it."

How insane that night was. I knew with my intelligence that it wasn't possible to trade one life for another, one set of years for another. But I wasn't being intelligent that night. I suddenly realized that having a baby would sever me from Charlie; we would no longer be the complete and satisfied couple that we were. I didn't stop to remember that I had not been a thoroughly satisfied half of that pair. I only sensed a great vast change ahead of me, and I was afraid of that change.

I couldn't sleep. I wandered through our large old colonial house, gazing out windows into the snowy night, running my hands over the familiar furniture. I drifted into the pantry and without turning on the light got down a bottle of Advocat; I had become enamored of this Dutch liquor in Holland, where they told me it was a good drink for pregnant women because it contained eggs. All the bottles and glasses in the pantry glinted silvery in the light from the window. I drank some of the thick yellow liquor and felt better, and poured myself another glass and wandered back into the living room. I was so restless I knew I couldn't go back to bed; that would only make me toss and turn and wake Charlie up. I sank down on the big white sofa in the living room and pulled an afghan down over me and cuddled up under it. For a while I was happy: warm and lonely and somehow self-sufficient in that big, dark, quiet room. The furniture seemed somehow benign and understanding. I had always wondered about the furniture at night, if it didn't move around a bit; it seemed strange that it sat where it was, day after day, night after night, without moving, when I felt it had a life of its own. The furniture as I watched did not move. Yet it radiated a friendliness that comforted me. I drank some more Advocat; I slept for a while.

When I woke up, it was still night, and I felt cozy and rather gay and all my fear was gone. The wind had stopped howling, and the sudden silence of the night was hauntingly prophetic. I thought of Charlie upstairs above me, sleeping, and I smiled to myself, thinking how ridiculous I had been earlier. Charlie would live forever with or without my love, I knew: he was strong and forceful and good, a great bear of a man, full of life. I had been foolish to worry. I couldn't imagine what had come over me. I snuggled back down under the afghan and closed my eyes.

My stomach hardened. It was as if it had become an enormous fist clenching, squeezing out coils of pain. I waited until it had softened, then turned over the other way and tried to go back to sleep. It hardened again.

"Oh, stop it," I said aloud, and rubbed my tummy. Several times during the past few days and nights it had hardened on me like this, though not quite so dramatically.

And not quite so often, for there it was again. It was amazing: down there were my bare feet and legs and up here were my arms and shoulders and neck and head, and there in the middle, detached from the familiar comfortable normal part of me was this vast round territory that had suddenly made up its own rules and started its own revolution. My stomach clenched like a giant fist, and the coils of pain squeezed out like a hot red acid, encircling me.

"Not now," I said, "not yet. I'm not ready. I'm not in the mood. I haven't slept for ages. Let me take a nap first."

My stomach clenched, and I heard myself cry out, a tiny involuntary moan. I sat up and looked around. It was still night, still dark out. Charlie was still upstairs, asleep. I was all alone, and it seemed a very strange time for my stomach to start this strange little act. It clenched again, hard, so hard that I thought, Well, good grief, do you suppose this is really it? I'd better not get the sofa wet.

I pulled myself up into a standing position, and after a few seconds' deliberation I wandered into the downstairs bathroom. When I pulled down my pants I saw they were covered with blood. In spite of everything, it was still a shock to know that my body, which of course I considered a part of me, was doing this, this bright indiscreet bleeding, without my knowledge or awareness. That blood, which could have been a stranger's, so independently had it flown, seemed full of existential significances. I would have stared at it forever, entranced in meta-physical wanderings, but my stomach clenched again, hard. I looked at my stomach. I could see the clenching, the tightening, as if both sides were trying to draw in to touch each other. I looked down again at the blood on my pants, and then at my huge hard belly, and then up at my startled face in the bathroom mirror. My hair was standing up all over in wild black curls. The center focused; it was all real. I grinned at myself in the mirror. I felt ab-solutely gay.

"Well, good for you, stomach!" I said at last, and patted myself. "What a good little stomach you are!" I shuffled out of the bathroom and back into the kitchen, wondering what I should do first. I felt giddy, I felt immeasurably pleased with myself. "Guess what, table," I said to the kitchen table, "I think it's starting. My stomach's as hard as you are."

I leaned on the table with both hands and panted as my stomach hardened again. Should I wake Charlie yet? I thought. Should I call the doctor? No, it would be a shame to wake her up. Should I bring my bag downstairs? Perhaps I should have another drink. Perhaps champagne. That would make the waiting easier. What a party I'd have drinking champagne and waiting for the contractions to become serious ones. I went back into the pantry and began to scrounge around in the wine rack, looking for champagne. I found a bottle, and shuffled to the refrigerator, and put it in to cool, and held onto the refrigerator door and panted. Everyone had assured me I would have hours and hours of this simple cadenced pain. I was supposed to go to the hospital when the contractions were regular and four minutes apart. I decided just for the fun of it not to wait for the champagne, to time the contractions right then. I turned on the kitchen light, sank down into a captain's chair, and let my legs slide out in front of me. I watched the thin red second hand go around the face of our big yellow kitchen clock.

The contractions were two minutes apart. I sat there for fifteen minutes until I could trust myself to believe it.

"Well," I said to my stomach, "aren't you clever. You just get right down to business, don't you." My stomach hardened in reply.

I was terribly pleased with myself and appreciated the delights of temporary schizophrenia. The baby hovered somewhere in the distance like a thought or the refrain of a song, but my stomach had suddenly become a real individual, a charming, entertaining, quite willful friend, and I found myself trailing along behind it like a child after an older, braver, slightly frightening playmate, one who was leading me to places I couldn't imagine.

I shuffled up the stairs, stopping now and then to bend and relax and pant when the contractions came, and then went on into my bedroom. I was amused at how soundly Charlie slept, so oblivious to all that was going on. I dressed myself in my favorite maternity clothes and cleverly put my pierced earrings in in the dark, then sat down on the bed next to Charlie and watched him sleep for a while. He seemed so sweet and innocent, so good and dear. I felt in contrast very capable, large, and important. Finally I woke him up.

"Charlie," I said, "wake up. It's happening."

Charlie opened his eyes and stared at me for a while, surfacing from his deep sleep. "What's happening?"

"The baby."

"You're sure?"

"Feel."

With his hand on my stomach the clenching did not feel quite so bad. I wondered if perhaps I had made a mistake. Perhaps it was only a false alarm.

"Two minutes apart," I said.

"Let's go to the hospital," Charlie said.

While Charlie dressed I made the bed, then sat on it and felt my stomach and panted. I wanted to call friends to tell them it was starting but I realized that I was supposed to wait until it was all over to call. Still, I was terribly excited and happy, as if I were about to go to a marvelous party.

Charlie helped me down the stairs, then went out to start the Jeep and warm it. He put my small overnight bag full of nursing bras and nightgowns in the jeep, then came for me. As I went out the door of my house I felt buoyant, as if I were stepping off the stoop into gravity-free air. I wondered who would be in my arms when I entered the house again.

I chatted gaily to Charlie all the way to the hospital. I felt I had never been quite so witty and enjoyable a conversationalist. Charlie had to concentrate on steering the jeep over the snowpacked roads, and we slid once or twice on ice, but it all seemed distant and easy to me, although an occasional bump made me gasp. Everything seemed out of my hands now. I felt that if Charlie had settled back in his seat the car would have gently moved itself along the snowy roads. It was beautiful out. Everything was white and soft and full of depth.

At the hospital I couldn't help smiling at everyone. So this is what the janitor who mops the floor here every night looks like, I thought. How nice it must be to work in such a place of drama, and so this will be my nurse. The labor room they put me in had a window, and I could see the sky lightening and the windows of a white clapboard church begin to glow. I liked it when the nurse slipped a crisp white institutional frock over me; it was as if someone were taking care of me, someone were dressing me, like a mother.

I climbed up on a high white bed and the nurses covered me with a soft beige blanket, and Charlie came in and held my hand. He looked out of place in his green sweater and old gray corduroy slacks while the rest of us were all in white.

"Charlie," I said, "you promised you'd come into the delivery room with me. You promised."

"I will," he said. "I will. I'll get the hospital garb on when the time comes. But you've still got a long way to go."

"How do you know?" I asked. I knew that Charlie had not been with Adelaide when Caroline and Cathy were born.

"The nurses told me," Charlie said. "They said that if you're still smiling and joking around, you've got a long way to go."

Hah, I thought to myself, will they have a surprise coming! I'm going to smile and joke through it all. Why not? It's easy. To Charlie, I said, "Do I need some more lipstick?"

Charlie said, "Oh, Zelda, I love you."

And of course the nurses were right. After a while I stopped smiling and joking and concentrated on breathing correctly and not screaming. After a while the nurses didn't seem so cute or sweet and Charlie seemed absolutely irritating. It occurred to me in a rush that I was going to have to surrender myself to something out of my control. It was as if my greedy hardening stomach was trying to pull myself—the

271

"I" of my self—out of my head, to pull it down to the center of my body, and when I finally realized that this was what was necessary I let go. And things began to move much more rapidly. I let go of myself, of my "I," the I who was Zelda, who was thirty years old and had curly black hair and a ready smile, who knew about T. S. Eliot, who loved to ride horses through the woods. I let go. And my I, my self, seemed to suddenly sink and surge downward into the center of my being. I lost myself, I surrendered myself to the passionate lustful pain. Charlie held my hand and rubbed my back, but I was not with Charlie. And I was not with the baby. I was with, blended with, something else, some greedy, fierce, ripping power. Suddenly the clenched fist socked me in the small of my back, and my back arched, and I cried out in a way that I never would have let myself cry before. They took me to the delivery room.

For a moment the glare of that bright clean room startled me. I came back. I said, "Charlie, I'm going to have a baby."

Charlie said, "Do you want something? For the pain?"

"I'm thirsty," I said. "If they could just let me have something to drink—"

Someone wet my lips with a moist cloth, and I said "Thank you," and then the fist inside my stomach reached up and pulled me down.

"Push," someone said. "Really push. Get mad."

Someone in white accidentally hit the mirror so that I saw my face. The sight shocked me. I was red

272

and shiny-looking, and it seemed I had two chins, for I was digging my chin down into my chest as I pushed. I saw that I was not Zelda; I had become something else, not even a woman, but a female creature, sister to cows and bitches and tornadoes and floods, a shining hot dynamo exploding life.

"DON'T LOOK AT ME!" I screamed, and I grabbed the handguards of the table, and let go of myself, and arched my back, and pushed. I felt that if I pushed with one more ounce of strength I would burst apart and set the delivery room and everyone in it on fire.

"Keep your butt pressed against the table. Keep your bottom down," a nurse said to me.

I pushed and screamed again.

Charlie said to the doctor, "Is she okay?"

The doctor said, "Look, the head is crowning."

I stood on a high red cliff and pushed myself off, and shouted with joy as I fell.

"Zelda, Zelda, it's all right," Charlie was saying, pressing his hands on my shoulders. I was shaking all over.

"Of course it's all right!" I shouted, and pushed again, this time with a final furious, elated force that welled up easily within me. My baby slid out. He cried.

When he cried, I became myself again. It was very strange. I became myself again, a queer, wild, slightly drunk self, but still Zelda. "He's here!" I shouted. "Let me hold him! Oh, too bad it's over, that was fantastic— Look. Look. What a funny-looking little thing he is."

So Adam was born. My son. Everything after that was reasonable and sweet: the tiny nightclothes and diapers, the trusting glazed gaze, the beautiful fist clenching my finger, and Charlie's tears running freely down his face as he watched the two of us together, as he held his new son. It was a special time, those first few days of Adam's life, and Charlie and I shared it together, like a fresh sweet fruit. I talked about feeding schedules and burping with nurses and other mothers and wrote letters to friends, and learned to nurse, and soon was a nice normal person again. Yet sometimes as I looked out my bedroom window on the fifth floor of the hospital, I would long to open it, to break it open, and to throw my body out into the cold wild air, so that I could experience it again: the terror, the pain, the wild spinning fall, the soaring on the back of some universal power that dipped me deep into the oceans of fear and joy, that soared me high into the skies of an agonizing joy where words can never go. I felt sorry for Charlie because he was a man. I knew I would have to have another child. I wanted to go soaring again.

SEVEN

"You are being ridiculous. You are being irrational. Zelda, get hold of yourself, for heaven's sake."

"I am getting hold of myself, dammit. And I am not being irrational. You're the one being irrational. You're being irrational and insensitive. Ouch—oh

274

shit; oh, that was a good one."

"If we don't leave right now, you'll have the baby in the car."

"Then call Mrs. Justin and ask her to come over."

"We don't need Mrs. Justin. Catherine and Caroline are here. Now, God dammit, stop it!"

"Charlie, please, Charlie, I'm begging you. I can't leave Adam alone with them. Please don't make me leave Adam alone with them. Oh, fuck shit shit; oh, it hurts. Charlie, please."

"Zelda, my love. Lie down a minute. Stop talking and do your breathing and listen to me a minute. Adam will be just fine with the girls. They'll take good care of him. You're being crazy."

"Charlie. We are a good ten-minute drive from the nearest person. Your daughters have come to visit us only two times in the past two years, and they have not spoken one word to Adam, or held him, or smiled at him, in all that time. Just because you are paying them for helping doesn't mean they'll be nice to him. He's just a little two-year-old boy, and he doesn't even know who they are, and his mommy and daddy are going away to get a new baby. He needs someone he trusts. He's got to have security today. Please. He loves Mrs. Justin. *Please call her.*"

"Zelda, you make the girls sound like monsters."

"Well, they *are* monsters. They are spoiled, selfish, inconsiderate, unloving, hateful, spiteful monsters."

"Zelda, calm down. We've talked about this before. There's bound to be some jealousy. You can't expect them to love your children."

"Who's asking for love? I'm asking for a smile now and then, maybe a hug or a nice hello? Jesus, Charlie, just think about how they were last night when they arrived. Have you ever seen two more sullen faces? Did they speak to Adam or smile at him? Did they offer to help me with anything? My God, they just sat there at the dinner table looking surly while I fixed the meal and set the table and did the dishes. When I brought Adam downstairs to say good night they didn't even look at him, they just kept staring at the television. You think they're going to cuddle and kiss him today? Not very damned likely."

"It's their age. And it's a tough situation. You've got to understand. It probably looks as though I love Adam more than I love them because I'm always holding him on my lap. He can say, 'Daddy, Daddy,' and run to me and I'll pick him up, and they can't do that anymore. They're bound to resent him."

"Well, dammit, Charlie, if you know they're bound to resent him, why in God's name did you ask them to come up here and help us now? If they resent Adam, they're going to hate taking care of him while we have a new baby."

"Look. We've been through this before. Caroline is in college and Cathy will start in another year. They need money. They need lots of money for tuition and books and clothes. I don't have lots of money. I can't afford to pay for help for you and the farm and Adam and take care of their needs, too. It is only sensible that they come up now; it's summer, they don't have jobs, they ought to earn some of the money I give them."

"Oh, Charlie, I understand all that, and I wanted it to be that way, too. But it's not working out that way, can't you see? Charlie, please. I hurt. Listen, let's do this, let's make a deal. I know you've got to go to that fucking conference, and I want you to go. I'll manage here somehow after the baby's born, when I can be here to watch the girls with Adam. But please, today, please let's have Mrs. Justin come. Let Adam be with someone he loves and trusts for this one day. Please."

I was sobbing. The sun was rising and I was rolling on the floor in my summer nightgown, sobbing. My contractions were coming every two minutes. The hospital was a good twenty-five minutes away, but I would not leave Adam, my helpless sleeping son, I would not leave him alone with my stepdaughters. I could not.

"Zelda . . ." Charlie began again.

"Charlie. Help me. I hurt."

Charlie went to the phone and dialed Mrs. Justin, our good old reliable baby-sitter. She was a grandmother who lived on the same farm she had been born on seventy years before, and she was the closest thing to a grandmother that Adam had, because Charlie's own mother was dead now and my mother was a snazzy businesswoman, not at all interested in coming back to a New Hampshire farm to help with diapers and housework and gardening.

"She's coming right away," Charlie said to me. "Now let me help you get up off the floor. Let's get you to the car."

"I don't want to leave until she's here."

"All right. Let's just get you down to the car."

"I want to go look at Adam before I go."

We shuffled slowly into his room. I bent and clutched the bedpost and panted through a contraction as I looked at him. He was wearing light blue summer pajamas, and his hair was curly from the heat, and his face was rosy and flushed.

"My little boy," I whispered.

"Don't wake him up," Charlie said. "Come on, Zelda. He'll be fine."

As we slowly made our way down the stairs, I thought how different the house looked this time: in the two years since I had had Adam, I had devoted myself entirely to the house. I had scraped off old paint and wallpaper in each room and repainted, re-wallpapered. I had learned to garden, to can and freeze, and cook and bake. I had the house looking lovely, perfectly lovely, and I had the cookie jar full of homemade oatmeal-raisin cookies, and the freezer full of nutritious casseroles. If I hadn't been roaringly happy during those two years, at least I had been content, fatly, gooeily content, loving my living child and then the new kicking secret in my tummy. I had done the best I could to live up to a certain fantasy, a certain image in my head of motherhood and the good life on a farm.

Charlie had been in paradise. He had taught at the university, and spent his free time chopping firewood for the winter or helping with the garden.

He enjoyed writing in his study and stepping out into the fresh country air whenever he needed a break. And Adam bloomed on the farm like one of its natural wild flowers. He toddled after butterflies, and ran splashing in the pond, and tried to catch frogs, and wandered through fields of grass higher than his head. I sat in the sun reading all the useless pleasurable novels I had deprived myself of during my Ph.D.-oriented years, and Adam dug in the sand or chased chickens or played with our cats. From time to time I surfaced enough to go around to the colleges within driving distance to see if they needed anyone to teach, and they didn't. It was 1975. The money was disappearing from colleges and universities. Jobs were getting harder and harder to find. I moved slowly, read and rested, took care of my little boy, fixed up the house, and grew a new baby inside me.

I was quite content. I felt myself in a sort of resting place, a holding pattern. I knew in a few years I'd get back out to the real world to study and work and teach, but I had had enough of that for a while. I was ready for babies and a farm. I accumulated loose milky flesh about my body, and a corresponding loose milky joy around my life. I relaxed. I expanded, my whole body expanded, as one does when lying in the warm sun on a summer's holiday.

And Charlie loved Adam.

I had been preparing myself for the opposite. Adam would be an interference, I knew, he would be noisy and bothersome and demanding. Charlie

279

was now forty-five; he had one family almost grown-up; he would be bored with babies, I thought. But a great fierce bond seemed to spring up between my son and my husband immediately, perhaps because Charlie held Adam the first few moments of his life, and looked into his dark satisfied eyes and felt the infinite perfection of the small body. I don't know. How can it be explained? Charlie loved his son, and I loved Charlie even more because he did love his son, and there we were, all of us in love with each other. Charlie carried Adam everywhere in a backpack as he planted trees that spring or dug the soil in the garden or went for walks in the woods. He put him on the floor in his study while he worked. He brought him little toys. He took him with him when he drove off to town for errands. He held him on his lap while he ate. He was truly in love with his child. Of course it helped that Adam was still a baby, not old enough to whine or talk back or tear up important papers. Later, love would he tempered by righteous irritation. But that first year we were all in love, and it was a sloppy, gooey year, perhaps the happiest year of our lives.

Caroline and Cathy did not come up to see Adam as a baby. We called them from the hospital the second day of Adam's life to tell them about him, and they both said the same thing: "Oh." No give-away tone to the voice, no other words. We thought, Are they happy? Sad? Bored? Charlie wrote each girl a long letter telling her how much he loved her, why she was special to him, how he would always love her. I sent two silver bracelets with a silver heart-shaped charm saying "I love you," on one side and "Adam Campbell, January 30, 1973," on the other to Caroline and Cathy. As far as I know, the girls received them, that is the bracelets never came back in the mail; but the girls never mentioned them and never wore them. We called and wrote several times, asking the girls to come up and visit that spring; we now lived so close. Charlie offered to go down to pick them up by car, or to send them bus tickets, but there were always excuses. School, tests, parties, the possibility of jobs. I felt bad that they didn't come up. I thought that if they could just *see* Adam, small innocent baby, they would like him, if not love him. And I missed the girls, missed their jokes and gossip and simply the sight of them, so tall and slim and pretty. They had become a part of my life, and their absence was noticeable. But I didn't want to force their presence, and Charlie didn't want to, either.

At the beginning of the summer Charlie received cool little letters from the girls saying that they would prefer not to come visit us that summer. They said they both had a lot of baby-sitting jobs, and their mother's mother, their grandmother, was coming up to visit that summer, and they wanted to spend as much time as possible with her now that she was growing old, and they wanted to spend as much time as possible with their friends. They were sensible letters. I was sad they weren't coming, but also relieved. I remembered the negative side of our

281

Amsterdam stay, when the girls turned bitchy at the sight of housework. The farm and Adam both required a lot of work. I didn't need the girls around, scowling at the sight of work.

It was the end of December and Adam was eleven months old before Caroline and Cathy ever saw him. They had finally condescended to come visit us at the end of the Christmas vacation; probably their decision was based on the fact that Charlie told them he was giving them a car. It had been my idea, the car; I thought such a grand expensive gift would prove to them that Charlie still loved them in spite of the fact that he had a new child. I also thought it would make it easier for them to come see us. And, truly, I thought it simply would be very nice for them to have. It would be in Caroline's name because she was the older and had a license, but Cathy would eventually be able to use it, too. Charlie and I spent hours looking through car lots at good used cars and finally settled on a very swanky red VW Beetle convertible. It was a cute car, squat and classy; lovable. I couldn't wait for the girls to have it.

Charlie drove down to Hadley to pick the girls up; he drove the red VW, and at my suggestion stuck a big red bow on the hood. Later he told me that the girls were appropriately thrilled, in their own quiet standoffish way; they seemed to be more upset that it was only one car and they would have to share it than happy that the car was theirs at all. This made Charlie feel sad and mad, and their drive back to our farm was not as gay as I had predicted it would be.

I stayed home that day, taking care of Adam and fixing a huge party dinner and wandering through the house admiring my work. I had had only a year there, and during that year I had had a baby, but I had still accomplished a lot of redecorating. The house, except for some old peeling ceilings and a few shabby rooms here and there, looked lovely. I had put fresh evergreens from our farm all around the house, tied with red ribbon, and we had cut our tree from our own land and it still stood in the front parlor, with Caroline's and Cathy's presents under it. Adam was starting to walk, and was full of giggles. He was plump and happy; he had a six-toothed smile that I thought no one could resist.

He was taking a nap when the girls arrived late in the afternoon with Charlie. I had put him down late especially for that reason, thinking it would be good for us four to have some time alone, without the new person around. Charlie's daughters came into the house and let me kiss them on their icy cheeks: they were taller, slimmer, and much lovelier than they had been in Amsterdam. They were young women. They were absolutely gorgeous. "How lovely you have become!" I kept saying to them, I couldn't help saying to them. "Oh, aren't you happy to be so beautiful!" I was really happy to see them. I almost cried out of sheer delight. These were my— my what? I had no word for it. Not daughters, not relatives, not friends, but *my* somethings, creatures that I had known for a long time and helped and influenced and cared for.

Caroline and Cathy turned eyes on me that were as cold as the December air. They held their bodies stiffly. They stared at me as if I were a stranger, as if they didn't know me, and didn't like me, and didn't plan to. They'll warm up, I told myself, but they didn't, not for a second of the two long days they were there.

I poured myself a stiff scotch and suggested we go in by the tree. It was too dark and cold to go out for a walk or a ride; too early to eat. I hoped that opening their other presents would brighten them up a bit. Charlie and I had both written the girls letters during that long year, and we had mentioned Adam only briefly. The girls had never answered any of the letters. I think I had regretted that the most, that Caroline, especially Caroline, who had written me such long intimate, openhearted young letters, had stopped writing to me completely. But when Christmas came around, a new problem presented itself: we did not know what the girls wanted as presents. We had written them to ask; they had not responded. We did not know their sizes, interests, desires. So their major present that year was the car. I bought them each an Indian cotton top, and two or three books, and crazy socks with each toe made and colored separately. Because I was into my earth mother stage, and because I thought handmade gifts would show love because they showed time instead of money given, I knitted them each long mufflers with matching caps.

We sat in the front parlor by a nice crackly fire that

I had made, and looked at the sparkling lights of the Christmas tree, and Charlie and I drank scotch and the girls drank eggnog with rum, and they opened their presents, and looked at each one with an infinitely bored expression, and said, "Thanks, Dad. Thanks, Zelda. And thanks again for the car." And that was it. Merry Christmas, everyone.

Things did not improve when Adam cooed out on awakening from his nap. I knew they certainly would not cry out, "Ooh, isn't he sweet!" when they saw him, although he was sweet; most eleven-month-old babies are. But I was not prepared for the brief stony glares he received when I brought him down.

"This is Adam," I said, not too brightly, not too gaily, as if I were bringing in the family dog or cat.

"Hi," Cathy said, not quite looking at him, not quite smiling.

"He's cute," Caroline said flatly, and that was that. They didn't try to talk to him or hold him, they didn't ask questions about him.

We sat in the parlor for a while, one big happy family. Adam played on the floor with the torn wrapping paper and bows. The girls desultorily thumbed through their new books. The house smelled of evergreens, and a big stew simmering in wine, and applewood in the fire. Adam giggled and blithered with glee as he shredded the wrapping paper. Caroline and Cathy had not, as usual, brought anyone presents, and they would not respond to questions except in monosyllables, and I thought my heart would break. How could they have turned this way, so suddenly, so completely? Only a year ago we had been happy together, friends in Amsterdam. I was miserable. And I was piqued. But Charlie was their father, and he sat through it all as if pleasantly content, and I thought that if he wasn't going to say anything I should hold my peace, too.

Finally I served dinner, and after dinner the girls glued themselves to the television set while Charlie and I did the dishes and Adam chewed on Arrowroot cookies and played in his playpen in the kitchen. "Hi, pie," I said to him now and then, or, "How's it going, love?" But I didn't say as much to him as I usually did; each word sounded too loud, too nauseatingly sweet, because Caroline and Cathy could hear.

The next day Charlie took them for a long walk around the farm, to show them how he had fixed up and cleaned up the horse barn, to show them the trees he had planted, and the berry bushes, and the spot—now laden with snow—where we planted our garden in summer. I asked each girl if she'd like to go riding with me on good ol' Liza and Gabe, but they both said shortly, no. So I served them a warm lunch, and then they got into their new red Beetle and drove unsmilingly away.

"Teen-agers go through stages like that," Charlie said to me as we watched them drive away. "I'm sure they act like that with their mother. They're trying to break off, to find their own life-style, to establish their own independence, and they have to cut all ties.

They're in that stage of life where they hate all people over thirty, all people who might have any claim on their lives. It's too bad, I know. It's an ugly stage. I hate it. I'd like to give them hell about it; I find them thoroughly unpleasant. I'm really pissed at the way they acted about the car. But they don't need criticism from me right now. It wouldn't help. In addition to their regular problems they've got you and Adam to contend with. But don't take it personally. Talk to anyone who's a parent of a teen-ager; they'll tell you. It's a rotten stage. All anyone can do is just sit back and try to keep loving them in spite of it all. They'll come out of it, you'll see. I'm not worried about it. I'm just glad for once in my life that I don't have to live with them."

We went through the spring and summer without seeing the girls or hearing from them, although Charlie drove down twice to take them out to dinner and returned to say that they were still pretty much, pretty bitchily the same. In a fit of hopefulness I sent Caroline a box of homemade cookies, but received no reply. Caroline and Cathy came up again for a day during their 1974 Christmas vacation, but again it was as unpleasant and uncomfortable as the one before. It didn't help much that I was almost four months' pregnant with my new child and beginning to show it, or that Adam was now almost two and walking and talking and trying to make contact with the girls. "Who you?" he would say, or, "See my train?" or, "You have a pretty on your neck." They replied to him as shortly as possible. For a while, when they were first there, he simply stood next to them, trying to figure out what kind of strange people these were who didn't smile or try to cuddle him. After a while he got bored with them and wandered away. It was not a successful visit, and I felt myself churning inside with longing to scream things at both sour-faced girls. But Charlie kept still, and so did I.

Then it was June, and my second baby was on her way.

The baby was due the first week in June. Charlie was due at a week-long conference the second week in June. The house was basically in good shape, but I wasn't eager to be alone out in the country with an energetic two-year-old and a new baby and a sore bum. And the grass needed mowing and the garden needed weeding and new seeds needed planting. The baby chicks Charlie had been incubating were due to hatch. Mrs. Justin, our favorite baby-sitter, had her own farm and family to run. Because we were on a farm, we were a good twenty-minute drive from our university friends, and the best of those friends were out of town on summer vacation. I would be isolated on the farm for seven days with Adam and a new baby. I needed help. It seemed logical that Caroline and Cathy help, especially since we would pay them. Charlie told them he would pay them each two hundred dollars for the one week's work. At first I thought he was giving them far too much, but then I decided that it would be worth it if only they would smile.

It had been almost six months since we had seen the girls. I thought of the past, all the years I had known them and loved them. It was true that they needed money; perhaps, I thought, they also needed to be included in Charlie's new family group, to feel that they were wanted and could be helpful. Perhaps it would make them feel happier and more comfortable with us if they realized they could give as well as receive. After all, I told myself, they were *Caroline* and *Cathy*, girls I had known and laughed with for years. And they were seventeen and twenty now, big girls; surely they were maturing. I told Charlie to go ahead and see if he could arrange the setup with the girls.

They said on the phone, in their new monotones, okay, fine, they would do it. And they arrived on June seventh, my due date, the day we had asked them to come. But they arrived with the same ungiving expressions that they had come with for two years. They didn't speak easily, they looked surly, they averted their eyes. I smiled, Charlie smiled, we both smiled till our jaws hurt; still they froze away from us. And froze away from Adam. They did not touch him, or speak to him, or look at him. What has happened? I longed to ask. Why are you both acting this way? Do you suddenly hate us all? What can we do to change things? But their faces invited no such intimate questions.

When my labor pains started that night, waking me from my sleep, I panicked. I said *No*, new baby, not yet. I'm not ready for you yet. I've got to figure a way out of this. I can't leave Adam here alone with these two ice maidens. Perhaps I was behaving irrationally; of course the girls wouldn't kill Adam. But I so wanted the new baby's birth to be a time of love and joy for everyone, including Adam. I didn't want him to remember it as a time of loneliness and strangeness and fear. Perhaps I was being irrational, fearing to leave him with the girls. But then Charlie was being too rational, I thought, and I had to counteract that. Not everything could be measured in money and logic, not at times like these.

It was almost five-thirty by the time Mrs. Justin came and we gave her her instructions. Caroline and Cathy were still asleep, in the pull-out bed in the front parlor. Adam was still asleep upstairs. My contractions were coming fast and hard. We got into the car. Charlie drove as fast as he dared.

"Have you tried to talk to them about it?" I asked Charlie between pants. "Have you tried to tell them how we feel?"

"I spoke to them a bit yesterday," Charlie said. "They said they feel funny here. They feel left out. We have our own little family and they aren't a part of it. They said they don't want to be a part of it, either. They just want to stay away from us. I guess they feel I've betrayed them and you have sort of tempted me into the betrayal. They don't like to talk about it much. They won't talk to me much, won't open up. When I told them how we still loved them and cared for them, how we miss them and miss their company and friendship, they didn't respond.

290

Finally both girls said that they thought if we hadn't had Adam we could have afforded to send them to better colleges, to private instead of state schools. Cathy said it didn't seem fair that I could go out and get myself some new children when she couldn't go out and get herself a nice new father."

"Oh, Charlie," I moaned.

"Well," Charlie said, "I have my hopes for this week. Maybe over a long period of time they'll relax, feel at home, talk with you. They're going through a tough time all around, you know. They told me that about a year ago Adelaide was offered a new job at the university. Quite a jump up from her former position. She is now executive secretary to the vice-president of the university. It's a demanding job; it pays well, and it's prestigious, and apparently she loves it. It's really a classy job, and a powerful one. She's gotten into it completely. She works full time and overtime, and often has dinner with the trustees or visiting biggies. I guess it's rather become her whole life. She was glad it came along just as the girls were getting ready to leave the nest, but I guess the girls weren't ready for it. On the one hand they've got their mother, who is too tired to cook dinner or to make home-made anything, and who is too busy and too involved with her new work to be really there for them, and on the other hand they've got us with our boring farm and new babies. They're feeling isolated and unprotected and estranged and bitter."

"But how great for Adelaide!" I cried out, louder than I meant to because of my contractions. "Did you talk to her when you picked the girls up yesterday? Did you see her?"

"Yes," Charlie said, "and she looked better than I've ever seen her in her life. She's kept her hair blonde and she's very slim and was wearing a simple tailored shirt and slacks instead of that frilly crap she used to wear. She is happy; that radiates from her all over. She is really happy. She looks elegant and totally complete. We didn't talk to each other very long, but it was quite pleasant. She had a classy leather briefcase under her arm. She looked great."

"God, I'm so glad!" I screeched. "Oh, Charlie, can you drive any faster? I think I've got to push."

"Puff and blow, for God's sake," Charlie said. "Don't push, Jesus Christ!" He pressed down hard on the accelerator.

I was afraid I would have the baby in the car. I was afraid Adam would cry when he woke up and found us gone. I was afraid the girls would be mean to him. I was afraid that in Charlie's eyes I was suddenly not as attractive as Adelaide was, slim and elegant and sporting a leather briefcase. I was afraid that I would never be slim and elegant and sporting my own leather briefcase. And it is true that one's psychological state has a lot to, do with one's physical state. Somewhere underneath it all I rationally knew what was going on, but I was so afraid of everything that each contraction seemed like a hard grip of fear. By the time we got to the hospital I was sobbing and shaking and out of control. We had of course forgotten to call the doctor to tell him we were on the way. I collapsed into a wheelchair and we went up to the maternity ward, where I was somehow shoved or thrown onto a table and hurried into the delivery room. By then I was pushing: I had to push. And I was screaming because of the pain, because I was so out of control, because my whole life was out of control. Never had anything hurt so much. The table was not ready. I grasped Charlie with my left hand and a nurse with my right hand, and another nurse ran around all flustered down where my legs were, trying to do something with white towels, and I yelled, "Please help me! Please give me something for the pain!" And in a lovely sliding whoosh my daughter was born.

I had two cozy, aching, leaking, loving days in the hospital with Lucy before I went home. I let myself forget Adam, little chubby Adam, for those two days because Charlie was still there and I knew that Charlie would take care of him. I gave myself over to the adoration and contemplation of my new child, to the enjoyment of my pains and wounds, to the routine care of others, to soggy, milky, bloody, hot and moist bliss. But the third day of Lucy's life I went home. The nurses and my physician warned me against it, but I didn't listen to them. I didn't care. I would not leave my son alone with my stepdaughters.

Charlie came to pick me up, and Adam was in the car. His hair was curly from the humidity of the New Hampshire day and his checks were flushed. I put the baby in a baby carrier in the back seat and rode in the front seat next to Charlie, hugging Adam and stroking his perfect tanned sturdy legs and burying my nose in his hair.

"How are Cathy and Caroline?" I asked him.

"Who?"

"Cathy and Caroline—"

"Oh, those ladies that are living at our house? They're okay." And that was all he said. At least, I thought, at least he doesn't seem afraid of them.

Charlie got us all settled at home. Cathy and Caroline were out weeding the garden, and when we drove in they turned to look at us, but did not leave their work to come up to see me and my new child. Charlie carried Lucy in and settled her in her bed. He brought me my overnight bag and unpacked it for me. He fixed me a bloody mary; he fixed himself and Adam and me lunch.

He said, "I'm sorry I have to go. A man my age has no business having babies. I'd like to stay home and simply hold Lucy and stare at her. She is so beautiful. But the conference is important."

"I know that," I said.

"I've talked with the girls. I told them to be nice to you and to Adam. I told them they are to do all dishes and housework while I'm gone. They've been working out in the garden pretty well. I think it will all be just fine. I really do think it will be better than leaving you here with some strange expensive public health nurse."

"Maybe," I said.

"I've got to go. I'll take Adam outside and have

the girls watch him while you nurse Lucy and take your nap. Don't worry. I promise it will all be okay."

Charlie left me then, leading Adam out the door, holding his dimpled hand. I shuffled up the stairs into my bedroom and tried to put on some lipstick, tried to brush my hair. I didn't want to look too boringly dowdy. I changed out of my maternity clothes into a soft blue nightgown that I had bought when Adam was born; it buttoned down the front so that I could open it easily for nursing. I shuffled down the hall to the bathroom and took care of some physical needs, and by the time I was able to shuffle back, Lucy was wailing her new baby wail. I changed her and nursed her and talked to her a bit, and soon she fell back asleep. It was a warm June day and the windows were open, and insects buzzed against the screen and there was no breeze. I lay back on my bed, listening hard for sounds of Adam, and before I knew it I was asleep.

When I awoke it was because Lucy was crying again. The light in my bedroom had changed and deepened. With horror I looked at my watch; it was almost six-thirty. I had slept for five straight hours, I had left my little boy alone in the world for five straight hours. Frantically I grabbed up Lucy and changed her, then held her to me and shuffled out of my room and down the stairs. "There, there," I murmured, "there, there, you'll get your dinner in a minute. Let's just find Adam first."

The door into the kitchen was shut. I opened it to see Catherine and Caroline sitting at the dinner table, eating the casserole I had made and frozen earlier that month. The television was on and they were entranced by it.

"Hello," I said. "Where's Adam?"

"In there," Cathy said, and jerked her head sideways.

Adam was lying in the playpen, sucking his thumb and rolling rhythmically from side to side. When he saw me he stood up and burst into tears.

"MOMMY!" he wailed.

Neither girl looked at him or at me; they continued to steadily watch the television. I put Lucy on the rug on the floor and went over to lift Adam out of the playpen. It hurt to lift him; he was so much heavier than Lucy, and I had to bend down into an awkward position to reach him. I felt things inside me pull. But he wrapped himself around me and buried his head in my neck and cried, so I could not put him down.

"Did you feed him?" I asked the girls.

They pointed to a plate full of food. "He didn't want it," they said. "He said he didn't like it."

"Oh, well, did you give him anything else?"

"No. He didn't say he wanted anything else. We just thought he wasn't hungry."

Lucy, who had apparently been shocked into silence for a few moments, now began to wail again, wildly now. It had been over five hours since she had been fed. Adam continued to clutch me and sob. Both girls continued to watch television.

"Look, sweet pie," I said to Adam, "Mommy will

put you in your high chair, and I'll sit right next to you and feed you your dinner, and you can watch baby Lucy drink her dinner just like you did when you were a baby."

"Out of your breasts?" Adam asked.

"Out of my breasts," I said.

The novelty of it appealed to Adam; he willingly got into his high chair. I picked Lucy up and pulled a chair over for myself to sit in next to Adam's high chair, and opened my robe and got Lucy's greedy mouth onto my left nipple. I held her with my left arm and fed Adam his food with my right hand. The girls continued to watch television. It was as if the three of us simply were not there. I felt a rage bubbling within me, but I tried to keep it down, not wanting to mix Lucy's milk with acid.

My stomach growled. I had not had anything to eat or drink since lunchtime, when Charlie had been there to fix my food; that protected friendly time seemed ages away. Now I felt like an unwanted stranger in my own home. There I sat, weary and aching and bleeding and leaking and longing for a kind and interested word. There I sat with my new baby, and Caroline and Cathy did not so much as turn their heads to see what Lucy looked like. There I sat, feeding Adam as I nursed Lucy, while Caroline and Cathy stared at the television, and ate the casserole I had made, and acted as if no one else were in the room. It was strange. It was awful.

"Do you suppose one of you could get me a plate of the casserole?" I asked. "I'm very hungry. And

297

could you please pour me a beer?"

Caroline and Cathy looked at each other, exchanged a long, bored, superior, put-upon look.

Then, "I'll get it," Caroline sighed. She rose and opened a beer and without pouring it into a glass plopped it down in front of me like a surly waitress. Then she glopped the casserole on a plate and shoved that in front of me. She sat back down again.

I was nearly in tears. I felt as though the world had gone mad. The hate that radiated from the girls was suffocating me. I could not understand what happened, but I knew that if I tried to discuss it with them I would burst into humiliating sobs and not be able to stop.

"Could I please have a fork?" I asked. I thought of all the times, the thousands of times, that I had cooked dinner for them, and set the table, and done the dishes.

Cathy rose this time, and got a fork from the drawer and laid it down near me. Then she, too, sat down to stare at the television.

I was so hungry that I somehow managed to eat my dinner and feed Lucy and feed Adam all at the same time. I switched Lucy to my right breast, put a mouthful of food in Adam's mouth, then quickly stuffed food in my mouth while Adam chewed. I had to ask the girls for another beer, for a napkin, for an apple for myself and a banana for Adam. Finally I felt satisfied, and Adam had eaten everything, and Lucy's mouth went slack around my nipple. I held her against my shoulder and patted her until she gave a loud, moist vulgar burp. The sound made Adam laugh, and I smiled, but Caroline and Cathy appeared not to hear it.

I pushed back my chair, and laid Lucy on the floor, and helped Adam out of his high chair. Then, without speaking to the girls (after all, what could I possibly say?), I picked Lucy up and took Adam by the hand and led him up the stairs. We went into his bedroom, and I spent two long hours there, playing toys with him, reading him books, while Lucy lay on the floor, looking up at the light. Now and then she would cry a bit, and I would hold her, and she would snuggle against me, not sleepy, but content. Finally I managed to get Adam into his summer pajamas, and into the bathroom to use the toilet and to brush his teeth, and finally, finally, he was in bed. I was exhausted. I felt like a prisoner in my house. I could hear sounds of the television below me. Lucy did not want to sleep, so I sat with her on my bed for a while and sang to her, and let her lie on her stomach on my rug while I tried to write a few birth announcements to friends. But I was tired, too tired. I craved rest and sleep. I longed for a hot bath, a stiff scotch, and twenty-four hours of uninterrupted sleep. I wished that someone friendly would call me to see how I was; I wished Caroline and Cathy would come up and ask how I felt, if there was anything they could do to help. I wondered why on earth they were behaving like such total rotten spoiled bitches; I didn't have the emotional or physical energy to try to figure it out myself. I decided that in the morning I would definitely screw up my courage and ask them what was going on. If I could be brave enough to ask point-blank right into their bitterly closed faces what was going on, surely they would have to answer.

I nursed Lucy again, earlier than she should have been, but I was hoping it would make her sleep, and it did. At nine-thirty I put her to bed and checked Adam, who was sleeping soundly, and then, passing up the hot bath I longed for, fell into my bed, into a thick and fitful sleep.

Lucy woke at two and decided to stay up the rest of the night. Apparently her five-hour nap during the day had given her energy; now, according to her system, it was time to wake up and play. She would not sleep. She nursed, and then messed around with my nipples awhile, and I sang to her softly and rocked her and talked with her and walked her around and rubbed her back, and she would not sleep. She was adorable, and I adored her, but I was tired. She was just over three days old. I needed sleep. I longed for sleep. I thought of going downstairs to ask one of the girls to hold her for me for just one hour but decided against it. I didn't feel that I could trust them with Lucy or face their hate in the middle of the night. So I took care of her myself. Luckily she was not crying, she had no colic, she was not upset, she was just awake and looking for some action, and the only time she cried was when I put her back down into her little wicker cradle. I felt like a candle melting, all my skin and flesh seemed to be drooping downward from exhaustion. I wanted to let go, to sink, to lose myself in sleep. Instead I held Lucy for three hours, studying her sweet delicate face, talking to her. Finally, at five, I put her down in bed next to me and nursed her again, and we both fell asleep, in our hot moist bed, together.

Adam woke me at six-thirty. He came pattering into my room, crying, "Mommy, Mommy, where are you?" His face was so brilliant with joy when he saw that I was there, really there in the bed, that I had not left him, that even though I was nearly sick with the need of sleep, I could not be angry with him for waking early.

"Come into my bed and snuggle with me awhile," I said, and I scooted Lucy over and made room for my son. We snuggled and talked for a while, and it was sweet. But all too soon Adam wanted to get up, he wanted to eat his breakfast, he wanted to go out to play.

Lucy still slept. I took Adam by the hand and led him downstairs. Little dots danced before my eyes as I walked; I was so tired. I was so sleepy. I ached with exhaustion. It hurt my knees to walk down the stairs. My breasts ached, my back ached, my bottom ached. Panic was rising within me. I could not cope alone. I was too tired.

I knocked on the parlor door. No one answered. I knocked again, more loudly. Still there was no answer.

"Girls?" I said. "Cathy? Caroline?"

There was no answer.

I pushed the door open and went into the room.

Both girls were in the sofa bed, twisted in the sheets, their heads hiding under their pillows.

"Girls," I said, "I'm sorry to wake you up, but it's seven-thirty, it's not too early. I was up all night with Lucy, and I am really exhausted. Could you please get Adam some breakfast and take him outside to play a bit? It looks like a beautiful morning."

There was no answer.

"They're sleeping," Adam said. He was holding onto my hand very tight and standing very close to me. "Let's go."

I moved close to the bed and gently shook a body—it was so hidden by pillows and covers that I couldn't tell whose it was.

"Please," I said. "Wake up. Please help me. Your father is paying you a lot of money to help me this week, and I need help right now. I'm going to be sick if I don't get some sleep. Please wake up and give Adam his breakfast and take him outside for a while."

Slowly the two girls surfaced from the bed. Their hair hung in their eyes. They sat up and stared at me as if I were some monstrous stranger asking obscene favors.

"Good morning," I said, and tried a smile.

"Let me get my clothes on and I'll get him breakfast," Caroline said, not returning my smile, not attempting to be pleasant in any way.

"Come watch cartoons, Adam," I said to my son. "You can watch television while the girls dress, and then you can have breakfast and they'll take you outside to play. Caroline, I'll get him settled in front of the television in the kitchen. Then I've just got to go back to bed. Lucy's still sleeping, and I've got to sleep, while I've got the chance."

Caroline said nothing.

I took Adam into the kitchen, put him on a chair, gave him his blanket to cover up with and to rub against his cheek, turned on the television, then shuffled back upstairs to my bedroom and the hot sinking luxury of my bed.

It was two hours later when I awakened to the sound of crying. It was not Lucy crying; she was still lying on my bed, awake now and sucking her fist, but looking at the sunlight on my wall and seeming quite content. The sound of crying came from downstairs. My body did not want to respond to the sound, every muscle and bone and nerve pulled me back down into the dark heart of necessary sleep. It hurt to open my eyes. It took effort to keep them open. But it was Adam crying, and he was crying very hard, forlornly, and I could not let myself sleep.

I rose and shuffled down to the bathroom. I noticed that I was still bleeding heavily; the blood was shocking to me, so bright, thick, messy. It irritated me that my body continued to do such things without my knowledge or consent at this time when I could not stop to understand the significance. I washed myself, and longed to sit for a while in a nice warm tub of water, and heard Adam crying still, and knew I could not. I rinsed my face with cold water quickly, hoping that would help me wake up. Then I hurried as fast as I could back to my bedroom to pick up Lucy, who was by now beginning to make little whimpering sounds. With her in my arms I made my way down the stairs.

The noise was coming from the kitchen. Adam was in there, lying on the floor and crying. Caroline and Cathy were there, too. Caroline was on the phone, talking, and Cathy was standing next to her. When they saw me come in, they turned their faces away.

I laid Lucy on the rug and knelt and took Adam in my arms.

"Adam, hon, what's wrong?"

"I want to go out and play. I'm tired of watching television. I want to ride my little car."

"Haven't you been outside yet?"

"No. I want to ride my little car."

I turned to look at the girls. Caroline had hung up the phone. They were both at the sink, pretending to rinse off the breakfast dishes.

"Adam said he wants to go out and play," I said. "Can't you take him outside for a while? You don't have to play with him, just be there."

There was a long silence, and then Cathy said, "It's so boring."

"What?"

"It's so boring," Cathy said. "Just watching him play."

Lucy began to cry. Adam was still sniffling against my nightgown. I hurt everywhere and felt weak and vulnerable; yet from some new source of energy anger was surging inside me.

"Oh, Cathy," I said. "Oh, Caroline. Lots of jobs

are boring. I'm only asking for a few days, a few hours of help. And we're paying you a lot of money. Why can't you help me a little? I am tired. I am hurt. I need rest. I need help. What has happened, what have I possibly done to make you two act this way? Can you tell me? Will you please try to talk to me about it? I just don't understand. I used to love you girls, and I thought at least we were friends, and friends help each other. But you two seem to hate me, and I don't understand it. What is going on?"

Cathy burst into tears and ran from the room.

Caroline said, "We don't like to be here. It's boring. It's a real drag. We want to go home."

There was no trace, no sign, that I had ever so much as passed the young woman on the street before. I did not know her. Her eyes were metallic, ungiving; what she was doing, the way she was staring at me, seemed a form of killing.

Squirming against me was Lucy, waving her tiny fists in the air and howling now, partially because of hunger, partially, I am sure, because she was feeling the waves of disbelief and anger and self-defense that surged outward from my body.

"All right," I said, and forced myself to rise from where I knelt with Adam on the floor. My knees were trembling so that I thought I would fall, but I wanted to rise to a full and wrathful height; standing somehow made me seem less powerless. "All right, then," I hissed, and I was suddenly angry beyond tears. "Go home. Get out. But don't either one of you ask me for anything again. I'll see to it that you don't get your goddamned two hundred dollars; you certainly haven't earned a penny of it. You're both just—just cruel and unkind and selfish. I've done a lot for you in the years I've known you; you can't imagine what I've done for you, but I will never do anything for you again."

"I don't care," Caroline said. Her face was white, but her eyes were still hard. She crossed the room, and I heard her go into the parlor.

Adam was hanging onto my legs with both hands and had his head buried into my bottom. Lucy was still whining, and I absentmindedly patted her back with a quivering hand. I stood there, frozen, shaking, and listened to the sounds: suitcases closing, the girls speaking in whispers, the front door opening, the front door slamming shut, and then the sound of the car, their Beetle, starting and driving away.

I went to the phone and called Mrs. Justin. When she answered it I was so out of control I could scarcely make myself understood over the sobs. "Mrs. Justin," I said, "could you please come up and help me for a little while right now?"

"I'll be right there," she said.

She came right away, and by then I had managed to get to a chair and to nurse Lucy, who had not been changed and who peed all over herself and my night-gown, and to stroke Adam's hair as he sat next to me, listening to me say over and over again, "It will be all right, honey, don't worry, it will be all right." I was trying to comfort myself as well as my son.

Mrs. Justin found an old farm woman to come help with the housework and the kitchen, and a young teen-age girl to come sleep overnight. The girl was not very bright and she was overweight and had thin hair and pimples, but she did wake up cheerfully, she did fix Adam breakfast, she did take him out to play. She smiled at Adam, and talked to him in a gentle tone of voice, and she chattered cheerfully to me, "How's the new baby this morning; oh, there she is; what a little doll; would you let me hold her? Oh, what a cutie pie." The girl asked me how Lucy was sleeping, and about nursing, and about Adam's birth, and she told me stories of the births of her brothers and sisters, and she brought me beers and lunch while I sat on the sofa nursing Lucy, and she took Adam for piggy-back rides around inside the house and for long walks outside. I loved her. Her name was Tina. She was a nice, warm, loving, cheerful human being, exactly what I needed at that point in my life. She was sloppy and dirty and messy and not very smart, but I was absolutely thrilled to have her around me. When she first walked in the door and smiled at me and picked Adam up in her arms, and nuzzled him and said, "My, aren't you a big boy for two!", I felt tears of gratitude spring into my eyes. I was so grateful to her I could have died of it on the spot. She stayed all week, and I do not know what I would have done without her.

When Charlie came back from his conference, I told him about the trouble I had had with the girls.

Charlie said he was sorry, that he didn't understand it, that he would call them to find out what was going on. But every time he called, the girls were out. The days passed. Finally he wrote them a long letter, which they never answered.

"Well," he said wryly, "let's wait until the end of the summer. Let's wait until they need college tuition and money for clothes. Let's wait till check time. We'll hear from them then."

And of course he was right. But we did have the whole summer without them, and for once I didn't feel sad not to have the girls around. I felt happy and peaceful. I didn't know what their particular problem was, but I was too busy to care. And it is true, I was more than too busy to care, I was angry and hurt and sad. I resented them for making the birth of my daughter and the first few days of her life into such a melodrama of anger and resentment and smothered negative emotions. At that point in my life I didn't know if I would ever be able to forgive Charlie's daughters. I didn't know if I would ever want them around again. I felt that something had been destroyed.

And now Lucy and Adam are two and four, and I take their lives for granted, I stomp around and curse them under my breath for taking up my time, for using up my life. I swat them and yell at them and make faces at them that would scare a grown-up, and they yell at me and make faces at me and whine and demand and clutter and wail and pull

308

and pull and drag. They gnaw at me. They eat me alive. Here in Helsinki it is the end of November and quite quite cold. It takes long, clumsy, muttering ages for me to get the children into their snow clothes: long underwear, three pairs of woolen socks, undershirts, shirts, sweaters, coats, mittens, knit scarves, hats, boots—and then someone has an itch, or has to pee, or has a bump in his boot. Finally we go down all the stairs, the surrealistic harsh gray stairs, and out of the apartment to the crisp white air. I take pictures with my little black camera: click, there you have it, the lie: two beautiful children looking bright and gay in red and blue winter clothes, their cheeks rosy, their smiles real, the landscape white and soft. Adam is eating snow. Lucy is trying to pull her orange plastic sled. No, it is not a lie, it is true. They are beautiful children, they are happy, they feel loved, it is winter, they will play in the snow and laugh and I will laugh with them. Now, with my own children, I am learning. I am learning daily, with our little fights and wars, with our daily misunderstandings, I am learning daily to forgive and forget. It doesn't matter that upstairs I yelled at Adam, "*Dammit,* when will you ever learn to put on your own clothes! This is driving me crazy. Now stick your foot in harder, dammit!" Now we are downstairs, the moment has passed, this is a new moment and we are happy together. It doesn't matter today that Adam said yesterday, "I don't love you anymore." He does love me. He loved me even then as he spoke, and I knew it. I love him even when I'm shaking him for writing on the walls, and he knows it. Underneath all the whirling, whisking light loud froth of daily hurts and angers stands the foundation of our love, too deep to ever be damaged, too solid, too significant to be even slightly chipped. This is what it means to be a mother with a child, to be a child with a mother. Such deep, satisfying security. Perhaps this is what makes the difference between mothering and stepmothering, between being a child and being a stepchild: the lack of that basic foundation of love and trust that stands solidly under the torrents of daily emotions, rage turning to laughter, smiles turning to frowns, hugs turning to spanks and snarls, hate melting to forgiveness and love. Probably that foundation can be built up, and depending on the people, it can probably be as secure as if it had sprung up naturally, like the earth beneath one's feet, as normal mothering and childing do. Perhaps it is easier, surely it is easier, if one has one's own children first and then accumulates stepchildren. One's own children will have taught one the lesson of instant forgiveness, instant hate and love. I don't know. I know only that I came to the knowledge of forgiveness, real forgiveness, late in life, after my own children were born, were there to teach me.

We walk around the apartment building now. Behind the apartment is a lovely wooded area. There are great gray rocks to climb on, and a swing set and sandpile, which of course is now covered with snow, and there is a miniature valley in the midst of the trees where an enormous gray rabbit lives. He is almost the size of a kangaroo, this rabbit, and very brave, and quite handsome in his rather frightening largeness. The children love to see him, we all love to see him; he hops here and there, avoiding us yet somehow playing with us, bouncing here and there to lead us away from his nest. He is gray, and the undersides of his feet which we see when he hops, are white. But now, as we approach his small wooded area, we have a wonderful surprise. There is the rabbit, "our" rabbit, perking up near a rock, studying us, ready to move, and he is no longer gray. He has turned snow-white.

"Mommy, Mommy, look at the bunny!" Adam calls. "He's all white!"

"It's marvelous!" I say, and kneel to put my arms around Lucy, to point out to her exactly where the rabbit is sitting. It's hard to see him against the white snow. "It's natural camouflage," I tell Adam. "In the summer he grows gray fur to be the color of the rocks, so that predators can't see him, and in the winter he turns white. Why do you think he turns white?"

"Because snow is white," Adam says impatiently, as if I've asked an obviously stupid question, which perhaps I have. "But what's a predator?"

"Something that would want to kill a rabbit and eat it," I say. "A cougar, or a wolf, or a dog, or perhaps a man." I'm not in the mood for a heavy discussion about predators and guns and death this morning. Wonderfully the rabbit obliges and begins to hop about, and both children shout with joy and chase after him clumsily, wading through the snow.

Off they go, happily. And it feels good to have them go, for a while. I know that the petty, trivial, yet wearing and down-pulling daily quarrels of ours are necessary, are a preparation. Someday these two little people, my children, will grow and change and want to be separate from me. They will want to leave me, suddenly they will want to leave me more than anything else. An uncontrollable force will push them from me just as fiercely and irrevocably as the force that pushed them from me at their births. The difference of course will be that I won't be ready for it, no matter when it comes. I will have gotten used to having them around; I won't want the separation. They will seem too young, or too vulnerable, or I will be needing their companionship, or something. Perhaps by the time they are grown our society will have developed even queerer refinements, and parents will be able to have accouchements during the days the children leave. How nice it would be, I can imagine it: let's say when Adam is finishing his freshman year in college. He'll want to leave me, to live on his own. He won't want to tell me whom he's dating or what he's smoking or where he's working, for a while. And I'll simply go into a hospital, and sit around in nightgowns eating chocolates and having nurses bring me meals on a tray and give me back rubs. I'll receive flowers from friends and cards in the mail; the cards will be a sly mixture of congratulations and sympathy. Perhaps by then the greeting card companies will have coy little rhymes for such things:

Hello, Mother dear, are you feeling queer?
Now that your child is leaving his home?
Is he acting unpretty, in fact downright shitty
Because he wants to be out on his own?
Don't worry, don't fret, and please don't forget
That all one's children must leave the nest.
Now he's acting rotten, but that will soon be
    forgotten
When he's learned how to fly along with the rest.
So don't worry, don't fear, your sweet little dear
Is trying his best to become a man.
Let him alone, he's got to leave home,
It's all just part of Nature's Plan.
These tough days won't last, they quickly will pass,
It's hard when a young one is learning to fly.
And he'll be your friend in the future; till then
Get a prescription for Valium and try not to cry.

They were going through it then, Caroline and Cathy, through the pains and pangs of coming-of-age. They needed the support of the adults in their lives at the very time that they most needed to break from those adults; they needed the adults to be nicest to them at the time when they, the children, needed to behave most horribly. And there was their mother, Adelaide, with her new important job and her leather briefcase, all happy and self-proud, suddenly like a mother hen that has become a bird of paradise. And there Charlie was with his work, his more and more all-encompassing work, and there I was, of course, with the babies. I know this now, I see this now. In fact, I began to understand when Adam was about three; I'm a quick learner. Once when I was very tired I almost screamed at Adam that I hated him. I didn't scream it at him, but I did stomp around the kitchen in the middle of the night muttering it to myself as I fixed him some warm milk. And after a while I knew that yes, Caroline and Cathy had acted hatefully toward me at the time of Lucy's birth; more than that, they had hated me. They had thoroughly and unreservedly hated me. As blood draws sharks and nightmares call up forgotten pain, so their new hatred summoned the old. They hated my new children, their father's new loves. They hated me for having the children. And finally, at last, they hated me for the old initial sin: for living with their father when they were little girls and needed him still. Finally, at last, it all came out, the grief and fury of their childhood years, the unremitting despair that things would never change; that their Daddy would never come back; that I was the woman in his house. Perhaps they were not conscious of their hate and its deeply rooted reasons; I certainly did not figure it out right away. It was all I could do to survive in the face of it, in the face of that destructive force that rose up from the past to confront me at the time I was most vulnerable, most unable to respond or understand. Because I was their stepmother, I was not able to love them through that time of hate.

But because I was their stepmother, I did come to love them again. And that, in the end, is the important thing.

Love. We didn't see Caroline and Cathy again until a year later. They called up unexpectedly one June morning to ask if they could come up for a visit and bring friends. We said of course. Charlie had written to them sporadically, and paid their bills, and we had sent them small checks for Christmas, but we had not asked them up to see us that summer. Cathy had turned eighteen; now the girls were no longer children who had to come stay with their father during the summer months because of court orders. Charlie was glad that they were coming up; I was not so sure. Lucy was now a year old, and walking and running and cooing and laughing, and Adam was a bright chubby three. I was nervous about seeing the girls again, nervous about having them see my children. I knew that Caroline and Cathy would not apologize for their actions the year before, but I still wanted some sign of regret on their part, some reparation. Yet I knew there would be none. I was not quite sure what to do. I was afraid to see them again, face to face. For all I knew, they still hated me, and I was not sure how I felt about them.

Lucy fell asleep in the early afternoon, and I put her down for her nap. Then, because I was restless and worried, I saddled Liza up and told Charlie to listen for Lucy, and took Adam up on the horse with me and went off for a slow, gentle ride. It was summer, and hot, and lush everywhere, green and fertile and juicy everywhere. We rode across the pasture and up a trail in the woods to a small stream. We stopped there a while, and waded in the water and listened to the silence. Finally we rode back. I unsaddled Liza and turned her loose in the pasture, and took Adam by the hand and led him to the house. The Beetle was parked near the barn; I knew the girls had arrived.

Our entry into the kitchen was complicated, as the rest of my life would be, by a child's urgent, uncivilized needs: Adam had to go to the toilet. We walked into the kitchen, saw five people standing there, and suddenly I had to rush off after Adam to help him on the john. When we returned, the introductions were made: Caroline had brought a young man with her. His name was John and he was very tall and rather nondescript, with long hair in a pony tail and blue denim clothes. Cathy had a boy with her, too, a shorter blond named Mike, who had magnificent green eyes. Both girls were slim and tanned and tall and shining. Both girls, it was at once obvious, were in love. Their men were chatting with Charlie about the joys of the country, and the girls listened with obvious, violent contentment. They said hello to me pleasantly, and even smiled and talked to Adam a little bit, and it was as if I were meeting strangers, seeing the girls for the first time. We all drank beers and then went out walking as Charlie showed everyone what he had done to improve the farm, and our garden, and the new chicken shed, and so on, and then we came in and I fixed dinner. Incredibly, unbelievably, Caroline and Cathy played with Lucy and Adam while I cooked. They did it as easily, as easefully, as if there had never been any tension, any hatred, any discord, the year before. They didn't kiss and cuddle the children, but they did treat them nicely, they did talk and laugh with them, they bounced Lucy on their knees.

John and Mike didn't last very long, not much more than a year, but I feel eternally grateful to them for what they did. They fell in love with my stepdaughters, they made Caroline and Cathy fall in love with them, and in the midst of all that strong, sweet joyful love everything else was smoothed over. We sat around the table that summer night, all of us happy: Charlie and John and Mike discussing the merits of farm life, Cathy and Caroline occasionally speaking but usually merely sitting back with proud pleased smiles, Lucy hammering on her high chair with her spoon, Adam playing under the table with a cat. The sky was still softly bright when the four young people left at eight-thirty to drive back to Hadley. Charlie had invited them to stay, but they all had jobs to get back to. I saw how eager the girls were to leave us, this time their eagerness because they wanted to slide into the dark intimacy of the car, to press up against the strong male flesh of the men they loved, to lean their heads against the men's chests, to stroke and kiss. They were so happy.

And Adam, sleepy in his father's arms, and Lucy, drowsing in mine, and Charlie, and I, were all happy, too. How magic love can be, like a spell, like a balm, spreading over everyone and everything, curing ills, healing wounds, wordlessly, silently soothing. That was a good year, the year that both Caroline and Cathy were in love.

EIGHT

The little notebook I am writing in is 5½ inches by 7½ inches; the back is turquoise in color, and on the front, framed in the same turquoise, is a color photo of a man, complete with goggles, helmet, racing clothes, and special boots, racing a motorcycle. In the photo it looks as though the man is coming right at me; if the action were to start with a burst of speed and sound, the man on the motorcycle would roar from the picture right over me, right up over my chest and face. Men are dangerous. But all I have to do is to open the little notebook to write in it, and there he is, the motorcycle man, face down, pressed against the kitchen table. If he came out now he could only smash into the wood, hurting no one but himself. I didn't choose this particular notebook. It was one in a set of three which I bought wrapped in cellophane at the local grocery store for five Finnmarks, forty pennies. Dear dumb little notebooks, they are like a sort of God to me, or at least an angel: they listen to my confessions and enable me to forgive myself and to understand. I don't attend church here in Helsinki, although I have gone to hear the *cantor minores* sing at the Temppeliaukio Church, the church carved out of a rock, and found it a sternly inspiring place to be. But I haven't attended church anywhere for several years. Since I became an adult I found church too hypocritical a place to feel comfortable in. Now that I am older, things become less sharply delineated, and I see that I am like the others; that I, too, do things wrong and need a sense of forgiveness and love. And metaphors: the church provides metaphors that help one if not understand his own life at least see it embellished, befriended, echoed, transcended. I like metaphors. I need one for myself, and I don't care how corny it is. The man on the motorcycle on the front of this book does not provide one for me; he is too artificial. I will have to make up my own, I suppose, here, now, in this dumb little, dear little confessional notebook. I will have to create something beautiful and simply structured to help me make some sense out of my life.

It is midnight. Charlie is somewhere in Sweden, sleeping, having delivered a lecture at the University of Lund. Adam and Lucy are in their little room, sleeping, innocent among their covers, faces flushed. Stephen is somewhere over the Atlantic Ocean, in a silver 747 heading for Boston and Logan International. Good-bye, Stephen; thank you and good-bye.

I feel guilty because of Stephen, because of how I was with him, I feel guilty because of the decision I have made about my life, guilty because it will undoubtedly hurt Charlie. I feel guilty because I'll be taking my children away from their father, at least for a while. But one way or the other I knew I would end up feeling guilty about something; I'm still a Methodist from Kansas. At least I have done it: I have made a decision. Strange how effortless that decision was. And this way, the way I have chosen, I feel least guilty about the most things and happiest about the most things. I think. I must be a very slow person. Meanings come to me after actions, after I have thought things out, as I am thinking them out here in my turquoise motorcycle-man book.

I had quite enough time to make decisions in advance. I had all the time, and all the information available, before I went to the hotel to meet Stephen. I am still amazed at how dazed and undecided I was right up to the moment I knocked on his bedroom door. I spent the days before his arrival, and the very minutes I sat on Bus 90 riding closer and closer to the Rautatientori and the Hotel Vakuuna, frantically asking myself questions. Did I love Stephen? Did I love Charlie? Did I want to sleep with Stephen? *Would* I sleep with Stephen? *Should* I sleep with Stephen? What about Ellen—she was my friend—what did I owe her? What about Charlie—he was my husband—what did I owe him? What did I want? How did I feel? What was important? What would I do?

Amazing. Amazing that a supposedly intelligent person could have such a thoroughly muddled mind on such clean-cut subjects.

I certainly acted as if I were going to sleep with Stephen, no matter what I thought I was going to do. I arranged for a baby-sitter to stay all day, *all day,* seven long hours, with my children, and I refused to think about the fact that she was an older woman with good recommendations from the American Women's League in Helsinki, but that I and my children had never seen her before. I took a shower, shaved my arms and legs, put on creams and lotions and perfume, dressed in my most elegant and attractive casual clothes, even bought myself mouthwash and breath mints, like an eager young lover on a television commercial. I wore fresh underwear, my best pair.

When Stephen called from the airport to tell me he had arrived, I told him to go to the Hotel Vakuuna. Other hotels might have been better, certainly less centrally located, farther away from places where I might run into Americans or Finns who knew me. But of course when Stephen called I hadn't thought of a place for him to stay, I hadn't found out about any faraway intimate hotels, and the Hotel Vakuuna just popped out when he asked for a suggestion. Later I decided that it was a good choice even though it is so close to the America Center and the United States Information Service, and so on. For one thing, it was easy for me to get to, it didn't involve time-consuming tram and bus changes or long walks in the cold. It was only a block from the large brick-paved square where the buses stopped. I had only to cut through the large marvelous railway station and cross the taxi island and another small street, and there I was. The other good thing was that the hotel was located next to Sokos, a large department store. If people who knew me saw me in the area, they would assume I was going into Sokos; in fact, on one side of the hotel there was a small door at right angles to a door leading into Sokos. If anyone saw me coming out of the Hotel Vakuuna, I thought I would simply laugh and say that I had gotten confused, had gone in through the wrong door.

But as it turned out, no one saw me.

I went in through the door of the Hotel Vakuuna and up the stairs; Stephen had called when he was settled in the hotel to tell me his room number: 561. The closer I got to his room, the more frantically my thoughts raced, the less sure I was of what I wanted. I felt I owed Stephen something simply because he had pursued me, because he had come, because he was there.

"Hello," he smiled, opening the door.

"Hello," I said, and entered the room.

Stephen was wearing a soft blue cotton oxford shirt, and the collar was open, and the sleeves were rolled up. He had apparently just washed and shaved; he looked and smelled clean. He was, there was no denying it, a marvelously handsome man, and I am susceptible to handsome things.

So, of course, after we smiled at each other a moment, we kissed. And kissed, and kissed.

"I need to take my coat and mittens off," I gasped at last. "I'm getting hot."

"Look," Stephen said as he helped me take off my big fur coat, "I ordered up some champagne. Would you like some?"

"Champagne at ten o'clock in the morning!" I laughed. "Of course."

Stephen crossed the room to the desk, where the ice bucket stood, and it was then, in the way that he lifted the champagne bottle from the bucket and poured it into the glasses, that I knew I still loved Charlie. Charlie is such a big man, but he does small things with a special grace. We have shared many bottles of champagne together, and the image of his large good hands lifting the bottle from its nest is imprinted in my mind. Stephen's hands were shaking slightly, and they were not as big as Charlie's; he did not care for the feel of the special bottle or for the sight of the champagne as it bubbled up in the glass. It was something he wanted to get over with, to hurry through, it was not a moment to be graced in itself. I saw in that instant how Stephen would pass over all things, expensive champagne in its rainbow iridescence, his wife, his children, my children, to get to me, to have me; whereas Charlie would not do that, Charlie would slowly treasure and value each thing at its best worth, give his time and attention to each thing, and then come at last to me, having chosen me as the best of all the good things in his life. Charlie is a Methodist from Kansas, too; he feels an obligation to give all things

323

their due, to handle all things with appropriate seriousness. I could see that pouring a glass of champagne on our fourteenth anniversary would be a more significant act to Charlie than pouring a glass of champagne before making love to me for the first time would be to Stephen. Stephen was aimed for the act, the accomplishment; he was first of all an ambitious man.

"Stephen," I said as I took the glass of champagne, "I want to talk about all this before I get snockered and do something I might regret. I think it's wildly romantic of you to come to Helsinki to see me, but it's just not right. It won't work out. It's the wrong thing to do."

"Well, sit down," Stephen said. "At least sit down for a while." He smiled at me. He had a gorgeous smile.

I sat down, on the edge of the bed. Stephen pulled a chair from the desk and turned it so that he sat facing me. Our knees did not quite touch.

"Zelda," he said, "I'm not trying to get you to do anything wrong. I want to marry you, you know, not just have a quick affair. Though God knows I'd love that, too."

"Oh, Stephen. I can't have an affair with you or marry you. I just can't. You've come all this way, clear across the Atlantic Ocean—"

"—and the Baltic Sea," Stephen said, smiling, being charming.

"—and it makes me feel I'm obligated to have an affair with you. And you are the most handsome man I've ever seen in my life, and you know, you can tell how I feel when I'm near you, in a way I do want you—"

Stephen's eyes grew serious as I spoke, and when I said that I did want him he put down his champagne glass and took mine from my hand, and I was so startled by that that I sloshed champagne over both of us, and that didn't matter; Stephen was next to me, on top of me, and pushing me back down on the bed.

Oh, how pleasurable it was. Everything seemed so mysteriously attractive hidden behind the layers of clothing, and as we rolled and kissed and fondled and pressed against each other I had the same frightened, exhilarating feelings I had had when I was in high school and going steady with my first real boyfriend. We spent so many hours of our lives, Dave and I, in the front seat of his '56 Chevrolet, kissing, touching, pressing, moaning, longing, and never quite completing the act. We were both Methodists from Kansas. Perhaps it is because of that that I have always found temptation much more exciting than completion. My mother had told me that if I had sex before I married I would go to hell. When I finally did sleep with Charlie, before marriage, it was the most exotic and grandiose gesture of my life, I felt I was giving up all the world, and more than that, all my hope of afterlife. How splendid it was! How doomed I felt, and how proud I was of my love, my love that meant more to me than heaven or eternal damnation. Strange, funny, that I didn't believe in hell anymore. Or even in the integrity of marriage. Surely, surely, I thought, I have gone this far in deceiving Charlie, surely the act itself does not matter, is not a way of deceiving him more. And yet, of course, to me, the act itself, the completion, did matter, did mean something.

I pushed Stephen away. In doing so I half slid, half fell off the bed. I scrambled to my feet, panting heavily, and backed up against the wall.

"Stephen, please," I said. "Please let me talk to you. Let me say what I have to say. Just give me a few minutes to talk. Then, I promise, if you still want to sleep with me, I will. But I need to settle some things first."

Stephen twisted away from me and sat on the edge of the bed, hiding his face in his hands, propping his elbows on his knees. His back was beautiful, heaving still as he tried to control his breath.

"Talk," he said to me, still not looking at me, still hiding his head in his hands.

"Stephen," I said, and thought, What am I going to say? What is it that is so important that I have to say? "Stephen, I'm all confused. I'm sorry. I want you physically; God, who wouldn't want you physically? But all that means something to me, it means more than just screwing around—"

"It means more than that to me, too."

"Let me finish. Please. Look, maybe I've been giving off some signals I wasn't aware of. Or maybe I was aware of them but didn't know what they'd lead to. Or whatever. Oh, I'm so sorry, I don't know

326

what I want to say exactly. Look, I'm over thirty. I have two little children whom I love but who bore me to tears sometimes. I want to teach and I can't, and that frustrates me unbelievably. I love Charlie and I love our marriage and I want to stay married to Charlie, and I want to do right by him. If I were in my own home, working somewhere, teaching, I wouldn't even be interested in you at all. Oh, I didn't mean that the way it sounded. It's just that my life has gotten so far out of control, and things mean so much to me, and if I sleep with you, then I'll have all that burden of meaning to deal with. And then there's Ellen. She's my friend. She's beautiful. I know you love her, I know you love your children. It's been fun flirting, I love flirting, but I don't want to do anything more than that. I'm so flattered that you came all the way to Helsinki, I'm so absolutely delighted that you want me. It's wonderful, it's a fantastic ego trip. I'll live off of it for years and years. But I'm greedy and selfish and bad; I just want the good part, the fun of flirting and the sweet knowledge that you want me. I don't want the rest of it, the guilt and the hurting of others and the mess. Oh, I don't know. I can't even think straight. Am I making any sense to you at all?"

"Zelda," Stephen said, and turned and stood and looked at me across the bed, "if you could wish for anything right now in your life, what would you wish for?"

"A job," I said. I smiled. "Isn't that ridiculous?"

Stephen looked at me a moment. "I have a job for

you," he said.

"You what? You have a job for me?"

"Not in my department. Not at the university. A local community college is looking for a full-time English instructor. Freshman English and some basic literature courses. I've already told them about you. If you finished your Ph.D., and if they liked you, you could get tenure and teach the upper-level courses. It's made for you. It's perfect. The only problem is that they need someone starting in January and you and Charlie are supposed to be here till May. Also, the college is located a good thirty-minute drive from your farm."

"Oh, Stephen," I said. "Oh, Stephen. Oh, oh, I can't believe it. You talked to them about me?"

"I gave them a copy of your résumé. I recommended you highly."

"Maybe they've hired someone else by now."

"No. I know Jim Steele, who's the chairman there. He's waiting to hear from me. I told them I'd contact you about the job. I know how much you've been wanting one."

"Well, well, what can we do? I mean, I'll take the job. I will. Oh, God, it's like a miracle. Can we call them now and tell them I'll take the job?"

"Don't you want to talk it over with Charlie first? Don't you want to know what the salary is?"

I thought for a moment. "Yes. Yes, I do want to know what the salary is, but that won't make any difference. And no, no, I don't want to talk it over with Charlie. I want the job. I've followed him around long enough; it's time I went someplace myself."

"Then we'll send them a cable. And as soon as I return to the States I'll call Jim Steele and reaffirm the cable. And you can do the rest yourself."

"Can we send the cable now?"

We went to the telephone and sent the cable. Stephen pulled the desk chair out and sat at the desk while he talked on the phone. I paced the room, making plans. I would have to make plane reservations, I would have to pack, I would have to make preschool arrangements for the children, I would have to. . . . Oh, God, I would have to tell Charlie.

When the cable was sent, Stephen turned back to me and looked at me awhile, smiling. Then he said, "You're really a crazy lady, Zelda, do you know that?"

"But I'm a hell of an English teacher," I said. I felt high. I hadn't even finished my glass of champagne, and I felt high, drunk, euphoric.

"That's what I told the people in Jim Steele's department," Stephen said.

"Now I really should sleep with you," I said, suddenly sobered. "Out of gratitude, if nothing else."

Stephen stood up, and crossed the room, and took me in his arms. He looked at me for a long time, and then he kissed me and held me against him. "Zelda," he said, "I don't want you to sleep with me out of gratitude. Or out of boredom, or out of confusion, or out of anything else than love. I want you to sleep with me because you love me. That's the only way it will be good for you, so it's the only way it will be good for me. Listen: I love you. So I'm going to go back home. I'm going to leave you alone. If you want me, you'll know where to find me."

"But, Stephen," I said, "you've come all the way across the Atlantic Ocean!"

"And the Baltic Sea," Stephen smiled. "But it was worth it just to see the look on your face when I told you about the job."

I looked up at Stephen and saw that there were tears in his eyes, and I looked away quickly, but not before the tears came into my eyes.

"Stephen," I said, speaking into his cotton shirt, "you're a good person."

"I know," Stephen said. "Isn't it a shame?"

"You've changed my life, you know," I said. "You've given me the two things I've needed most: a job and the knowledge that someone as great as you are could love me. I can't ever repay you. How can I ever repay you?"

"Fall in love with me," Stephen said, and smiled to show he was saying it pleasantly.

"What will you do now?"

"Me? I'll go back home and run my department and live with Ellen and the children."

"Ellen is wonderful. Joe and Carrie are beautiful. Your department has fantastic potential. You could have it worse."

"I know, I know all that. You don't have to feel sorry for me. Oh, Zelda, you're so funny. You're so happy over a stupid, low-paying, demanding job.

Look at you. You're all wrapped up in it already. You think you're the luckiest person in the world."

"I AM the luckiest person in the world. I have everything I've always wanted, children, Charlie, and now a job—"

"—and a friend on the side."

"A *friend*. Oh, Stephen, oh, Stephen, I do love you."

We hugged again, and kissed again, and it happened again, the chemistry, the explosion, the desire. I was tormented. I wanted to sleep with Stephen, now for every reason in the world, except for one: my bonds to Charlie. And, having finally made a decision, I felt bound to keep it. I pushed away from Stephen, put on my coat, and went out of his room.

I stood outside Room 561 for a few minutes, simply staring at the walls and the light blue rug. I felt as though I had just stepped off a spaceship. Things had gone too fast for me. Too much had happened, and the meaning was still light-years behind. I was happy, but not satisfied. Something more was needed to confirm and enrich what had just happened.

I turned and knocked on the door again. When Stephen opened it, I said, "Stephen, look, I've hired a baby-sitter for the whole day. You said you were my friend, and you are, you are my *friend*. Let's do things that friends do. Let me show you Helsinki. It's an interesting city, the Ateneum has an exhibit of Russian art, the Café Manta has exquisite pas-

331

tries. You've come all this way, you should at least see the city."

"What if people see us together?"

"I don't care," I said. "I'll say you're a friend. And it will be the truth."

So Stephen washed his face and put on his coat and hat and gloves, and we went out together to spend the day walking around Helsinki. We went to galleries and museums, we walked up and down the beautiful Esplanade, looking in at shop windows, we sat on the steps at the harbor, leading down to the ocean, and looked at the boats and the ships and the gulls and the curving line of land meeting sea. It was a cold day; we held hands when we walked, and I was amazed that chemistry could be so strong as to zing itself right through his leather gloves and my wool mittens. We ate a late delicious lunch at the Café Manta, and drank beer and then tea, and talked about ourselves. We talked about our pasts, and our hopes, and our problems, and our desires. It was certainly one of the most wonderful after-noons of my life, being with this handsome strange male friend in a handsome strange city, feeling free for a moment of the responsibilities of husband, children, and job, yet knowing that they were all there for me to return to.

Finally I had to go home; I had promised the baby-sitter I would be there at four. Stephen waited with me for the bus, then stood smiling and waving good-bye as I rode off. I sat on the blue plastic seat of Bus 16 as if I were in a chariot made of pink clouds pulled by blue dragons. I felt as though I were the luckiest woman in the world.

Adam and Lucy were clingy and whiny when I came in the door; the apartment was a mess. I didn't care. I paid the babysitter and sat down on the floor in my good clothes to hold my children. I let them jump on me, roll on me, fall against me. I kissed them and hugged them and held them and bounced them. I was an angel of patience and good humor. Finally I fed them and bathed them and read them stories and cajoled them into helping me pick up the apartment, and one hour later than their usual bedtime I got them into bed. Then I put on my nightgown and robe, and fixed myself some Maalva rose hip tea, and turned off all the lights but the one here in the kitchen, and sat down here at the window to write in this little motorcycle-man book, to think. As I look out the window, I see that it has begun to rain.

And thank you, Helsinki, and thank you, funny little notebook; you've given me my metaphor, you've made it all come clear. Though it is trite, corny, overused, still I've thought of a metaphor for my life. Let's say, as I sit here, solid and warm and comfortable, still resonating from the pushes and sounds and hugs of my children, let's say that I am, hilly, solid thing that I am, the earth. Well, we are all that, aren't we, each person a separate, complete, fascinating sphere, a world composed of inner unfathomed activity and outer layers of beauty or ugliness. We sleep and wake like the earth, we experience seasons of warmth or cold, we revolve through time, we burst forth from our mothers, we grow and erupt, and finally die and dissolve, spinning off into space. The earth metaphor is just fine; it will do. And if I am the earth, then my love for my children is the ocean, deep and wide and endlessly profound. My love for my children washes over me, it composes the greater part of me, it tugs and drags at me, it lifts up gifts to me, it storms and shines at me, it is truly the other half of myself. It is inseparable, undeniable; it has formed me. My love for my children is the ocean, vast, as eternal as any earthly thing can be eternal, beautiful; making me complete.

My love for Charlie then is a river, perhaps all rivers, because my love for him is such a varied thing. My love for my husband is a river, flowing from the heart of me, entering into and sustaining the ocean, a part of me and the ocean. My love for Charlie is a river, a river that has cut itself deep into me, a river that is calm and broad and good. And probably necessary, if I am to grow as well as I can.

And my work is then the rain. My work, teaching English to young college students, is the rain of my life: it is necessary for my existence. It nurtures me, fills me, replenishes me, cleanses me, makes me grow, causes me to remain open and receiving, helps me to give.

That is all true. True, but not perfect. No, it's not perfect. It won't work. It won't hold. It's a lousy metaphor. I've had too much scotch again and am not thinking straight. When I first knew and married Charlie, of course he was the ocean to my earth, and all the rivers and all the rain. It's not fair to relegate him to one place; he'll keep changing, and I'll keep changing, and our relationship will not remain the same. No, it will certainly not remain the same, not after I tell him about my job. *My job.* Charlie, please understand.

The metaphor breaks down in other places, too: what, if I continue it, are my friends? What are Alice, Linda, Ellen, Rija, Gunnel—Stephen—what are my friends? Perhaps they are the fountains of my life: dazzling, refreshing, delightful, gracing and brightening my life. But then what about Caroline and Cathy? If I cast myself as the earth and everyone else must be some form of water, I guess I can only cast Caroline and Cathy as small lakes in my life, and nothing more. I have supported them, as the earth does support lakes, but I cannot say they are a part of me, I could never say that, and I am sure they would never say that, either. So I'll have to leave them as lakes, pretty, superficial, sometimes sparkling, sometimes sullied; there.

Last year, last fall, after the peacemaking summer visit from Charlie's girls, we received our first unexpected letter from Caroline. It was a long, friendly, chatty letter, written to both of us, telling about Caroline's new apartment and her three girl friends and how hard her courses were and whom she was dating. There was no request for money. And the last sentence was: "Hope you two and the children are fine. Love, Caroline."

Charlie was happy. "I knew this would happen eventually," he said. "She wants to get back in touch again. She's grown up a bit. The worst of it is over, thank God."

He wrote back to Caroline, and after a while, I wrote, too. My letter was shorter, more cautious, and I mentioned Adam and Lucy only briefly. I realized how dull my letter might sound to a college girl; I wrote only about the farm, and our new kittens, and how many apples I had managed to slice and freeze or make into applesauce and apple cider. I longed to say in the letter, "Look, this is just a phase I'm going through, motherhood and calm farm life; it doesn't make me very interesting, I know, but it makes me quite content. You went through a phase, God knows; I deserve to go through one, too." As I wrote the letter, I knew that the farm, my children, my gentle, calm, safe plodding life, would not satisfy me much longer.

Caroline wrote back another long, friendly letter. She said that Cathy said hi. We wrote back to Caroline. Several letters were exchanged between us, and suddenly it was Christmas and both girls came up to spend two days of their Christmas vacation with us.

It was a good visit. There were no enthusiastic hugs and kisses, in fact there was no touching at all, and we were all rather reserved, rather careful. But we ate and drank and laughed and talked together. The girls helped me clear off the table without waiting for me to ask. They smiled and said thank you when they opened their presents. They even brought little presents for Adam and Lucy, and although they did not hold either child, they did talk to them a bit, they did smile at them. It was as if a storm were over, as if a nightmare had ended. By the end of their two days there, we were almost comfortable with each other.

In February, Caroline wrote to ask if Charlie and I could come down to New Haven to visit. It was her last year of college, and she wanted to show us her apartment and her roommates before everything changed. She had mentioned that she wanted us to come down during the Christmas visit, but we had thought she was perhaps only being polite. Now she seemed to be seriously, honestly inviting us.

"I can't go down," Charlie said. "I just don't have the time. Why don't you go?"

"Me? Alone? She doesn't want me, she wants you, you're her father, for heaven's sake," I said.

But later, when Charlie called Caroline to tell her that he was too busy to go down for even an overnight visit, Caroline said, "Well, then, can Zelda come?"

"Well, then, can Zelda come?"

Those were the words Caroline said, and those five simple words made my heart jump up in my throat and made tears spring to my eyes. "She wants me to come," I whispered to the air, as if saying it aloud, repeating it, made it more believable, more real. It was then, when I realized how happy I was that Caroline wanted me to come, that I also realized how sad I had been, in some hidden part of my heart, not to be part of her life, not to have her as part of mine.

I went. It was a great trip, for many reasons. It was the first time I had ever been away from Adam and Lucy and Charlie. Charlie and I had managed to squeeze out a weekend here and there to go down to New York to see a play and visit friends, and of course Charlie had gone off to his everlasting conferences many times, leaving me alone with Adam and Lucy. But now it was my turn: I was going on a trip by myself, without husband or children. I packed like a bride, took a new thick juicy paperback to read on the bus down, bought Caroline and Cathy new shirts, and took enough cash to buy plenty of wine and beer.

How free I felt as I stepped off the bus in New Haven! It was intoxicating simply to stand there, without having to lift a baby or push a stroller or answer a high-pitched question. And when I saw Caroline in her jeans and down jacket coming toward me, I felt young again for the first time in years.

That night, Friday night, the girls drove me to the dorm, so that I could see Cathy's room and meet her roommate, and then we stopped at a liquor store and I bought beer, wine, vodka, scotch, tonic, and soda, so that everyone would be happy, and then we went to Caroline's apartment and had a great drunken dinner party. One roommate had cooked the appetizers, one had done the salad, one the meat, one the desserts. By the time we had gotten to the desserts I was probably too tipsy to taste anything, but even so the food all tasted exquisitely good, perhaps simply because for once I wasn't fixing it or cleaning up the mess. I did offer to help, but the apartment kitchen was so small that only two people could fit into it at one time, and two of Caroline's roommates did the dishes, and Caroline and Cathy and I sat and drank.

I loved the apartment. It was like a three-dimensional collage; so many diversely colored and designed pieces were thrown into it by the four roommates to make a bright, gay room. There was the usual cheap ugly green Salvation Army sofa, but it was covered by an afghan knitted by someone's mother. There was a purple velvet Chippendale chair and a sleek Danish plastic chair and a bright yellow beanbag chair. There were plants hanging everywhere in wonderful macrame hangers, and there were paintings and photographs covering every inch of the wall. There were lewd posters of rock stars, and save-the-ecology posters of whales. Even the bathroom walls were covered—with clipped cartoons and jokes about men, vibrators, women's lib, sex, college life, unemployment. I could have spent hours in the bathroom alone; I never did manage to read all the jokes.

We sat in the living room, drinking, talking, laughing. The talk faded like smoke; the next day I could not remember a word of it. About an hour after dinner Cathy's date for the evening, a tall sexy blond boy named Chris showed up and took her away. Two of Caroline's other roommates left with dates, and then there were just the three of us, Caroline, I, and the other roommate, Lynn. Lynn had made us tea, which sobered us up a bit, and we talked about courses, grades, the bad job market, the uncertainty of the future. We sank deeper into our chairs.

Finally I heard myself say, "Is this what you two usually do on a Friday night? Sit at home and get depressed?"

It turned out that no, they didn't usually sit at home and get depressed, they were sitting at home on my account; usually they had dates or went out to Louie's.

"Louie's? What's Louie's?" I asked.

Caroline looked mischievous. "You wanna see Louie's? Hey, you *oughta* see *Louie's*. Come on. It'll be good for you."

So we put on lipstick and got into our coats and went off to Louie's. It turned out to be a big, dark noisy bar where a live band was playing and kids sat crushed elbow to elbow at tiny rickety tables, drinking cheap beer and overpriced mixed drinks. When we entered, the beat and the noise after the cold calm outdoors hit me like a wall and I had to stand still for a few moments to let my eyes get adjusted. It was, I suppose, any typical bar where college kids hang out, only perhaps a little smokier and a little louder, but then again, it was a Friday night.

Caroline and Lynn seemed to know their way around, and led me through a maze of legs and tables and moving bodies to what seemed the only available table in the place, one back in the corner against the wall. As I squeezed and slid my way after the girls I noticed that no one in the bar was over thirty, or even close to it. I shrank a bit inside my clothes, wishing I could hide. I felt old, maternal, out of place. I *was* out of place; how long had it been—years!—since I had been in a bar without my husband. I was glad we were going to a corner table.

"This is it," Caroline said to me as we sat down. I chose the chair that was most in the dark. "Look, Lynn," she went on, "Ed's over there with Andrea. Can you believe it?"

"I hope John shows tonight," Lynn said.

I listened to Caroline and Lynn gossip about people I didn't know, people who were not having babies and working on farms and holding down jobs, but who were breaking up with steadies or flunking upper-level courses or wrecking MG's or going off skiing for the weekend. The waitress finally showed up at our table, and brought us all beers, which I paid for, and then I sat there, suddenly very happy, very content, to be simply sitting there, at Louie's, listening to my stepdaughter and her friend talk. Caroline had had her hair cut that fall, in a simple Dutch-girl style with bangs. She was wearing jeans and an unmemorable blue jersey, and small gold pierced earrings. She had put blue shadow on her eyes and blusher on her cheeks, but wore no lipstick. She looked sophisticated and very lovely, completely different from the little buck-toothed girl I had first met, the little girl who had been all angles and sharp, breakable places. I wondered if Adelaide had ever come to Louie's with Caroline; it didn't seem like a place to bring one's mother; in a surge of intuition I knew that Caroline would never bring her mother here, just as Lucy, when she grew up, would never want to show up at a bar with her mother. I felt warmed, special, privileged: I was getting to see a part of Caroline's life that Charlie and Adelaide couldn't share. I sat there, drinking, getting drunk again, smiling fondly at Caroline, thinking how lovely she was, wondering if I had had any influence at all in her growth.

"Would you like to dance?"

The boy said it three times before he got my attention and managed to make me realize he was talking to me.

Even so I said, "What?" I couldn't have been more shocked if a frog had dropped into my lap.

"Would you like to dance?" the boy shouted.

Through my fog of booze I quickly registered: one tall, dark-haired, good-looking boy, slim, perhaps twenty, leaning on the table, looking at me. I also registered the looks of total surprise on Caroline and Lynn's faces.

I didn't know what to do. I felt totally startled and helpless. I looked at Caroline. "I think he asked me to dance with him," I said.

"Well, dance with him," she replied.

"Okay," I said to the boy. He turned then, and walked out to the dance floor, and I followed, pushing my way through chairs and warm bodies.

My heart was suddenly fluttering insanely, my hands were sweating, and I was afraid that my whole body would break out into one great twitchy tic of nervousness. I thought, all at once, in a rush of horror, I can't dance with this boy! I'm a mother. I live on a farm. (My God, I'm married.) (My God, that's my husband's daughter back there, watching me.) I don't know how to dance. I'll make a fool of myself. What do I do? How does one dance? How could this person have asked me to dance; can't he see I'm old and married? What a good-looking boy!

Of course I knew how to dance. Charlie and I had danced at parties, and at dances, and I had played the radio and held my children in my arms and danced with them. I had danced to rock music every day in the winter simply to fight off the boredom. I knew how to dance, but out there on the dance floor with a strange boy and Caroline watching I suddenly felt paralyzed. Every movement and gesture seemed difficult and clumsy. If I hadn't had so much to drink, I wouldn't have been able to move.

But I do like to dance. And the music was good and loud, and I had had a lot to drink, and the boy had a super smile, and all of a sudden I was dancing. All of a sudden there I was, wife and mother and farm lady, dancing in a bar in New Haven, Connecticut, with a gorgeous young boy. I was happy. I danced. I loved myself for having worn jeans and a sweater to visit Caroline instead of my dressier slacks.

I had forgotten how good it felt to dance while smiling at a good-looking stranger.

"Thank you," I said politely when the music ended, and started to go back to the table.

But the boy caught me by my hand; he actually took my hand in his. "Wait," he said. "They'll play another in a minute."

God forgive me, I believe I giggled. I couldn't believe this boy was holding my hand. "That's a married hand you're holding," I wanted to say, but fortunately the music did start again, right away, and he let go of my married hand, and we danced.

We danced for perhaps a half hour without stopping. The boy had a great long back and long, slim legs and his movements were easy and slow and smooth, not frenetic or wild, like some of the others. He had blue eyes, I began to decide, at least they looked blue in the dim light of the dance floor. At first I found it very difficult to look him in the eyes. I kept looking away, feeling somehow embarrassed and guilty, and then I did look him in the eyes, and he smiled, and I smiled, and once that contact was established it seemed too pleasurable to break.

When the band took intermission they put on some recorded music, but I decided to sit down. I didn't want to admit it, but I was very much out of breath. The boy followed me back to the table and sat down next to me without being asked. Caroline and Lynn had been dancing, too, and were slowly making their way through the crowd back to the table.

"It's wild tonight!" Caroline said happily, and sat down. She lifted her hair up off her neck. Her cheeks were flushed from the heat of dancing; she looked terrific.

"What's your name?" The boy said to me.

"What?" I said. I had heard him, but I couldn't believe the question. It seemed such an odd thing to ask. Also I wasn't quite sure what to answer. I knew that "Mrs. Campbell" wouldn't do.

"Zelda," I said, and smiled.

"Zelda?" he asked. "No kidding? Zelda? I've never met a Zelda before. What a crazy name! Like Fitzgerald's wife."

"That's it," I said. "Yeah, it is a crazy name. My sister's name is Audrey. My mother liked strange names." I didn't say—why didn't I say?—"and my daughter's name is Lucy and my son's name is Adam, and this girl sitting next to me, my step-daughter, is named Caroline."

"My name's Charles," the boy said.

"You're putting me on," I said.

"No, I'm not," the boy said. He looked surprised. "What's wrong with Charles? It's a perfectly normal name."

"Does anyone ever call you Charlie?" I asked.

"Nope. And no one ever calls me Chuck, either. I hate nicknames."

I watched him carefully as he spoke. He wasn't putting me on. It wasn't a joke. His name really was Charles.

"This is Caroline," I said, and motioned toward my step-daughter, "and this is Lynn."

"Hi," they all said, and looked each other over. Suddenly a new fear hit me: that they would all start

345

discussing where they went to college and what year they were, and I would have to reveal what had somehow become a shameful secret: my old marriedness.

"I've got to go to the john," I said to Caroline. "Where is it?"

She told me, and I rose and wound my way toward it. I hoped that by the time I was back the boy Charles would have left the table. Perhaps, I thought, perhaps Caroline would tell Charles who I was, what I was. In the bathroom I began to laugh softly and drunkenly. I was after all having fun. It was after all a good joke, especially on that poor boy. If only he knew how I had to suck in my stretch-marked stomach in order to zip up my jeans! Still, I could see in the dim light of the rest room that I looked good, younger than I really was, with a glow on. I looked happy. I was proud of myself, I admit it, and I was glad that Caroline was there, to see that her boring stepmother was still zippy enough to be asked to dance by a college boy.

I took my time in the john, hoping the boy would be gone when I got back to my table, and when I did get back to it, the boy was still there, and he had ordered beers for all of us. He and Caroline and Lynn were discussing some current New Haven scandal.

I slid into my place and sat back and chugged at my beer, hoping for more courage to get through the crazy night.

"What do you think of Cataloni?" the boy asked, looking at me.

I stared back. I didn't know whether he was talking about a person or an Italian noodle.

"She's from out of town," Caroline said, and went on talking. I realized then that she wasn't going to give me away, she wasn't going to say, "She doesn't know who Cataloni is because she's my stepmother and she lives on a farm with her husband and children." I also realized what a great couple Charles and Caroline would make, the two of them so tall and slim, one so dark, one so fair.

The music started and Charles asked me to dance again.

"I'm tired," I said. "I'd like to finish my beer. Why don't you dance with Caroline?" There, I thought, I have done my respectable deed. Off you go, you two young lovers.

"I'll just wait with you," Charles said. He leaned back and put his arm around the back of my chair. I looked at him, astonished. He looked at me. He was gorgeous. I smiled. He smiled. It was ridiculous. I was sexually attracted to him, right there in front of my husband's daughter, and I felt as embarrassed and guilty as if I had just wet my pants. I looked away from Charles, although simply taking my eyes away from his ended a warm pleasure I was beginning to feel. I looked at Caroline. Her face was expressionless: she was staring out at the dance floor, watching for someone, absorbed in her thoughts. At least, I thought, she didn't seem ashamed of me. A boy came through the crowd to ask her to dance, and she smiled when she saw him, and I realized that she wasn't all that interested in what I was doing.

So I danced again with the boy. I danced all night with the boy. With Charles. Not Charlie, my husband; Charles, my twenty-year-old one-night stand. We danced till two-thirty in the morning. We danced to fast music, and we danced to slow music. He held me quite tightly against him, and I thought I would turn into one long drop of sheer pleasure and puddle onto the floor. It felt so good to be in the slim unfamilar arms of a strange male. After a while I stopped telling myself that this boy could have been a student of mine, I was old enough to be his teacher, and that my stepdaughter was watching. After a while I stopped telling myself anything. I gave myself over to the experience. How very sweet it was.

The boy held me close when we danced. He smelled good, like pine soap and clean cotton and sweat, and I liked the smells, having been so long conditioned to baby powder and baby poop and disinfectant. I let myself go. I melted against him. I breathed in his smell. I relished the feel of his long, slim body against mine.

"Listen," the boy said, whispering in my ear and sending chills all over me, "can I take you home?"

Take me home? I thought. Take me *home?* I live in New Hampshire, I've got a husband and children at home. And a stepdaughter here in New Haven.

But I had gone past the joking stage. I could no more say, flippantly, "Oh, I'm staying with my stepdaughter tonight," than I could have laughed in his face. I didn't know what to say.

"I—I'm staying with a friend," I said. "We all came together, Caroline and Lynn and I."

"Let me take you home," the boy said. He looked at me. "Please," he said.

God, it was like old college days, a night full of drinking and dancing and then the desire at the end of the evening, the desire not to go away from the good warm body, the desire to go further into some dark, warm delicious space with the person in your arms. And I had a nice trusty IUD, something I hadn't had in college.

"I'll check with Caroline," I said.

But I couldn't get to Caroline. She was on the dance floor with the boy she had been with all evening, and Lynn was dancing with someone, too. Charles had followed me, holding my hand, and when I said, helplessly, "I guess we'll just have to wait till they're through dancing," he said, "let's sit down and finish our beers."

We went back to our table and sat down, and I realized then how sleepy I was, how tired, but how sensually pleased. I sipped my beer and gazed out at the dance floor, watching for Caroline, and the boy said:

"Zelda . . ."

And I looked at him, and he leaned over and quite gently kissed me.

It was surely one of the lovelier kisses in my lifetime, rating right up there with some of Charlie's better ones, and those of Lucy and Adam. It was a sweet, good, strong kiss, and he put his hands on my

349

shoulders and I could tell he wanted me sexually. And I wanted him.

"Zelda," someone said, and I looked up into Caroline's smiling face.

"Are you ready to leave?" I asked. I was surprised to find that I could still speak in a normal tone of voice.

"Yes," Caroline said, "I'm leaving, but I'm not going back to the apartment. Lynn's going home, though; she can drive you back now if you want. And Jim will take me back to our apartment in the morning, so I'll see you then. Okay?"

"Okay," I said. What else could I say?

I watched as Caroline and her boyfriend, whose name I now assumed was Jim, left Louie's. It was late, and many couples had already left, so Caroline and Jim were able to walk out together, arms wrapped around each other, hips and thighs touching as they walked.

"Hi," Lynn said, coming up to the table. "Ready to go?" She looked tired and sad.

"Yes, sure," I told her. "Give me just a minute, will you?"

"Okay," she said. "I've got to go to the john, anyway."

I turned toward Charles, who had been sitting patiently next to me, his arm resting on the back of my chair, his hand resting on my shoulder.

"I've got to go," I said to him.

He leaned over and kissed me again. "Then go with me," he said. He smiled. "I don't think Caro-

350

line will miss you tonight."

The thought stunned me; he was right. Caroline wouldn't miss me; she didn't seem to care whether I went off with the boy or not. So I didn't have to be good for her sake. Still, still, even without an audience, even with the security of secrecy, going off with Charles was something I just could not do.

"Look," I said, "I can't go with you. I'm married."

"So?" the boy said.

"So?" I repeated, amazed. "So I'm married. I mean I'm really married. I mean my husband and I have an agreement; it's called fidelity. It's old-fashioned, and at times like this I'm not sure it's the best thing, but well, there it is. I can't go with you. But I want to thank you, you have been—beautiful. I've had a fantastic evening with you. You can't imagine what it means to me, I'll never forget you."

The boy looked at me for a while. "You're serious, aren't you?" he said.

"I'm serious."

"Well," he said, "it's a hell of a shame. But my name is Charles Hall, and I live on Chestnut Street, here in New Haven, and my name's in the phone book if you ever want to see me again."

Oh, it was wonderful, it was wonderful to have him tell me that. "I'll remember," I said.

We kissed again, and then Lynn was standing there, and I said good-bye to Charles and got up and went out of Louie's with Lynn. Lynn had apparently had a bad night and was in a bit of a sulk. I tried to talk with her; I asked her what was wrong, but all she would say was, "Oh, boy trouble," and nothing else. So we rode home in a sleepy silence and went right to bed. In the morning, when I awakened, Caroline was there, wearing the same jeans and sweater from the previous night, curled up in a living room chair, drinking tea.

I wandered around the apartment in my night-gown, enjoying the luxury of a lazy morning without children to feed and diaper and hold.

"Water's hot if you want some tea," Caroline said. "I'll fix you an omelette in a minute."

I fixed myself some tea, then sat down in the living room with Caroline. It was a sunny morning, and the sun warmed a spot on the old Salvation Army sofa; I sat there and pulled a green afghan over my knees and shoulders.

"Did you have a good night?" I asked Caroline.

"Ummmm," Caroline smiled.

"Is that a special guy?" I asked. "I mean the guy you went off with."

"Yeah," Caroline said. "A very special guy."

"Do you think you'll marry him?"

"I know I won't."

"But if he's so special . . ."

"Oh, Zelda, he is special, I'm in love with him. But he's so ambitious; he wants to be a lawyer, and he wants a sweet little wife in the background to decorate the house just the right way and to cook just the right meals for the important guests and to wear just the right clothes, all that crap. He's upward mobile. He wants to be a big somebody someday, and he needs a wife who will dedicate herself to his success. I just can't do that."

"I can understand that. You want to dedicate yourself to your own success."

"No, not even that. I don't care about success, not the way Jim does. I mean he wants to be a senator someday, he wants lots of money, and his name in the daily newspapers. I don't want that. I just want to find someone good to live with, and a good job that will mean something to me. I want to go to grad school, I want to see if I can work with the U.S. Department of Forestry someday. I don't even care about marriage as long as I can find someone who will be willing to let me live my life the way I want to. I mean I'm willing to share and compromise and all that, but I'm not willing to go under."

"Do you want children?"

"Children?" Caroline smiled and looked sad at the same time. "Oh, I don't know. I used to think that I wanted a lot of children. I suppose I still would like to have a child, but not for a long, long time."

We sat for a moment, in pensive silence, and I tried to think of what I would say if Caroline asked me if I was glad I had had children. Instead she surprised me by saying, "Did you go home with that guy last night?"

"Caroline!" I said. "Of course not. Good grief, I'm married, you know. Why, did you think I would?"

"I didn't know. I don't know what kind of arrangements you and Dad have."

I had to think that one over for a minute. "Would you have cared?" I asked finally. "I mean, would you have thought it was right or wrong?" I was eager to hear her answer.

But at that Caroline's eyes shifted away and the blank, bored expression of her teen-age years slid over her face. "I don't know," she said. "I really don't know."

"I'm faithful to Charlie," I said. "I always have been." We sat there for a moment while I decided whether to deliver a speech on the importance of fidelity in marriage. I decided not to; Caroline was a big girl now. I opted for lightheartedness. "But he sure was cute, wasn't he?" I smiled.

"He was a real ice cream sundae," Caroline said. We both laughed.

"You can't imagine how great it felt to have him ask me to—dance—and so on," I said. "I mean after all these months of motherhood and farm life. I was beginning to feel boring and ugly." I paused, waiting for Caroline to tell me that I wasn't boring and ugly.

But she again didn't offer me what I wanted. Instead she seemed to have sunk back into some deep, sad mood of hers. She sat for a while, staring into her tea cup. Then with a surge of energy she said, "Hey, I'm going to make you that omelette now!"

She made the omelette, which was delicious, thin and light and full of cheese and herbs, and we talked about safer topics, whales and Jacques Cousteau, graduate school and old professors. When it was time for me to go, to get back on the Greyhound bus that would take me back to my farm and my husband and my babies and my everyday life, I felt sad. I wondered if she had any idea what the visit had meant to me. But as we coolly kissed each other's cheek before I boarded the bus, I realized that she had already sent me on my way, and was not thinking about me and the meanings of my life at all. She had too much to work out with her own. I belonged to her childhood, to her past; she apparently couldn't use me in working out her future. Still for me it had been a successful visit. I felt we had somehow gone through a barrier and entered a new phase in our lives together. We had been comfortable together, there was that, and we had eaten together, she had fixed my meals, we had sat and talked and laughed together, and that was nice. It seemed that perhaps we might after all be friends. And as I rode back through the snow-covered countryside of New England, I realized that for me it would be very nice, that that was what I wanted: to be friends with the pretty young woman with the long blonde hair. Perhaps I had influenced her life, perhaps not, that did not matter. What was important was that I knew her, I cared for her, I liked her. I liked what she had become, and I liked what she wanted to be. Caroline had become interesting, discerning, competent, thoughtful. She was a young woman I was glad to know, to be related to. I liked being connected to her. I was glad, after all, to have a stepdaughter.

NINE

Joy and frustration.

Frustration and joy.

It is Christmas here in Helsinki, and that brings the joy. But Lucy has the chicken pox, and that brings the frustration.

Having children is like giving hostages to Fate; one can never relax, never let down the guard. And meanings get mixed up, confused: pleasure becomes a source of worry because it could cause pain. I must always think: If I am happy now, will this somehow, on some weird universal scale, cause my children to suffer later? If I suffer now, will this protect me and my children from suffering later? Does Lucy have the chicken pox because I almost had an affair with Stephen, because I am leaving my husband for a job?

They came at the same time, Christmas and the chicken pox. Adam picked them up from his school where there was a sudden outbreak of chicken pox, and was sick with them ten days before Christmas exactly, so I knew what to expect. However Adam's had been a light and easy case, only seven tiny pox marks, and no fever, and although I kept him in the apartment for five days straight I could tell it wasn't necessary; he was bursting with energy. I gave him several cornstarch baths, but they were unnecessary; he said he did not itch. With Lucy, however, it is different. Poor little girl, it is quite different. She has a fever, and she feels fussy and cranky and she itches everywhere, and she is irrationally afraid of the bath now and won't let me rinse her with the cornstarch water that is supposed to soothe her. The baby book says, "Do not let the child scratch the pox." It sounds reasonable enough, but is an almost impossible thing to do: she itches, she has to scratch. I've cut her nails, and hold her and entertain her constantly to distract her from the itching, but still she scratches. A few pox are turning red, perhaps they are infected. Oh, my baby, poor baby, how awful for you. I empathize with her so much that I itch all over, behind my car, under my breast, on my check. I refuse to scratch anywhere, as if tolerating these little irritations will make Lucy's illness easier for her.

And yet, through it all, bad mother that I am, I keep thinking, Oh, PLEASE, Lucy, get well, get it over with. I want to go home, and I can't get on a plane until all her pox are crusty and dry. Good Lord, if all these pox get crusty and dry, they probably won't let us on a plane, they'll probably want to quarantine us somewhere. The baby book says that the pox are not contagious or dangerous after they have crusted, but what a terrible sight it will be. What a terrible sight it is now, my daughter's perfect face and body, covered with these ugly spots. They are round and red at the base, and white and pimply at the top, and I hate them. I sit rocking Lucy, saying I hate them, I hate these bad ol' chicken pox.

At least there is the tree to look at. Dear Gunnel,

our landlady, and her husband, Klaus, went to their summer home up in the middle part of Finland and brought us back a Christmas tree. It is exquisitely shaped, perfectly triangular, with branches that lilt gracefully down like ballerina's arms. I almost cried with delight when I saw it, and smelled it: the fresh pine fragrance freshened these gray rooms remarkably. Adam had made cardboard and foil and construction-paper decorations at his little school and brought them home, and when we hung them on the tree they looked so charming that we decided not to buy any other decorations this year, but make all our own. The house looks like a trash basket now, for I have ignored cleaning it so that I could hold and comfort Lucy and occupy Adam by making more decorations. We have cut and glued and colored and pasted and sprinkled gold and silver sparkles on angels' wings and paper candy canes. Red and green odds and ends and scraps have piled up around the kitchen table like a crazy gay enormous dust. We tried to make a popcorn chain, but it was such difficult work, what with Lucy sitting on my lap, making it hard for me to reach around her to push the needle through the popcorn without stabbing her or myself, that I gave it up and we ate it all instead of stringing it. And now the tree stands there, in the corner of our apartment, like a bit of magic in the midst of the everyday world. I miss having sparkling lights, but not very much. The tree seems so right somehow, this way, so primitive, childish, natural, merry. The Finns do not celebrate

Valentine's Day, and they used red hearts as Christmas decorations everywhere, and we have hung some on our tree, too, and they seem right, those symbols of love, dangling from the tree next to the stars and bells. I will use hearts again next year, I know; there are some things I am learning here that I will keep with me always.

Two sets of friends—acquaintances?—*friends*—have surprised us by stopping by with gifts for us and the children. Bright solid painted wooden toys for Adam and Lucy, pictures of Finland for Charles, jewelry from Arikka for me. Charlie and I were surprised and touched, and felt had that we had nothing here to offer them in return. But really, it is strange. One couple we have seen only two times in the four months we have been here. They are shy and quiet and distant, and although they have always said that we were to call them if we ever needed anything, we have never really gotten to know them. And here they were, ringing our doorbell, arms full of presents. Perhaps they are, as the travel guides say, basically a warm people, the Finns. Certainly one could never accuse them of being greasily, insincerely overquick to friendship. Perhaps it has something to do with faces; their faces are by and large attractive, but do not have the easy mobility I am used to. They seem expressionless, passionless, and really rather dull, but apparently underneath it all there is a thoughtfulness and generosity that runs deep and true. At one of the formal cocktail parties we went to, where we all sat with our backs straight, balancing our plates and glasses on our knees and solemnly discussing income tax and education, I happened to compliment another guest on her striking metal and wooden necklace. We discussed the shop where she had bought it, and Finnish jewelry in general, and I had thought that was the end of it; but here, in a small elegant brown box, was the necklace for me, a gift from the hostess of the party. I had not known she had even heard, but she had, and remembered. In comparison it seems that Americans seem to talk incessantly and intimately; we have fun with our words, we don't take the spending of them seriously. The Finns on the other hand seem to weigh and measure each word; their conversation seems heavy, but it is a heaviness of good value.

Last Sunday we went as a family to our host family's home for the traditional Finnish Christmas dinner. It was beautifully done. The house was full of flowers, poinsettias and hyacinths, and candles were lighted everywhere, and a small fire was burning in the square corner fireplace. The meal was enormous and delicious: the first course was herring served in seven different ways with a marvelous *sillsalad* of beets and herring and potatoes and sour cream. There were potato casseroles and sweet potato casseroles, ham, peas, a green salad, a dessert of homemade tarts smothered in whipped cream. And lots and lots of booze: glogg, wine, cloudberry liqueur. The warmth of the sweet, spicy glogg filled me before the dinner started, and so I was able to float, suspended in the insulation of alcohol, through the rest of the time, when I had to help my children act like human beings through the meal. The food interested them only moderately, and since there were no other children or toys around, they found themselves bored rather quickly. I had the sense to bring a box of building bricks, and they played fairly happily for a while with them. Oh, children make so many things difficult—marriages, foreign countries, elegant dinners. Still, I will remember the Christmas dinner in the warm Finnish home, and I think my children will too. I am glad they were there. After the meal our host, a high-level government official, took Lucy on his knee and sang her a Finnish children's song and bounced her. I was surprised, pleased. Perhaps my children *will* take something warming away with them from this sojourn in a cold land. Perhaps we have all learned something, Charlie and the children and I, about making it through the tough times with a bit of persistence and grace.

Now it is Christmas night. We have gone to the America Center for a Christmas party complete with champagne, and to other Fulbrighters' homes for cocktails and canapés, and people have been kind. But still there is a sense of isolation here on this day; still I feel lonely, and miss everything: the Christmas parades on television, football games, friends, relatives, *home*. Christmas has made the time go faster, at least, but still not fast enough. I have made plane reservations for the fourth day of

January, but I see obstacles growing up around that day like bramblebushes around a sleeping princess. Perhaps Lucy will not be well enough to travel then—I must always watch out for "complications" from the chicken pox—or Adam might be ill with something else, or there might be a blizzard to stop all air travel and postpone things for days. Any number of things could happen; I hardly dare leave the apartment to go get groceries for fear that I'll slip and fall down the stairs and break my leg. I do so want to go home.

"My bum hurts, my bum hurts," Lucy cries as I sit rocking her in front of the Christmas tree. She is restless and whiny and miserable, and she rubs at her chest where scores of pox have popped out under her pajamas.

I open her pajamas to look at her bum and see that more, even more pox have broken out. It seems impossible for more to come, her skin will be completely covered. I try to rub cornstarch and water on it as a salve, but it seems to make her only more miserable. And some of the pox are clearly broken open and infected; an angry red. How can this happen, how can my modern child be so riddled with something as antiquated as pox?

"Charlie," I say, "we have to call a doctor."

"It's Christmas night," Charlie says. "Can't it wait till morning?"

"Look, I was up with her all night. We didn't sleep at all; you know that. I'm exhausted. She's exhausted. We can't go through another night. She is miserable."

Charlie calls several friends who recommend physicians, but we are unable to reach them, and finally we call Gunnel. She tells us of an emergency clinic near the large open market at Hakaniementie, and wonderfully she offers to drive us there. Adam is contentedly playing with the toys Santa brought him, and it is senseless to take him out into the cold dark night, so Charlie stays home with him. But as I walk down the stairs with Lucy squirming in my arms I feel a horrible sense of dread. I want Charlie, his tall, strong presence, near me, to protect me, to make everything right. "I can't do it by myself," I want to scream.

Gunnel's presence in the car is like a balm. She talks sweetly to Lucy, and tells me of the times when her own boys, who are now grown, were sick. She doesn't seem Finnish to me, Gunnel, for she talks and laughs so readily, radiates such warmth. The strange car and bright city lights distract Lucy for a while from her itching, and soon we arrive at the clinic.

It is seven in the evening, and the clinic has several sets of people sitting in the waiting room. Some are coughing; one little boy looks quite sick, and a new sense of panic floods me: what if Lucy, so weakened now by her pox, becomes infected with one of the illnesses floating around this room? I was probably wrong to bring her here. I am endangering her even more. I twist in my chair, and bounce and cuddle Lucy, and smile and chat with Gunnel, but inside I am screaming loud and shrill with fear. Will the physician be able to speak English?, I wonder. Will he know the Finnish word for chicken pox, will he be able to do anything, will "complications" develop? We wait and wait and wait, and Lucy fusses, and my stomach grinds into itself.

Finally we are admitted into the inner office, where a surprisingly young doctor waits. Yes, he speaks English.

"She has chicken pox," I say.

"And they are infected," he tells me.

I feel like a child at a confessor: "She hasn't slept for two nights, I've walked her and rocked her constantly, but she can't sleep. I've kept her clothes on, but she still scratches."

"I will give her an antihistamine for the itching," the doctor says, "and an internal antibiotic for the infection, and also a local antibiotic which you must apply to the infected poxes. The local antibiotic will turn her skin blue, but after a few days it will wear or wash off."

It is a religious experience, going to the doctor: the sense of fear and dread and guilt, and then the hot glory of being saved. I pay the physician his seventy Finnmarks (about sixteen dollars) for the office call, and then Gunnel and I rush back out into the night to find an open pharmacy.

I give Lucy her medicine in the car, and before we are home she falls asleep. I thank Gunnel and lug my sleeping daughter up the four flights of stairs and into our apartment. She lies sprawled on the bed while I dab the blue antibiotic on her infected pox, and I see how deep and blissful her sleep is; she feeds on it like a starved animal.

And now the tears well up and fall. The physician has given us medicine, she will get better, she will get well. Already she is better, she is sunk in a healing sleep. At times like this I think how intolerable it is to be a mother, to have to see a child suffer, and I feel endlessly, helplessly grateful for the medicine that saves both my children and me. At times like this I feel a huge and resounding pity for all the mothers who lived before this century, who had to watch their children suffer without the cure of penicillin, antibiotics, miracle drugs. I wish compassion were retroactive; I wish I could somehow send some sense of strength and consolation back through the past into the endless dark nights, to help those other mothers as they rock and grieve over a sick child.

Lucy sleeps, and in the other bed Adam sleeps. I leave the room so that my crying, which has become exhausted sobs, will not wake them. Charlie takes me in his arms and holds me for a while, and kisses the top of my head.

"Come have a drink," he says. "I made something especially for you."

It is hot tea with brandy in it. He has also fixed a light snack left over from the Christmas dinner which I dutifully cooked earlier but was too worried and nervous to eat.

We sit in silence for a while, looking at the tree, enjoying our meal.

"Charlie," I say at last, "how will I ever be able to live without you? I can't."

"You can," Charlie says. "Of course you can. You will be in your own home, you'll have friends to help you, and if there is an emergency I'll be able to fly home to you. I'll only be twenty-four hours away. It will be good for you; it will make you even stronger."

"It's going to be hell for us both, isn't it?" I say, smiling.

"Yes, but it will be a nice, clean, healthy hell, with a light at the end."

It *is* Christmas. It is snowing outside, both my children are sleeping and out of harm, and my husband, with his words, has just given me the best present he could possibly give me.

Until now December had been a terrible month. When Charlie came home from his Swedish lecture tour in November, I arranged for a baby-sitter and made him take me out to dinner. We hadn't eaten out very often in Helsinki simply because we could not afford it, but that night in November we went to the Havis Amanda, one of the more expensive restaurants in Helsinki. It is located at the south end of the Esplanade, across from the famous fountain-statue of the naked woman, and the restaurant bears her name, but it shares nothing of her voluptuous and open sensuality. It is a dark, low-ceilinged serious restaurant, with first-class service and excellent, painstakingly prepared food.

During the meal we ate and talked lightly. Charlie told me about his trip; I told him about the children. But over dessert and liqueurs I told Charlie what I had gone there to tell him: about Stephen and our almost affair, about the job I was going to take in January.

Perhaps I was wrong to tell him about Stephen. I am certain that Charles will never be his friend again, and although he has agreed not to make a scene, not to kill him or hit him or tell Ellen about it all, still I know he will never be able to accept Stephen as his friend. That is one consequence of all this: we—Stephen and I—have ruined a friendship. It was strange that to Charlie that was the most important thing, the past, that I had almost had an affair with another man. When all the time it was the future that I felt guilty and tremulous about, that I was going to leave Charlie alone in Helsinki and go back to the States with my children so that I could work again.

It got to be embarrassing in the restaurant, that cool, reserved place, where the waiters moved as stiffly as if they were automated and everyone else laughed softly if they laughed at all, and spoke in German and Swedish. There we sat in our corner booth, Charlie and I, hissing at each other, trying not to yell. Finally we had to leave. It was difficult to argue on the streets, and worse on the bus, for most Finns know enough English to understand us, but we could not keep still. Once it was out, my secret, it was like a monster that we had to continually flail and fight with in order to beat down and away from our lives.

I had not thought it would be so bad. I had not thought it would take so long. We yelled and cried and argued all night long, while the children slept. Charlie could not believe that I had not actually slept with Stephen, and he could not believe that I wanted to go home only for the job; he thought I wanted to go home to continue my affair with Stephen. I felt helpless. There seemed no way to convince him that what I said was true; there was no proof I could give him.

Through the end of November and into December we raged at each other. We led a strange schizophrenic life after that first night. It was obvious that we couldn't continue the discussion all the time, obvious that we could not settle it immediately, and so we were kind and cool and formal with each other in the daytime when we had to work, tend to the children, buy the groceries, attend Fulbright functions, and so on. But at night, as soon as the children were asleep, I would kiss both their smooth, sweet foreheads, and tuck their blankets about them, and leave their room, pulling the door shut behind me so they would not hear. And zap: there would be Charlie, standing there, his words ready.

"I can't believe Stephen would spend the time and money to fly all the way here if you weren't sleeping with him," he would say, or:

"Come on, Zelda, let's sit down and finish this. Tell me the truth."

"But I *am* telling you the truth," I would wail, and we would be off. We would talk frantically, furiously,

368

deep into the night, only to give up in disgust or despair and to fall into our beds into a tossing, bothered sleep.

I described every encounter I had had with Stephen in great detail. I told Charlie to call Stephen on the phone and ask him. Of course, Charlie said he knew that Stephen would lie about it. I could see Charlie's point; it was ridiculous that we had done all the sneaking and bugging and trembling but not actually had intercourse.

"But that's the POINT," I would scream at Charlie, "that's the whole POINT! I didn't sleep with him. I was faithful to you!"

Toward the middle of December, Charlie changed. He stopped being angry and became instead saddened, heavy with despair. "I haven't given you what you want in life," he would say. "I haven't satisfied you. You should go to someone else."

"Look, Charlie," I would plead, "don't be that way. Look, look at my side, please. You have me, and your children, and your work. I don't feel guilty because your work is so important to you. I know your work is a part of you. Can't you see that my work is just as important to me?"

"I thought you wanted children, you wanted to be a mother," he would say.

"I did. I do. I want my children, I want to be a mother, I want to be a wife. But I also want to be a teacher. I also want my work. I want everything. You have everything; why can't I?"

"I've never had a lover," Charlie said. "All these

369

years, I've never held another woman in my arms. I've been satisfied by you, but I haven't made you happy. You've needed another man."

"Charlie, Charlie, stop. I haven't needed another man. I haven't even *had* another man. Probably I do need someone to look at me a certain way from time to time, it feels so good, it's an ego trip. Everyone needs that. But I don't need Stephen, I don't want him, I didn't sleep with him. I've been faithful to you. And yes, you have been faithful to me, I believe that, but good heavens, you've had Adelaide and how many other women before me! I've *always* been faithful to you."

It got to be humorous, absurd. We would be together in Stockmann's department store, looking at dolls and Lego sets for Santa to give Lucy and Adam for Christmas, and Charlie would look up from a battery-operated train and say, "You should go to him, Zelda. You really should. You should divorce me and go marry Stephen."

And once on Bus 16, coming home, surrounded by grim housewives with fur hats and shopping bags, we got into an argument over the meaning of faithfulness: Charlie argued that I was not faithful to him because I had *wanted* to sleep with Stephen; I argued that the important point was that I *hadn't*. "Jesus Christ," I whispered, tears coming into my eyes, "I wish I had slept with him, I really do. At least then I would have the experience to remember. I'm getting the same punishment, the same anger, whether I've done it or not." Several Finnish women sat staring at me, impassive, as the tears rolled down my cheeks.

The crisis came just four days before Christmas, as we were walking along the Esplanade. It was a clear, painfully cold day, but pretty even so. There were seven grand tall evergreen trees along the center path of the Esplanade, all covered with lights and Scandinavian flags. Bright orange tents rimmed the circle around the tall central square statue, and fur-coated women from different charity groups huddled inside the warmth of the tents to sell hand-made toys and hand-knit scarves and mittens to give as Christmas gifts. We had brought Adam and Lucy downtown with us to show them the Christmas window at Stockmann's and Sokos and Elanto-Centrum. The large window at Stockmann's was full of Snoopy dogs of all sizes, which made Adam squeal with delighted recognition. Lucy fell asleep in her stroller, and Adam walked along beside us, eating a fat sweet pretzel. As we came to the orange tents in the Esplanade, a handsome young man passed us and smiled, and I smiled back: it was Christmas. I suppose it was the young man's smile that Charlie noticed.

"Now that there's been one lover, how do I know there won't be more?" he asked.

"How do I know you haven't had hundreds of lovers on all your damned week-long conferences?" I replied. It was an offhand comment, not a serious one. I was thinking of Christmas, enjoying myself.

Charlie was silent for a moment. "You're right,"

he said. "I see your point. Actually, I could have slept around at the conferences; certainly a lot of people do. And I've had plenty of offers."

"Have you really?" I asked, stunned. I looked up at my husband. The Esplanade vanished, and I suddenly saw only Charlie's face. He was older now, of course, with gray in his hair and a thick heard, but he was still monumentally attractive. He was large, virile, wise. "Graduate students, right?" I asked. "I'm sure. They hear you talk, they know about you. Why, they're like academic groupies; they want to sleep with the great Charles Campbell. Right?" For some reason I was excited.

Charlie smiled. "Right," he said. He smiled almost foolishly, and I could tell he was remembering. "But I haven't slept with anyone else but you, not since the day I met you," he said. "And I won't."

"And I haven't and won't, either. Sleep with anyone else but *you*," I said. "Oh, Charlie, I've trusted you, and trusting is a way of loving. Can't you trust me? I've told you *everything*. And the important thing to me is not that Stephen wanted to sleep with me, but that he acted like a friend. He helped me get a job. He was my *friend*. The *job* is the important thing to me."

"Mommy, can I have one of those little Santas?" Adam, oblivious to our discussion, pulled at my hand. He pointed to an orange stand where little red-hatted Santas made out of pine cones and wooden balls dangled from bright yarn strings.

I gave him a mark and said, "Be a big boy, go up

372

and buy it yourself." Adam walked off toward the tent. I took Charlie's arm. "Please," I said, "don't be my enemy anymore. Be my friend."

Charlie wrapped me in his arms and hugged me tightly to him. "Oh, God, Zelda," he said, "it's so painful to think of you in someone else's arms."

"Charlie," I said, "believe me. He held me, but we never even had our clothes off. He never saw so much as my belly button."

"Oh, Zelda," Charlie said. "Oh, Zelda."

Adam came back then, radiant with delight that he had been able to communicate to the Finnish woman and buy his pine cone Santa. Lucy whimpered. in her stroller, and Adam said, "I'm brrrr," and Charlie and I unwrapped from each other enough to realize that it was time to get on a bus and go home, night was falling, our feet and fingers were cold. As we walked out of the circle on the Esplanade, we noticed several people staring at us, probably because we had been standing out in the open hugging each other, which is not *comme il fault* in Helsinki. Charlie walked ahead of me, holding Adam's hand and talking to him, and I followed behind, pushing the stroller. My heart felt lighter, easier. There on the Esplanade something had happened between us, some sort of unspoken settlement had been made. It occurred to me to wonder if Charlie had had an affair during one of his conferences, or if he slept around; he had certainly backed down once I brought the topic up. But I sensed that he had been telling me the truth, that he had been approached, but had never followed through, that he liked the approaches, the pleasure of desire, the sensations of longing and lust, but that he had, like me, not wanted or needed anything more. At any rate, I knew it would be crazy to start worrying about whether or not he had been unfaithful. I wanted him to trust me. I would have to trust him. *Trust.* In the next few months, I realized, we would have to trust each other as never before.

That night, after the children were in bed, we sat up late into the night again, but talking sensibly this time rather than arguing. That day an envelope had come in the mail for me from the little college where I was to teach; it contained a one-year teaching contract. There was a friendly accompanying letter from Jim Steele; he said he was eager to meet me and to have me join the department. Second-semester classes would not begin until the first of February, he wrote, but it would be good if I could come in before then, to learn about their system of teaching freshman comp, to get acquainted with the texts, and so on. I told Charlie that I wanted to go home after the first of the year, so that I would have time to get the children settled and into nursery schools, so that I would have time to get organized for my work.

"Zelda," Charlie said, "are you sure you want to do this? Are you sure you need to do it *now?*"

"I'm sure," I said. "I'm absolutely sure."

"We could go to Greece in January," he said. "I have to lecture there. We could take the children and spend two weeks sitting in the sun on some warm island."

"I don't want the sun and some warm island," I smiled. "I want a classroom full of pimply-faced kids who aren't sure of the difference between a semicolon and a colon."

"What will we do for sex?" Charlie asked.

"I don't know what you'll do," I said. "But I know what I'll do. I'll sublimate. I don't want sex with anyone but you. And I'm craving work so much that it will be a real substitute for me until we're together again. I feel very strongly about this. It will be hard working full time and taking care of the children without you. I'll be too tired for sex. I've discovered I don't even want sex with anyone but you. And, Charlie, I promise you, I won't see Stephen. I don't want to see him. And in spite of all that's happened, I think he is a good and honorable man. I know he won't try to see me anymore. He's my friend now. But what about you? What will *you* do for sex?"

"I don't know, Zelda," Charlie said. "I really don't know. I feel very committed to you, even now. Especially now. Perhaps I'll see if the Fulbright people will let me finish early. I could be home in April. And I can always go back to the States once or twice to lecture somewhere. I could stop by in February or March for a quick screw." We both laughed, and then he went on, his voice more serious, "What I don't know how I'll handle is missing the children. It will be awful not having Adam and Lucy around. It makes me want to weep to think about it."

"Are you kidding me?" I asked, amazed, astonished, overjoyed. "You'll miss those noisy, messy, troublesome little kids?"

"God, yes, of course I will," he said. "They give me the happiest moments of my day."

"Oh, Charlie, oh, Charlie," I cried. "Thank you!"

"Thank you?" he echoed. "For loving my own children? *Zelda.*" He looked at me.

I looked at him, really looked at him, this man I had seen almost daily for thirteen years, and I saw him. He loved my noisy children; he loved me. He was doing the best he could, he was letting me go free while still admitting that we were dedicated to each other.

"God," I said, "I love you so much. You're so *good!*" I went into his arms and began to cry. "I don't want to be away from you," I said. "I don't want the children to be away from you, and they'll miss you terribly. But, Charlie, I feel this is my one big chance, to teach at a college near a place where you teach, to have it all, my career, my children, and you. I want it so much."

"Then don't cry," Charlie said. "It looks like you've got it."

We made love that night for the first time in a long time, and it was rich and warm and affectionate, and touched with a bit of new strange exhilaration, as if we were making love with someone slightly new. After that we mentioned Stephen less and less and discussed our future more and more. And Christmas came, and Lucy had the chicken pox, and I felt better deep inside; I realized that life would never be perfect, there would always be trouble and trials, and that, in my superstitious point of view, was right. Perfection is cold and clear and unmoving. Life is warm and muddled and complicated. And good.

It is January 4, 1978, and these things have happened:

Lucy has completely recovered from her chicken pox. A few scabs spot her body here and there, but she doesn't mind them, nor do I. We all laugh at the patch of blonde hair that has turned green from the medicine I had to dab on a pox in her scalp. She will look a bit odd, but she will be able to make the trip home. And Adam is healthy; we all are.

Cathy, who is now twenty, has dropped out of university in the middle of a semester and run off to California with a handsome boy who plays the guitar.

Caroline has been accepted by the biology department at the graduate school where Charlie teaches. She says she is sick of New Haven and feels she needs to get back into contact with the "real" world. She wants to know if she can come live with us on the farm in January.

Adelaide has remarried. Her new husband is vice-president of a bank and apparently has lots of money, but Adelaide has decided to keep working; she is proud of her position at the university now, and feels that she is rather indispensable, and intends to work there until retirement. She and her new husband, whose name is Bob, have bought a smart town house, and alternate cooking gourmet meals there in the evenings when they come home from work. They were married over the Christmas vacation, and honeymooned in Bermuda. Adelaide is happy, and calm.

We know these things have happened because in the past few days we have been bombarded with letters and telegrams and telephone calls. We know that Adelaide is calm because of the way in which she handled Cathy's disappearance with the guitar player.

"She's *ruining* her life," Adelaide said to Charlie on the phone during a transatlantic phone call. The call had been placed at eleven o'clock Massachusetts time; Adelaide had waited up that late so that we would not be awakened before six Finnish time. There was only a slight hint of hysteria in her voice. "Do you suppose there is anything you could do about it?" she asked Charlie. "She always did want to please you."

"Perhaps this is the right thing for her to do," Charlie said.

"Oh. Charlie, you always were so exasperating," Adelaide wailed. "You're a *college professor*. How can you believe that dropping out of college is the right thing for your daughter to do! I wish to God I had had a college education; then my life wouldn't have been such a nasty grind when you left me."

"Maybe she'll finish college later," Charlie said. "I can't say I'm pleased that she's dropped out after the tuition's been paid, but Cathy's not a dumb girl, and this must have been what she needed to do."

"Oh, Charlie," Adelaide sighed.

"Well, I'll write to her. I'll call her and find out what's going on. Do you have her address or phone number?"

"No," Adelaide said. "All I know is California."

"California is a pretty big place," Charlie said. "Why don't you just relax? And when she gets in touch with you again, ask her to get in touch with me."

"She's only twenty," Adelaide said. "My baby. But I suppose you're right. There isn't much we can do until she lets us know where she is."

"Caroline wrote us that you're married now, Adelaide," Charlie said. "Congratulations. I hope you're happy."

"I am. I am happy, Charlie. *Very* happy. Although this Cathy business does get me down. I was hoping that I'd never have to talk to you about anything again, but this worries me, not knowing where she is or what she's doing."

"I'll do what I can to help," Charlie said. "I promise. As soon as she gets in touch with you—or Caroline or me—I'll try to find out what's going on. In the meantime, relax. Okay?"

"Okay," Adelaide said. Then she said, "Charlie? Thank you."

"Thank you," Charlie said.

The children were still sleeping when Adelaide's phone call came, and I sat in my nightgown and robe, drinking hot tea, fighting down irrational jealousy and trying to be glad that at least Adelaide and Charlie could talk pleasantly to each other.

"As the world turns," I said to Charlie.

"When you get home," Charlie said, "perhaps you can talk to Caroline and find out more about what Cathy's up to. There might be some friends who would know where she's gone, or what her plans are."

"I'll try," I said. "I'll write you if I find out anything."

"And you'll have to decide about Caroline," Charlie said. "If you want her to come live with you."

"That's easy," I said. "Of course I want her to come. I like Caroline. It will be fun having her there with me, great just to have another adult in the house. I'm going to have a lot of long, lonely nights."

"You can sit up grading your precious freshman comp essays," Charlie said. "That should keep you happy."

I smiled. "I think you're absolutely right. Charlie, I can't wait to be home, to teach again."

And now, on this cold January morning, I am doing the final necessary things so that I can go back home. I will let the children sleep a few more minutes. Last night I laid out all their clothes and packed their little backpacks full of books and toys and raisins and gum so that our long flight home will be tolerable. I scarcely slept all night, and have been up and dressed for almost an hour. While Charlie shaves in the bathroom, I pace one more time these small gray rooms, checking to see that I have not forgotten anything. I pause in each room to stare out the window at the gray Helsinki sky, at the stern modern apartment buildings and the autoroute, at the shivering birch and spruce and pine trees. In a while Gunnel, my friend, will come to drive us all to the airport, and all this will be behind me. I am not sorry to be leaving, but really I am not sorry that I was here.

I see that I have forgotten something. My Finnish fortune. It is a small, twisted, silvery piece of lead which created itself for me at a Finnish New Year's Eve party just a few nights ago. It is a custom in Finland to tell one's fortunes on New Year's Eve by melting a small block of lead in a special long-handled pan over a fireplace fire, then quickly throwing the melted lead into a pail of cold water. The melted lead immediately congeals into a solid shape, and the shape is symbolic of one's fortune for the next year. The final product is actually extremely pretty, like a small sculpture, glistening and silver, feathery and delicate and charming. Our hosts at the Finnish New Year's Eve party helped Charlie and me cast and read our fortunes, and we took turns with all the other guests holding up the sculptures and guessing what they meant. Some were easier than others: several fortunes looked like sailboats, which delighted the Finns, who love to sail. One was full of dark spots, which indicate money, and of course that made that person happy. Charlie's, if we all used our imagination, resembled an airplane, which was fitting, for he had more lecture trips lined up for the coming year than ever before.

My lead fortune, everyone agreed, looked like a series of steps. Twisted, knobbed, convoluted, ornate steps.

"It's not to predict your future," one Finn said to me. "It's to help you remember your past here—all those steps you had to climb to get to your apartment!"

We had all laughed. Earlier that New Year's Eve, when the clock had struck midnight and we watched out the window as the sky filled with bright fireworks, I had cried. I had cried out of happiness and exhaustion and fear and hope. Charlie had put his arms around me and held me tightly, and I had cried all the more, knowing how I would miss the comfort of his arms in the months to come.

And now here I stand, rubbing my twisted piece of Finnish lead, staring at the sky, crying again. I am sad to be leaving Helsinki and the friends I've made here; I am very sad to be leaving Charlie, even for this little while. But I am going to go; it is what I want to do, it is what I have chosen to do. I have made a decision; I am going to carry it out. Still, I think I never will get over how relationships and people and meanings change.

Last fall, in early September, just two days before we came to Finland, Caroline came up to the farm to see us and say good-bye. It was a Saturday, sunny and mild. She had Brad, her newest boyfriend, with her, and she was happy. She had graduated from college that spring and was now working for the government on a short-term federal project, studying gypsy moths, trying to find a way to keep them from destroying the trees and shrubs around New Haven. She had cut her hair to just below the ears, and given it a side part, and she looked much more mature, and less ordinary, than she had when she had had her hair long and straight and parted in the middle. She had been wearing jeans and a sweat shirt, and she had walked about the house and farm easily, relaxed, relaxed with the wonderful ease that comes from having a weekend off from a likable job and an enjoyable man to spend the weekend with.

I was frantically packing. The dining room was layered with open half-full suitcases, jars of peanut butter and pop-corn, and cartons of granola bars and Jell-O. I kept putting dresses and sweaters in and taking them out again, not sure what to take, not wanting to take too much or too little. I felt pressured and grouchy; I had been sad that I was losing the chance to teach again. People kept dropping by the farm spontaneously: the mathematician who was renting it for the year, wanting to go over the water system and fireplaces with Charlie; friends bringing good-bye gifts; adoring graduate students of Charlie's. The children ran around outside in unmatched too small clothes; everything decent was packed. The beds were unmade, the dishes were undone, the washer and dryer were running, people were coming in and going out, piles of necessities accumulated around the suitcases, and I could tell I was forgetting something. There was no way in the world I could manage to take everything we would need in a strange country for nine months.

Toward late afternoon Charlie went down to the cellar and came up with a few bottles of champagne. People kept coming and drinking a glass or two, but there was still enough for me to get slightly tipsy on, and that helped. Someone decided I shouldn't have to cook dinner that night (I wasn't planning to, anyway), and Caroline and her boyfriend volunteered to drive the long drive into town to get it. Adam asked to go along because he wanted to ride in Brad's car, which was a great old wine-colored jeep with a raccoon tail hanging from the antenna, and Lucy wanted to go because Adam wanted to go, and Charlie decided to go, too, so that he could drop some last-minute mail at the post office. I chose to stay home and take a long hot bath.

Suddenly everyone was gone. The place was silent. Our dog fell asleep on the kitchen rug. The sun began to set. The champagne bottles were empty. I stripped off my jeans and sank into a luxurious bubble bath, soaking in the heat, the pleasure, the silence. Then I dressed again and went back downstairs. I couldn't stand to stay in the house— there was too much demanding chaos in every room—so I went outside to walk around.

The silence of a farm, of the countryside, without people, is a profound and mysterious thing. I can understand the people who become hermits and mystics, for being alone in the countryside exposes one to the powerful sense of life that shimmers in inhuman things. I walked about the farm, my farm, my home, looking at the orange and brown mums I had planted, at the last roses, at the apple trees now laden with fruit, the berry bushes now beginning to show spots of rust and scarlet and flame. Birds chittered in the trees, the trees themselves breathed almost audibly. There was a tension in the air, between the excitement of fall approaching and the restfulness of the more quickly approaching night.

I walked up our dirt drive to the barnyard, where the horses stood. Dear Liza, dear Gabe. They were now nineteen and seventeen years old. They were standing together at one end of the barnyard, eyes half closed, doing nothing with that marvelous sense of significance that animals have. I went inside the barnyard and walked over to Liza and leaned up against her. It had been days since I had had the time to ride her. I hoped she would make it through the cold New England winter. I wished there were a way to make her understand that I was going to be gone, but that I was going to come back. I stroked her neck. She was still in good shape, although the hairs around her mouth and in her mane had grown humorously gray.

"I love you, Liza," I said.

She knocked her nose into my shoulder in reply. Gabe began to sniff around my hands and pockets, and sensing no sugar or carrots, stamped and snorted and walked away.

I stood there leaning on Liza as the light failed in

the sky. I felt a marvelous sense of loneliness; no, not of loneliness, but of aloneness, of individuality. The horse I was leaning on was truly a friend, a creature on this earth that knew me and loved me and responded to me and trusted me, a creature I knew and loved and responded to and trusted. I had known her longer than I had known Charlie or Charlie's children or my own. It seemed amazing. I calculated years in my head, and no, given even the most optimistic measures, I knew it would not be possible for her to still be around to comfort me when my children had grown and left home. She, Liza, would leave us first.

"I love you, Liza," I said again, and wrapped my arms around her neck.

Liza tolerated my affection for a moment, and then, bored with it, bent her neck away from my grasp and began to nibble at the stubbles of barnyard grass.

The wine-colored Jeep came bouncing back to the farm just then. As I walked from the barnyard I saw the people get out; they were like bright-colored beads of life exploding from a box. Big Irish Brad, wriggling noisy Adam, large strong Charlie, and then Caroline, slim and blonde, with Lucy in her arms. Lucy had fallen asleep and lay against Caroline, totally limp, lips open, sighing in her sleep.

It was a strange sight to see the two of them: Charlie's daughters, one twenty-three-years old, the other only two, one asleep in the other's arms. I wondered if it seemed to Charlie that Caroline looked like Lucy's mother more than I. They had the same coloring, the same bone structure, the same features; both girls were long and slim, fair-haired, green-eyed, white-skinned. At Lucy's birth I had been afraid that she was dead, because she was so pale, as white as a sheet of paper. But she had been perfectly healthy; she simply had managed to have Charlie's coloring. I remembered the time in Michigan when I had held Alice's little girl and longed for a little girl of my own, one who looked just like me. Now I had a little girl of my own, and she looked just like, exactly like, my stepdaughter. How strange life is.

We all went into the house, and because it was growing cool Charlie made a fire in the kitchen fireplace. Brad went downstairs and found more champagne. "Champagne and pizza!" we all cried. "How weird!" But it was delicious.

"Let me take Lucy up and put her in her crib," I said to Caroline.

"That's okay," Caroline said, settling into a kitchen chair. "I'll hold her. She might wake up if you move her. She's fine. I've got a free hand to eat with."

We sat about the round oak table, eating pizza, drinking champagne, watching the fire. Irish Brad entertained us with stories, but I didn't listen carefully. I kept looking at Caroline, holding sleeping Lucy, eating her pizza carefully, so that she wouldn't joggle Lucy too much and awaken her. I wondered if Caroline was perhaps sitting in the same chair she had been sitting in two years before, right after Lucy's birth, when I had sat holding Lucy at my breast, and feeding Adam and myself with my one free hand, and hating Caroline and Cathy with all my heart.

Oh, love. It is not a constant thing, though we would all prefer it to be so; it would certainly make for a calmer life. Love and time; love needs time; love must climb time as if time were a series of beautiful, twisted, convoluted stairs, with landings to rest at, and window seats looking out over the past, and railings to hold to against a fall into nothingness, and perhaps, one hopes, a room of wisdom and knowledge at the last step, at the top.

Here in Helsinki, I am not anywhere near the wisdom of that last step, but I have come this far, I do see now that I love Charlie, and that I always will. He loves me. We have come this far, quite far, together. I realize now that it is okay, it is allowable, to love other things at the same time I love him; my love for him is not diminished. And he realizes now that I must do the things I want to do or become a stunted person. In our case the way of separation enriches our love; the way of togetherness would have destroyed it. He will travel and lecture, and I will teach and play with the children, and we will write letters to each other. In a few short months we will be together again. It will be nice, coming together again. Perhaps there will be more comings and goings in our lives now that we are mutual people, both of us standing on our own personal ground. I will love him better for being independent of him. He will love me better, I think, because I will become a better person to love. It seems exciting. After thirteen years of marriage it seems that we are starting all over again.

And I love my children. I will love them enough to know, to accept the knowledge, that there will be times when I will hate them, when they will hate me, when we will make each other grieve and cry. But for the most part I will happily soak in the love, the beauty, the joy, of living with these young people.

I love my stepdaughters. Yes, I've climbed this far; I can say with honesty that I love them. It will be an interesting experience living with Caroline. Will she expect me to be her mother and keeper and cook and maid, or will she want to live as if we are friends? What will Adam think of having her in the house with us? He is almost five now, beginning to ask questions, sense relationships, put things together. He has never asked Charlie or me why Caroline calls Charlie "Dad" or why Caroline's last name is the same as ours, but I know the time will come when be will. What will I, or Charlie—it's his problem after all—say to Adam, innocent Adam, about Caroline and Cathy, these first children of his? What will we say to Adam about marriage and divorce and children then? Will Adam be afraid then that Charlie will leave him? Well, if so, he'll just have to be afraid; there is always that possibility. This is the twentieth century, and even though we live on a farm now, we are caught up in the values of our time. All in all, I think Caroline and I will have a good time together this semester. I am looking forward to talking and laughing and sharing life with her. It's obvious that I care for her—love her—more than I do Cathy. It always has been that way. But I feel no grudge against Cathy, and I think she carries no grudge against me. Out there in California with her guitar-playing boyfriend, she probably doesn't think of me at all. She's never needed me, leaned on me at all; it's always been men she's preferred, right from the start, Well, Adam is turning out to be a handsome and charming boy; perhaps when Cathy comes back this way she will enjoy his company.

Perhaps someday Cathy will take Adam and Caroline will take Lucy to a movie, and they'll sit and eat popcorn and laugh together, and perhaps, since they can never live as brother and sisters, perhaps they'll live as friends. Perhaps they will somehow enrich each other's lives. That is the most I could hope for. That would be a very fine thing.

But this much I know: it does not end here. We will not ever be at peace. Nothing will be definite. Our relationship will not now or ever become constant settled, fulfilled. It will always change. I will have to remember that, and not hold grudges. It is just as possible that my stepdaughters and I will die hating each other as it is that we will die loving each other. In this relationship nothing is assured. I can only enjoy the good times and let the other times go by.

Charlie has never seemed to worry about the relationship between his two sets of children. Perhaps that is because he is a historian, and a realist. He seems to know that children will get sick, and then get well, and that people will learn to love each other, or not, no matter how much we fret and yearn. It would not *bother* him if Caroline and Cathy did not love or care for Adam and Lucy; I wonder why it would bother me. I think it is more than merely that I have been a housekeeper for so long and want things tidy. No, it is that these are four people that I care for and enjoy, and I would like them to care for and enjoy each other. But I will let the matter rest, go free, I will not try anymore to work things out myself. Lucy fell asleep in Caroline's arms when I was not around.

Now, on this cold January morning, I pick up the twisted piece of lead, my Finnish fortune, and put it in my pocket. There's no place else to put it; all the bags are packed and locked. I could throw it away, the small unnecessary piece of metal; it is certainly worthless to everyone but me. But I want to take it back with me, as a memento, a *souvenir*, a talisman. I want to remember all that went on here, all I thought about and learned, all the steps I climbed, physically and in my mind. I want to keep it near me, up high somewhere on a desk or fireplace mantel, some everyday place where my eye will fall on it occasionally. I want it to help me remember how far I've come.

And I want it, in its severe and shining way, to continually bless and protect me. With love I am climbing the steps of time; I have so far to go.

Center Point Publishing
Brooks Road • PO Box 1
Thorndike ME 04986-0001 USA

**(207) 568-3717
US & Canada:
1 800 929-9108**